ABOUT THIS PUBLICATION

FOR SERVICE ASSISTANCE

Customer Service
1.704.898.0770

North Carolina General Statues is published by The Muliti-Media Group of Greater Charlotte in Charlotte, North Carolina. Copyright 2015 by the Multi-Media Group of Greater Charlotte. This book or parts thereof may not be reproduced in any form, stored in a retrieval system, or transmitted in any form by any means—electronic, mechanical, photocopy, recording or otherwise—without prior written permission of the publisher, except as provided by United States of America copyright law.

The records required by U.S. Code 2257(a) through (c) and the pertinent regulations 28 C.F.R. Cli. 1, Part 75 with respect to this publication and all materials associated with such records are maintained by The Multi-Media Group of Greater Charlotte, Publisher and available for review by Attorney General.

www.visionbooks.org

TID: 5105684
ISBN (10) digit: 150322855X
ISBN (13) digit: 978-1503228559

123-4-56789-01239-Paperback
123-4-56789-01239-Hardback

First Edition

090520140547

Printed in the United States of America

1

2015 EDITION

North Carolina Criminal Law And Procedure-Pamphlet # 70

Printed In conjunction with the Administration of the Courts

North Carolina Criminal Law and Procedure
Pamphlet Reference Guide

7

8

11

13

14

§ 128-28. Administration and responsibility for operation of System.

(a)   Vested in Board of Trustees. - The general administration and responsibility for the proper operation of the Retirement System and for making effective the provisions of this Article are hereby vested in the Board of Trustees: Provided, that all expenses in connection with the administration of the North Carolina Local Governmental Employees' Retirement System shall be charged against and paid from the expense fund as provided in subsection (f) of G.S. 128-30.

(b)   Board of Trustees a Body Politic and Corporate; Powers and Authority; Exemption from Taxation. - The Board of Trustees shall be a body politic and corporate under the name Board of Trustees of the North Carolina Local Governmental Employees' Retirement System, and as a body politic and corporate shall have the right to sue and be sued, shall have perpetual succession and a common seal, and in said corporate name shall be able and capable in law to take, demand, receive and possess all kinds of real and personal property necessary and proper for its corporate purposes, and to bargain, sell, grant, alien, or dispose of all such real and personal property as it may lawfully acquire. All such property owned or acquired by said body politic and corporate shall be exempt from all taxes imposed by the State or any political subdivision thereof, and shall not be subject to income taxes.

(c)   Members of Board. - The Board shall consist of (i) five members of the Board of Trustees of the Teachers' and State Employees' Retirement System appointed under G.S. 135-6(b): the State Treasurer; the Superintendent of Public Instruction; the two members appointed by the General Assembly; and one of the two members appointed by the Governor who are not members of the teaching profession or State employees; and (ii) eight members designated by the Governor:

(1)   One member shall be a mayor or a member of the governing body of a city or town participating in the Retirement System;

(2)   One member shall be a county commissioner of a county participating in the Retirement System;

(3)   One member shall be a law-enforcement officer employed by an employer participating in the Retirement System;

15

(4)   One member shall be a county manager of a county participating in the Retirement System;

(5)   One member shall be a city or town manager of a city or town participating in the Retirement System;

(6)   One member shall be an active, Fair Labor Standards Act nonexempt, local governmental employee of an employer;

(7)   One member shall be a retired, Fair Labor Standards Act nonexempt, local governmental employee of an employer; and

(8)   One member shall be an active or retired member of the Firemen's and Rescue Squad Workers' Pension Fund.

The Governor shall designate eight members on April 1 of years in which an election is held for the office of Governor, or as soon thereafter as possible, and the eight members designated by the Governor shall serve on the Board in addition to the regular duties of their city, town, or county office: Provided, that if for any reason any member appointed pursuant to subdivisions (1) through (6) of this subsection vacates the city, town, or county office or employment which the member held at the time of this designation, the Governor shall designate another member to serve until the next regular date for the designation of members to serve on the Board.

(d)   Compensation of Trustees. - The trustees shall be paid during sessions of the Board at the prevailing rate established for members of State boards and commissions, and they shall be reimbursed for all necessary expenses that they incur through service on the Board.

(e)   Oath. - Each trustee other than the ex officio members shall, within 10 days after his appointment, take an oath of office, that, so far as it devolves upon him, he will diligently and honestly administer the affairs of the said Board, and that he will not knowingly violate or willingly permit to be violated any of the provisions of law applicable to the Retirement System. Such oath shall be subscribed to by the member making it, and certified by the officer before whom it is taken, and immediately filed in the office of the Secretary of State: Provided, that where a local governmental official designated by the Governor has taken an oath of office in connection with the local governmental office that he holds, the oath for his local governmental office shall be deemed to be sufficient, and he shall not be required to take the oath hereinabove provided.

(f)   Voting Rights. - Each trustee shall be entitled to one vote in the Board. A majority of affirmative votes in attendance shall be necessary for a decision by the trustees at any meeting of said Board. A vote may only be taken if at least seven members of the Board are in attendance, in person or by telephone, for the meeting at which a vote on a decision is taken.

(g)   Rules and Regulations. - Subject to the limitations of this Chapter, the Board of Trustees shall, from time to time, establish rules and regulations for the administration of the funds created by this Chapter and for the transaction of its business. The Board of Trustees shall also, from time to time, in its discretion, adopt rules and regulations to prevent injustices and inequalities which might otherwise arise in the administration of this Chapter.

(h)   Officers and Other Employees, Salaries and Expenses. - The Board of Trustees shall elect from its membership a chairman, and shall, by a majority vote of all the members, appoint a director, who may be, but need not be, one of its members. The Board of Trustees shall engage such actuarial and other service as shall be required to transact the business of the Retirement System. The compensation of all persons engaged by the Board of Trustees, and all other expenses of the Board necessary for the operation of the Retirement System, shall be paid at such rates and in such amounts as the Board of Trustees shall approve.

(i)   Actuarial Data. - The Board of Trustees shall keep in convenient form such data as shall be necessary for actuarial valuation of the various funds of the Retirement System, and for checking the experience of the System.

(j)   Record of Proceedings; Annual Report. - The Board of Trustees shall keep a record of all of its proceedings which shall be open to public inspection. It shall publish annually a report showing the fiscal transactions of the Retirement System for the preceding year, the amount of the accumulated cash and securities of the System, and the last balance sheet showing the financial condition of the System by means of an actuarial valuation of the assets and liabilities of the Retirement System.

(k)   Legal Adviser. - The Attorney General shall be the legal adviser of the Board of Trustees.

(l)   Medical Board. - The Board of Trustees shall designate a Medical Board to be composed of not less than three nor more than five physicians not eligible

17

to participate in the Retirement System. The Board of Trustees may structure appointment requirements and term durations for those medical board members. If required, other physicians may be employed to report on special cases. The Medical Board shall arrange for and pass upon all medical examinations required under the provisions of this Chapter, and shall investigate all essential statements and certificates by or on behalf of a member in connection with an application for disability retirement, and shall report in writing to the Board of Trustees its conclusion and recommendations upon all the matters referred to it.

(m)   Duties of Actuary. - The Board of Trustees shall designate an actuary who shall be the technical adviser of the Board of Trustees on matters regarding the operation of the funds created by the provisions of this Chapter and shall perform such other duties as are required in connection therewith. For purposes of the annual valuation of System assets, the experience studies, and all other actuarial calculations required by this Chapter, all the assumptions used by the System's actuary, including mortality tables, interest rates, annuity factors, and employer contribution rates, shall be set out in the actuary's periodic reports or other materials provided to the Board of Trustees. These materials, once accepted by the Board, shall be considered part of the Plan documentation governing this Retirement System; similarly, the Board's minutes relative to all actuarial assumptions used by the System shall also be considered part of the Plan documentation governing this Retirement System, with the result of precluding any employer discretion in the determination of benefits payable hereunder, consistent with Section 401(a)(25) of the Internal Revenue Code.

(n)   Immediately after the establishment of the Retirement System the actuary shall make such investigation of the mortality, service and compensation experience of the members of the System as he shall recommend and the Board of Trustees shall authorize, and on the basis of such investigation he shall recommend for adoption by the Board of Trustees such tables and such rates as are required in subsection (o), paragraphs (1) and (2), of this section. The Board of Trustees shall adopt tables and certify rates, and as soon as practicable thereafter the actuary shall make a valuation based on such tables and rates of the assets and liabilities of the funds created by this Chapter.

(o)   In the year 1945, and at least once in each five-year period thereafter, the actuary shall make an actuarial investigation into the mortality, service and compensation experience of the members and beneficiaries of the Retirement System, and shall make a valuation of the assets and liabilities of the funds of the System, and taking into account the result of such investigation and valuation, the Board of Trustees shall:

(1)   Adopt for the Retirement System such mortality, service and other tables as shall be deemed necessary; and

(2)   Certify the rates of contributions payable by the participating units on account of new entrants at various ages.

(p)   On the basis of such tables and interest assumption rate as the Board of Trustees shall adopt, the actuary shall make an annual valuation of the assets and liabilities of the funds of the System created by this Chapter.

(q)   Notwithstanding any law, rule, regulation or policy to the contrary, any board, agency, department, institution or subdivision of the State maintaining lists of names and addresses in the administration of their programs may upon request provide to the Retirement System information limited to social security numbers, current name and addresses of persons identified by the System as members, beneficiaries, and beneficiaries of members of the System. The System shall use such information for the sole purpose of notifying members, beneficiaries, and beneficiaries of members of their rights to and accruals of benefits in the Retirement System. Any social security number, current name and address so obtained and any information concluded therefrom and the source thereof shall be treated as confidential and shall not be divulged by any employee of the Retirement System or of the Department of State Treasurer except as may be necessary to notify the member, beneficiary, or beneficiary of the member of their rights to and accruals of benefits in the Retirement System. Any person, officer, employee or former employee violating this provision shall be guilty of a Class 1 misdemeanor; and if such offending person be a public official or employee, he shall be dismissed from office or employment and shall not hold any public office or employment in this State for a period of five years thereafter.

(r)   Fraud Investigations - Access to Persons and Records. - In the course of conducting a fraud investigation, the Retirement Systems Division, or authorized representatives who are assisting the Retirement Systems Division staff, shall:

(1)   Have ready access to persons and may examine and copy all books, records, reports, vouchers, correspondence, files, personnel files, investments, and any other documentation of any employer. The review of State tax returns

shall be limited to matters of official business, and the Division's report shall not violate the confidentiality provisions of tax laws.

(2)   Have such access to persons, records, papers, reports, vouchers, correspondence, books, and any other documentation that is in the possession of any individual, private corporation, institution, association, board, or other organization which pertain to the following:

a.   Amounts received pursuant to a grant or contract from the federal government, the State, or its political subdivisions.

b.   Amounts received, disbursed, or otherwise handled on behalf of the federal government or the State.

(3)   Have the authority, and shall be provided with ready access, to examine and inspect all property, equipment, and facilities in the possession of any employer agency or any individual, private corporation, institution, association, board, or other organization that were furnished or otherwise provided through grant, contract, or any other type of funding by the employer agency.

With respect to the requirements of sub-subdivision (2)b. of this subsection, providers of social and medical services to a beneficiary shall make copies of records they maintain for services provided to a beneficiary available to the Retirement Systems Division, or to the authorized representatives who are assisting the Retirement Systems Division staff. Copies of the records of social and medical services provided to a beneficiary will permit verification of the health or other status of a beneficiary as required for the payment of benefits under Article 3 of this Chapter. The Retirement Systems Division, or authorized representatives who are assisting the Retirement Systems Division staff, shall request records in writing by providing the name of each beneficiary for whom records are sought, the purpose of the request, the statutory authority for the request, and a reasonable period of time for the production of record copies by the provider. A provider may charge, and the Retirement Systems Division, or authorized representatives who are assisting the Retirement Systems Division staff, shall, in accordance with G.S. 90-411, pay a reasonable fee to the provider for copies of the records provided in accordance with this subsection.

(s)   Fraud Investigative Reports and Work Papers. - The Director of the Retirement Systems Division shall maintain for 10 years a complete file of all fraud investigative reports and reports of other examinations, investigations, surveys, and reviews issued under the Director's authority. Fraud investigation work papers and other evidence or related supportive material directly pertaining to the work of the Retirement Systems Division of the Department of State Treasurer shall be retained according to an agreement between the Director of Retirement and State Archives. To promote intergovernmental cooperation and avoid unnecessary duplication of fraud investigative effort, and notwithstanding local unit personnel policies to the contrary, pertinent work papers and other supportive material relating to issued fraud investigation reports may be, at the discretion of the Director of Retirement and unless otherwise prohibited by law, made available for inspection by duly authorized representatives of the State and federal government who desire access to and inspection of such records in connection with some matter officially before them, including criminal investigations. Except as provided in this section, or upon an order issued in Wake County Superior Court upon 10 days' notice and hearing finding that access is necessary to a proper administration of justice, fraud investigation work papers and related supportive material shall be kept confidential, including any information developed as a part of the investigation.

(t)   Fraud Reports May Be Anonymous. - The identity of any person reporting fraud, waste, and abuse to the Retirement Systems Division shall be kept confidential and shall not be maintained as a public record within the meaning of G.S. 132-1. (1939, c. 390, s. 8; 1941, c. 357, s. 6; 1945, c. 526, s. 7; 1961, c. 515, ss. 3, 4; 1965, c. 781; 1969, c. 442, s. 15; 1973, c. 243, s. 8; 1985, c. 479, s. 196(o); 1987, c. 539, s. 1; 1993, c. 539, s. 944; 1994, Ex. Sess., c. 24, s. 14(c); 2006-64, ss. 1.1, 1.2; 2012-130, ss. 2(a), 9(a); 2012-185, ss. 2(c), 4(a); 2013-287, s. 4(b).)

§ 128-29. Management of funds.

(a)   Vested in Board of Trustees. - The Board of Trustees shall be the trustee of the several funds created by this Article as provided in G.S. 128-30.

(b)   Annual Allowance of Regular Interest. - The Board of Trustees annually shall allow regular interest on the mean amount for the preceding year in each of the funds with the exception of the expense fund. The amounts so allowed shall be due and payable to said funds, and shall be annually credited thereto by the Board of Trustees from interest and other earnings on the moneys of the Retirement System. Any additional amount required to meet the interest on the funds of the Retirement System shall be paid from the pension accumulation fund, and any excess of earnings over such amount required shall be paid to the pension accumulation fund. Regular interest shall mean interest at the rate of four per centum (4%) per annum with respect to all calculations and allowances on account of members' contributions and at the rate of three per centum (3%) per annum with respect to employers' contributions, with the right reserved to the Board of Trustees to set a different rate or rates from time to time.

(c)   Custodian of Funds. - The State Treasurer shall be the custodian of the several funds and shall invest their assets in accordance with the provisions of G.S. 147-69.2 and 147-69.3. All payments from said funds shall be made by him only upon vouchers signed by two persons designated by the Board of Trustees. The secretary of the Board of Trustees shall furnish said Board a surety bond in a company authorized to do business in North Carolina in such amount as shall be required by the Board, the premium to be paid from the expense fund.

(d)   Cash Deposits for Meeting Disbursements. - For the purpose of meeting disbursements for pensions, annuities and other payments there may be kept available cash, not exceeding ten per centum (10%) of the total amount in the several funds of the Retirement System, on deposit in one or more banks or trust companies of the State of North Carolina, organized under the laws of the State of North Carolina, or of the United States: Provided, that the sum on deposit in any one bank or trust company shall not exceed twenty-five per centum (25%) of the paid up capital and surplus of such bank or trust company.

(e)   Selection of Depositories. - The Board of Trustees shall select a bank or banks for the deposits of the funds and securities of the Retirement System in the same manner as such banks are selected by the Treasurer of the State of North Carolina. Such banks selected shall be required to conform to the law governing banks selected by the State. The funds and properties of the North Carolina Governmental Employees' Retirement System held in any bank of the State shall be safeguarded by a fidelity and surety bond, the amount to be determined by the Board of Trustees.

(f)   Immunity of Funds. - Except as otherwise herein provided, no trustee and no employee of the Board of Trustees shall have any direct interest in the gains or profits of any investment made by the Board of Trustees, nor as such receive any pay or emolument for this service. No trustee or employee of the Board shall, directly or indirectly, for himself or as an agent in any manner use the same, except to make such current and necessary payments as are authorized by the Board of Trustees; nor shall any trustee or employee of the Board of Trustees become an endorser or surety or in any manner an obligor for moneys loaned or borrowed from the Board of Trustees. (1939, c. 390, s. 9; 1941, c. 357, s. 7; 1945, c. 526, s. 5; 1957, c. 846, s. 1; 1959, c. 1181, s. 1; 1961, c. 397; 1967, c. 978, s. 8; 1971, c. 386, s. 3; 1973, c. 243, s. 10; 1979, c. 467, ss. 12, 13.)

§ 128-29.1. Authority to invest in certain common and preferred stocks.

In addition to all other powers of investment, the Board of Trustees, within the limitations set forth in this section, is also authorized to invest Retirement System funds in stocks, preferred or common, issued or guaranteed by a corporation created or existing under the laws of the United States or any state, district, or territory thereof, provided:

(1)   That for a period of five fiscal years for which the necessary statistical data are available next preceding the date of investment, such corporation as disclosed by its published fiscal annual statements shall have had an average annual net income plus its average annual fixed charges (as herein used, fixed charges shall mean interest on funded or unfunded debt, contingent interest charges, amortization of debt discount and expense and rentals for leased property and, in the case of consolidated earnings statements of parent and subsidiary corporations shall include all fixed charges and preferred dividend requirement, if any, of the subsidiaries) at least equal to one and one-half times the sum of its average annual dividend requirement for preferred stock and its average annual fixed charges for the same period; however, during neither of the last two years of such period shall the sum of its annual net income and its annual fixed charges have been less than one and one-half times the sum of its dividend requirements for preferred stock and its fixed charges for the same period;

(2)   That such corporation shall have no arrears of dividends on its preferred stock;

(3)   That such common stock is registered on a national securities exchange as provided in the Federal Securities Exchange Act, but such registration shall not be required of the following stocks:

a.   The common stock of a bank which is a member of Federal Deposit Insurance Corporation and has capital funds, represented by capital, surplus and undivided profits, of at least twenty million dollars ($20,000,000);

23

b.   The common stock of a life insurance company which has capital funds represented by capital, special surplus funds and unassigned surplus, of at least fifty million dollars ($50,000,000);

c.   The common stock of a fire or casualty insurance company, or a combination thereof, which has capital funds represented by capital, net surplus and voluntary reserves, of at least fifty million dollars ($50,000,000);

(4)   That the preferred stock of such corporation, if any be outstanding, shall qualify for investment under this section;

(5)   That such corporation, having no preferred stock outstanding, shall have had earnings for the five fiscal years next preceding the date of investment of at least twice the interest on all mortgages, bonds, debentures, and funded debts, if any, after deduction of the proper charges for replacements, depreciation, and obsolescence;

(6)   That such corporation shall have paid a cash dividend on its common stock in each year of the 10-year period next preceding the date of investment and the aggregate net earnings available for dividends on the common stock of such corporation for the whole of such period shall have been at least equal to the amount of such dividends paid;

(7)   That in applying the earnings test under this section to any issuing, assuming, or guaranteeing corporation, where such corporation, shall have acquired its property or any substantial part thereof within a five-year period immediately preceding the date of investment by consolidation, merger, or by the purchase of all or a substantial portion of the property of any other corporation or corporations, or shall have acquired the assets of any unincorporated business enterprise by purchase or otherwise, net income, fixed charges and preferred dividends of the several predecessor or constituent corporations or enterprises shall be consolidated and adjusted so as to ascertain whether or not the applicable requirements of this section have been complied with;

(8)   That the total value of common and preferred stocks shall not exceed twenty-five per centum (25%) of the total value of all invested funds of the Retirement System; provided, further:

24

a.   Not more than one and one-half per centum (1 1/2%) of the total value of such funds shall be invested in the stock of a single corporation, and provided further;

b.   The total number of shares in a single corporation shall not exceed eight per centum (8%) of the issued and outstanding stock of such corporation, and provided further;

c.   As used in this subdivision (8), value shall consist of the par value or unpaid balance of all unmatured or unpaid investments requiring the payment of a fixed amount at payment date and the cost price of all other investments.

In order to carry out the duties and exercise the powers imposed and granted by this section, the chairman of the Board of Trustees is authorized to appoint an investment committee consisting of five members, three of whom shall be members of the Board of Trustees designated ex officio by the chairman and two of whom shall not be members of the Board. Such investment committee shall have such powers and duties as the Board of Trustees may prescribe. The members of the investment committee shall receive for their services the same per diem and other allowances as are granted the members of the State Boards and commissions generally. (1961, c. 626; 1965, c. 415, s. 2; 1973, c. 243, s. 10.)

§ 128-30. Method of financing.

(a)   Funds to Which Assets of Retirement System Credited. - All of the assets of the Retirement System shall be credited according to the purpose for which they are held to one of five funds, namely, the annuity savings fund, the annuity reserve fund, the pension accumulation fund, the pension reserve fund and the expense fund.

(b)   Annuity Savings Fund. - The annuity savings fund shall be a fund in which shall be accumulated contributions from the compensation of members to provide for their annuities. Contributions to and payments from the annuity savings fund shall be made as follows:

(1)   Prior to July 1, 1951, each participating employer shall cause to be deducted from the salary of each member of each and every payroll of such employer for each and every payroll period four per centum (4%) of his earnable

compensation. On and after such date the rate so deducted shall be five per centum (5%) in the case of a Class A member or a Class C member, and four per centum (4%) in the case of a Class B member; provided, however, that with respect to any member who is covered under the Social Security Act in accordance with the agreement entered into during 1955 in accordance with the provisions of Article 2 of Chapter 135 of Volume 17 of the General Statutes, as amended, such deduction shall, commencing with the first day of the period of service with respect to which such agreement is effective, be at the rate of three per centum (3%) of the part of his actual compensation not in excess of the amount taxable to him under the Federal Insurance Contributions Act as from time to time in effect plus five per centum (5%) of the part of his actual compensation not so taxable; provided that in the case of any member so eligible and receiving compensation from two or more employers such deductions may be adjusted under such rules as the Board of Trustees may establish so as to be as nearly equivalent as practicable to the deductions which would have been made had the member received all of such compensation from one employer. Notwithstanding the foregoing, the Board of Trustees may in its discretion cause such portion as it may determine of deductions made between January 1, 1955, and December 1, 1955, to be transferred into the contribution fund established under G.S. 135-24, such amounts so transferred shall in that event be deemed to be taxes contributed by employees as required under Article 2 of Chapter 135 of Volume 17 of the General Statutes, as amended, and shall be in lieu of contributions otherwise payable in the same amount as so required. In determining the amount earned by a member whose compensation is derived partly or wholly from fees, such member shall submit a sworn statement to his employer monthly, or at least quarterly, each year as to the amount of fees received by such member as compensation during the period, and each month, or at least quarterly, such member shall pay to his employer the proper per centum of such compensation received from fees, which shall be considered as deductions by the employer as provided in subdivisions (1) and (2) of this subsection.

Notwithstanding the foregoing, effective July 1, 1965, with respect to the period of service commencing on July 1, 1965, and ending December 31, 1965, the rates of such deductions shall be four per centum (4%) of the portion of compensation not in excess of forty-eight hundred dollars ($4,800) and six per centum (6%) of the portion of compensation in excess of forty-eight hundred dollars ($4,800); and with respect to the period of service commencing January 1, 1966, and ending June 30, 1967, the rate of such deduction shall be four per centum (4%) of the portion of compensation not in excess of fifty-six hundred dollars ($5,600) and six per centum (6%) of the portion of compensation in

26

excess of fifty-six hundred dollars ($5,600); and with respect to the period of service commencing July 1, 1967, and ending June 30, 1976, the rate of such deductions shall be five per centum (5%) of the portion of compensation not in excess of five thousand six hundred dollars ($5,600) and six per centum (6%) of the portion of compensation in excess of five thousand six hundred dollars ($5,600). Such rates shall apply uniformly to all members of the Retirement System, irrespective of class.

Notwithstanding the foregoing, effective July 1, 1976, with respect to compensation paid on and after July 1, 1976, the rate of such deductions shall be six per centum (6%) of the compensation received by any member. Such rates shall apply uniformly to all members of the Retirement System, irrespective of class.

(2) The deductions provided for herein shall be made notwithstanding that the minimum compensation provided for by law for any member shall be reduced thereby. Every member shall be deemed to consent and agree to the deductions made and provided for herein and shall receipt for his full salary or compensation, and payment of salary or compensation less said deduction shall be a full and complete discharge and acquittance of all claims and demands whatsoever for the services rendered by such person during the period covered by such payment, except as to the benefits provided under this Article. The employer shall certify to the Board of Trustees on each and every payroll or in such other manner as the Board of Trustees may prescribe, the amounts to be deducted; and each of said amounts shall be deducted, and when deducted shall be paid into said annuity savings fund, and shall be credited, together with regular interest thereon to the individual account of the member from whose compensation said deduction was made.

(3) The accumulated contributions of a member drawn by him, or paid to his estate or to his designated beneficiary in event of his death as provided in this Article, shall be paid from the annuity savings fund. Upon the retirement of a member his accumulated contributions shall be transferred from the annuity savings fund to the annuity reserve fund.

(4) The Board of Trustees may approve the purchase of creditable service by any member for leaves of absence or for interrupted service to an employer for the sole purpose of acquiring knowledge, talents, or abilities and to increase the efficiency of service to the employer. This approval shall be made prior to the purchase of the creditable service, is limited to a career total of four years for each member, and may be obtained in the following manner:

27

a.   Approved leave of absence. - Where the employer grants an approved leave of absence, a member may make monthly contributions to the annuity savings fund on the basis of compensation the member was earning immediately prior to such leave of absence. The employer shall make monthly contributions equal to the normal and accrued liability contribution on such compensation or, in lieu thereof, the member may pay into the annuity savings fund monthly an amount equal to the employer's normal and accrued liability contribution when the policy of the employer is not to make such payment.

b.   No educational leave policy. - Where the employer has a policy of not granting educational leaves of absence or the member has unsuccessfully petitioned for leave of absence and the member has interrupted service for educational purposes, the member may make monthly contributions into the annuity savings fund in an amount equal to the employee contribution plus the employer normal and accrued liability contribution on the basis of the compensation the member was earning immediately prior to the interrupted service.

c.   Educational program prior to July 1, 1981. - Creditable service for leaves of absence or interrupted service for educational purposes prior to July 1, 1981, may be purchased by a member, before or after retirement, who returned as a contributing employee or teacher within 12 months after completing the educational program and completed 10 years of subsequent membership service, by making a lump sum payment into the annuity savings fund equal to the full cost of the service credits calculated on the basis of the assumptions used for purposes of the actuarial valuation of the system's liabilities and shall take into account the retirement allowance arising on account of the additional service credit commencing at the earliest age at which the member could retire on an unreduced retirement allowance as determined by the board of trustees upon the advice of the consulting actuary, plus a fee to be determined by the board of trustees.

Payments required to be made by the member and/or the employer under subparagraphs a or b are due by the 15th of the month following the month for which the service credit is allowed and payments made after the due date shall be assessed a penalty, in lieu of interest, of one percent (1%) per month or fraction thereof the payment is made beyond the due date; provided, that these payments shall be made prior to retirement and provided further, that if the member did not become a contributing member within 12 months after completing the educational program and failed to complete three years of subsequent membership service, except in the event of death or disability, any

28

payment made by the member including penalty shall be refunded with regular interest thereon and the service credits cancelled prior to or at retirement.

(b1)   Pick Up of Employee Contributions. - Anything within this section to the contrary notwithstanding, effective July 1, 1982, an employer, pursuant to the provisions of section 414(h)(2) of the Internal Revenue Code of 1954 as amended, may elect to pick up and pay the contributions which would be payable by the employees as members under subsection (b) of this section with respect to the service of employees after June 30, 1982.

The members' contributions picked up by an employer shall be designated for all purposes of the Retirement System as member contributions, except for the determination of tax upon a distribution from the System. These contributions shall be credited to the annuity savings fund and accumulated within the fund in a member's account which shall be separately established for the purpose of accounting for picked-up contributions.

Member contributions picked up by an employer shall be payable from the same source of funds used for the payment of compensation to a member. A deduction shall be made from a member's compensation equal to the amount of his contributions picked up by his employer. This deduction, however, shall not reduce his compensation as defined in subdivision (7a) of G.S. 128-21. Picked-up contributions shall be transmitted to the System monthly for the preceding month by means of a warrant drawn by the employer and payable to the Local Governmental Employees' Retirement System and shall be accompanied by a schedule of the picked-up contributions on such forms as may be prescribed. In the case of a failure to fulfill these conditions the provisions of subsection (g)(3) of this section shall apply.

(b2)   Retroactive Adjustment in Compensation or an Underreporting of Compensation. - A member or beneficiary who is awarded backpay in cases of a denied promotional opportunity or wrongful demotion in which the aggrieved member or beneficiary is granted a promotion or a demotion is reversed retroactively, or in cases in which an employer errs in the reporting of compensation, including the employee and employer contributions, the member or beneficiary and employer may make employee and employer contributions on the retroactive or additional compensation after submitting clear and convincing evidence of the retroactive promotion or underreporting of compensation, as follows:

29

(1)   Within 90 days of the denial of the promotion or the error in reporting, by the payment of employee and employer contributions that would have been paid; or

(2)   After 90 days of the denial of the promotion or the error in reporting, by the payment of the employee and employer contributions that would have been paid plus interest compounded annually at a rate equal to the greater of the average yield on the pension accumulation fund for the preceding calendar year or the actuarial investment rate-of-return assumption, as adopted by the Board of Trustees.

For members or beneficiaries electing to make the employee contributions on the retroactive adjustment in compensation or on the underreported compensation, the member's or beneficiary's employer, which granted the retroactive promotion or erred in underreporting compensation and contributions, shall make the required employer contributions. Nothing contained in this subsection shall prevent an employer from paying all or a part of the interest assessed on the employee contributions; and to the extent paid by the employer, the interest paid by the employer shall be credited to the pension accumulation fund; provided, however, an employer does not discriminate against any member or beneficiary or group of members or beneficiaries in his employ in paying all or any part of the interest assessed on the employee contributions due.

In the event the retroactive adjustment in compensation or the underreported compensation is for a period that occurs during the four consecutive calendar years that would have produced the highest average annual compensation pursuant to G.S. 135-1(5), the compensation the member or beneficiary would have received during the period shall be included in calculating the member's or beneficiary's average final compensation only in the event the appropriate employee and employer contributions are paid on such compensation.

An employer error in underreporting compensation shall not include a retroactive increase in compensation that occurs during the four consecutive calendar years that would have produced the highest average annual compensation pursuant to G.S. 135-1(5), for reasons other than a wrongfully denied promotional opportunity or wrongful demotion where the member is promoted or the demotion is reversed retroactively.

(c)   Annuity Reserve Fund. - The annuity reserve fund shall be the fund in which shall be held the reserves on all annuities in force and from which shall be paid all annuities and all benefits in lieu of annuities, payable as provided in this Article. Should a beneficiary retired on account of disability be restored to active service with a compensation not less than his average final compensation at the time of his last retirement his annuity reserve shall be transferred from the annuity reserve fund to the annuity savings fund and credited to his individual account therein.

(d)   Pension Accumulation Fund. - The pension accumulation fund shall be the fund in which shall be accumulated all reserves for the payment of all pensions and other benefits payable from contributions made by employers and from which shall be paid all pensions and other benefits on account of members with prior service credit. Contributions to and payments from the pension accumulation fund shall be made as follows:

(1)   Each participating employer shall pay to the pension accumulation fund monthly, or at such other intervals as may be agreed upon with the Board of Trustees, an amount equal to a certain percentage of the actual compensation of each member, to be known as the "normal contribution" and an additional amount equal to a percentage of his actual compensation to be known as the "accrued liability contribution." The rate per centum of such contributions shall be fixed on the basis of the liabilities of the Retirement System as shown by actuarial valuation. Until the first valuation for any employer whose participation commenced prior to July 1, 1951, the normal contribution shall be three percent (3%) for general employees and five percent (5%) for firemen and policemen, and the accrued liability contribution shall be three percent (3%) for general employees and six percent (6%) for firemen and policemen. Until the first valuation for any employer whose participation commenced on or after July 1, 1951, the normal contribution shall be four percent (4%) for general employees and six and two-thirds percent (6 2/3%) for firemen and policemen, and the accrued liability contribution shall be four percent (4%) for general employees and eight percent (8%) for firemen and policemen.

(2)   On the basis of regular interest and of such mortality and other tables as shall be adopted by the Board of Trustees, the actuary engaged by the Board to make each valuation required by this Article during the period over which the accrued liability contribution is payable, immediately after making such valuation, shall determine the uniform and constant percentage of the actual compensation of the average new entrant throughout his entire period of active service which would be sufficient to provide for the payment of any pension payable on his account and for the pro rata share of the cost of administration of the Retirement System. The rate per centum so determined shall be known as

the "normal contribution" rate. After the accrued liability contribution has ceased to be payable, the normal contribution rate shall be the rate per centum of the earnable salary of all members obtained by deducting from the total liabilities of the pension accumulation fund the amount of the funds in hand to the credit of that fund and dividing the remainder by one per centum (1%) of the present value of the prospective future salaries of all members as computed on the basis of the mortality and service tables adopted by the Board of Trustees and regular interest. The normal rate of contribution shall be determined by the actuary after each valuation. A normal contribution rate shall be determined separately for general employees as a group and for law enforcement officers as a group, these rates to be applied to the respective group payrolls of each employer in determining the normal contribution required of each employer.

(3)   The "accrued liability contribution" shall be set for each employer on the basis of the prior service credits allowable to the employees thereof, who are entitled to prior service certificates, and shall be paid for a period of approximately 30 years, provided that the length of the period of payment for each employer after contributions begin shall be determined by the Board of Trustees as the result of actuarial valuations.

(4)   At the end of the first year following the date of participation for each employer, the accrued liability payable by such employer shall be set, by deducting from the present value of the total liability for all pensions payable on account of all members and pensioners of the System who became participants through service for such employer, the present value of the future normal contributions payable, and the amount of any assets resulting from any contributions previously made by such employer. Then the "accrued liability contribution" rate for such employer shall be the per centum of the total annual compensation of all members employed by such employer which is equivalent to four per centum (4%) of the amount of such accrued liability. The expense of making such actuarial valuation to determine the accrued liability contribution for each employer shall be paid by such employer. The accrued liability contribution rate shall be increased on the basis of subsequent valuation if benefits are increased over those included in the valuations on the basis of which the original accrued liability contribution rate was determined.

(5)   The total amount payable in each year to the pension accumulation fund shall not be less than the sum of the rate per centum known as the normal contribution rate and the accrued liability contribution rate of the total earned compensation of all members during the preceding year: Provided, however, that the amount of each annual accrued liability contribution shall be at least

32

three per centum (3%) greater than the preceding annual accrued liability payment, and that the aggregate payment by employers shall be sufficient, when combined with the amount in the fund, to provide the pensions and other benefits payable out of the fund during the year then current.

(6)   The accrued liability contribution shall be discontinued as soon as the accumulated reserve in the pension accumulation fund shall equal the present value, as actuarlally computed and approved by the Board of Trustees, of the total liability of such fund less the present value, computed on the basis of the normal contribution rate then in force, of the prospective normal contributions to be received on account of all persons who are at that time members, as separately determined for general employees and law-enforcement officers.

(7)   All pensions, and benefits in lieu thereof, with the exception of those payable on account of members who received no prior service allowance, payable from contributions of employers, shall be paid from the pension accumulation fund.

(8)   Upon the retirement of a member not entitled to credit for prior service, an amount equal to his pension reserve shall be transferred from the pension accumulation fund to the pension reserve fund.

(9)   Notwithstanding the foregoing provisions of this subsection, beginning with the December 31, 1985 valuation, the actuary shall determine an additional "accrued liability contribution" on account of each employer's law enforcement officers. This contribution shall be that percentage of law enforcement officer compensation necessary to liquidate the "existing unfunded accrued liability" over a period of years to be determined by the Board of Trustees. The "existing unfunded accrued liability" for each employer shall be equal to the sum of two liabilities. The first is that portion of the unfunded accrued liability of the Law Enforcement Officers' Retirement System as of December 31, 1985, attributable to the accrued liability for each employer's law enforcement officers participating in that System, all based on actuarial assumptions and methods applicable to that System. The second is the accrued liability for additional benefits payable to each employer's law enforcement officers who are members of this Retirement System on December 31, 1985. The "accrued liability contribution" determined on the basis of this paragraph shall be added to that determined under subdivision (3) and shall be included in the total amount payable under subdivision (5).

(e)   Pension Reserve Fund. - The pension reserve fund shall be the fund in which shall be held the reserves of all pensions granted to members not entitled to credit for prior service and from which such pensions and benefits in lieu thereof shall be paid. Should such a beneficiary retired on account of disability be restored to active service with a compensation not less than his average final compensation at the time of his last retirement the pension thereon shall be transferred from the pension reserve fund to the pension accumulation fund. Should the pension of such disability beneficiary be reduced as a result of an increase in his earning capacity, the amount of the annual reduction in his pension shall be paid annually into the pension accumulation fund during the period of such reduction.

(f)   Expense Fund. - The expense fund shall be the fund from which the expenses of the administration of the Retirement System shall be paid, exclusive of amounts payable as retirement allowances and as other benefits provided herein. Contribution shall be made to the expense fund as follows:

(1)   The Board of Trustees shall determine annually the amount required to defray such administrative expenses for the ensuing fiscal year and shall adopt a budget in accordance therewith. The budget estimate of such expenses shall be paid to the expense fund from the pension accumulation fund.

(2)   For the purpose of organizing the Retirement System and establishing an office, the Board of Trustees may provide as a prerequisite to participation in the Retirement System that each participating employer or employee or both shall pay an additional contribution to the Retirement System for the expense fund not to exceed two dollars ($2.00) for each employee, such contribution of the employee to be credited to his individual account in the annuity savings fund at such later time as the Board of Trustees shall determine, and/or the Board of Trustees may borrow such amounts as may be necessary to organize and establish the Retirement System.

(g)   Collection of Contributions. -

(1)   The collection of members' contributions shall be as follows:

a.   Each employer shall cause to be deducted on each and every payroll of a member for each and every payroll subsequent to the date of participation in the Retirement System the contributions payable by such member as provided in this Article. Each employer shall certify to the treasurer of said employer on each and every payroll a statement as vouchers for the amount so deducted.

34

b.   The treasurer of each employer on the authority from the employer shall make deductions from salaries of members as provided in this Article and shall transmit monthly, or at such time as the Board of Trustees shall designate, the amount specified to be deducted, to the secretary-treasurer of the Board of Trustees. The secretary-treasurer of the Board of Trustees after making a record of all such receipts shall deposit them in a bank or banks selected by said Board of Trustees for use according to the provisions of this Article.

(2)   The collections of employers' contributions shall be made as follows: Upon the basis of each actuarial valuation provided herein the Board of Trustees shall annually prepare and certify to each employer a statement of the total amount necessary for the ensuing fiscal year to the pension accumulation fund as provided under subsection (d) of this section. Such employer contributions shall be transmitted to the secretary-treasurer of the Board of Trustees together with the employee deductions as provided under sub-subdivision b. of subdivision (1) of this subsection.

(3)   In the event the employee or employer contributions required under this section are not received by the date set by the Board of Trustees, the Board shall assess the employer with a penalty of 1% per month with a minimum penalty of twenty-five dollars ($25.00). If within 90 days after request therefor by the Board any employer shall not have provided the System with the records and other information required hereunder or if the full accrued amount of the contributions provided for under this section due from members employed by an employer or from an employer shall not have been received by the System from the chief fiscal officer of such employer within 30 days after the last due date as herein provided, then, notwithstanding anything herein or in the provisions of any other law to the contrary, upon notification by the Board to the State Treasurer as to the default of such employer as herein provided, any distributions which might otherwise be made to such employer, or the municipality or county of which such employer is an integral part, from any funds of the State or any funds collected by the State shall be withheld from such employer until notice from the Board to the State Treasurer that such employer is no longer in default.

(h)   Merger of Annuity Reserve Fund, and Pension Reserve Fund into Pension Accumulation Fund. - Notwithstanding the foregoing, effective at such date not later than December 31, 1959, as the Board of Trustees shall determine, the annuity reserve fund and the pension reserve fund shall be merged into and become a part of the pension accumulation fund, provided that such merger shall in no way adversely affect the rights of any members or

35

retired members of the System and further provided the Board of Trustees shall be and hereby is authorized to make such changes in the accounting methods and procedures of the System from time to time as, in its opinion, are in the interest of sound and proper administration of the System. (1939, c. 390, s. 10; 1941, c. 357, s. 8; 1943, c. 535; 1945, c. 526, s. 6; 1951, c. 274, ss. 7-9; 1955, c. 1153, s. 7; 1959, c. 491, s. 9; 1965, c. 781; 1967, c. 978, ss. 9, 10; 1971, c. 325, ss. 17-19; 1975, 2nd Sess., c. 983, ss. 129, 130; 1981, c. 1000, ss. 1, 3; 1981 (Reg. Sess., 1982), c. 1282, s. 9; 1985, c. 479, s. 196(p)-(r); c. 539, ss. 1, 2; 1991, c. 585, s. 2; 1995, c. 509, s. 68; 2003-359, s. 20; 2009-66, s. 7(b); 2010-72, s. 8(b); 2012-178, s. 3.)

§ 128-31. Exemptions from execution.

Except for the applications of the provisions of G.S. 110-136, and G.S. 110-136.3 et seq., and in connection with a court-ordered equitable distribution under G.S. 50-20, the right of a person to a pension, an annuity, or a retirement allowance, to the return of contributions, the pension, annuity or retirement allowance itself, any optional benefit or any other right accrued or accruing to any person under the provisions of this Article, and the moneys in the various funds created by this Article, are exempt from levy and sale, garnishment, attachment, or any other process whatsoever, and shall be unassignable except as in this Article specifically otherwise provided. Application for System approval of a domestic relations order dividing a person's interest under the Retirement System shall be accompanied by an order consistent with the system-designed template order provided on the System's Web site. Notwithstanding any provisions to the contrary, any overpayment of benefits to a member in a State-administered retirement system, the Disability Salary Continuation Plan, or the Disability Income Plan of North Carolina may be offset against any retirement allowance, return of contributions or any other right accruing under this Chapter to the same person, the person's estate, or designated beneficiary. (1939, c. 390, s. 11; 1985, c. 402; c. 649, s. 5; 1989, c. 665, s. 3; c. 792, s. 2.4; 2005-91, s. 11; 2013-405, s. 4(b).)

§ 128-32. Protection against fraud.

Any person who shall knowingly make any false statement or shall falsify or permit to be falsified any record or records of this Retirement System in any

36

attempt to defraud such System as a result of such act shall be guilty of a Class 1 misdemeanor. Should any change or error in the records result in any member or beneficiary receiving from the Retirement System more or less than he would have been entitled to receive had their records been correct, the Board of Trustees shall correct such error, and as far as practicable, shall adjust the payment in such a manner that the actuarial equivalent of the benefit to which such member or beneficiary was correctly entitled shall be paid. (1939, c. 390, s. 12; 1993, c. 539, s. 945; 1994, Ex. Sess., c. 24, s. 14(c).)

§ 128-32.1. Failure to respond.

If a member fails to respond within 120 days after preliminary option figures and the Form 6-E or Form 7-E are mailed, or if a member fails to respond within 120 days after the effective date of retirement, whichever is later, the Form 6 or Form 7 shall be null and void; the retirement system shall not be liable for any benefits due on account of the voided application, and a new application must be filed establishing a subsequent effective date of retirement. If an applicant for disability retirement fails to furnish requested additional medical information within 90 days following such request, the application shall be declared null and void under the same conditions outlined above, unless the applicant is eligible for early or service retirement in which case the application shall be processed accordingly, using the same effective date as would have been used had the application for disability retirement been approved. The Director of the Retirement Systems Division, acting on behalf of the Board of Trustees, may extend the 120-day limitation provided for in this section when a member has suffered incapacitation such that a reasonable person would not have expected the member to be able to complete the required paperwork within the regular deadline, or when an omission by the Retirement Systems Division prevents the member from having sufficient time to meet the regular deadline. (2005-91, s. 12; 2009-66, s. 4(a); 2010-72, s. 6(b).)

§ 128-33. Certain laws not applicable to members.

Subject to the provisions of Article 2 of Chapter 135 of Volume 3B of the General Statutes, as amended, no other provision of law in any other statute which provides wholly or partly at the expense of any county, city or town for pensions or retirement benefits for employees of the said county, city or town, their widows, or other dependents shall apply to members or beneficiaries of the Retirement System established by this Article. (1939, c. 390, s. 13; 1955, c. 1153, s. 8.)

§ 128-34. Transfer of members.

(a)   Any member of the North Carolina Governmental Employees' Retirement System who leaves the service of his employer and enters the service of another employer participating in the North Carolina Governmental Employees' Retirement System shall maintain his status as a member of the Retirement System and shall be credited with all of the amounts previously credited to his account in any of the funds under this Article, but the new employer shall be responsible for any accrued liability contribution payable on account of any prior service credit which such employee may have at the time of the transfer, and such employee shall be given such status and be credited with such service with the new employer as allowed with the former employer.

(b)   Any member of the Local Governmental Employees' Retirement System shall be entitled prior to his retirement to transfer to this Retirement System his credits for membership and prior service in the Teachers' and State Employees' Retirement System: Provided, the actual transfer of employment is made while he has an active account in the State System and such person shall request the State System to transfer his accumulated contributions, interest, and service credits to this Retirement System; provided further, the State System agrees to transfer to this Retirement System the amount of reserve held in the State System as the result of previous contributions of the employer on behalf of the transferring employee.

(c)   Any member whose services are terminated for any reason other than retirement or death who becomes employed by an employer participating in the Teachers' and State Employees' Retirement System shall be entitled to transfer to the State System his credits for membership and prior service in this Retirement System in accordance with G.S. 135-18.1: Provided, the actual transfer of employment is made while he has an active account in this Retirement System and such persons shall request this Retirement System to transfer his accumulated contributions, interest, and service credits to the State System. When such request is made by a member who is entitled to make it and who becomes a member of the State System after July 1, 1969, this Retirement System will also transfer to the State System the amount of reserve

38

held by this System as a result of previous contributions of the employer on behalf of the transferring employee.

(d)   The accumulated contributions and creditable service of any member whose service as an employee has been or is terminated other than by retirement or death and who, while still a member of this Retirement System, became or becomes a member, as defined in G.S. 135-53(11), of the Consolidated Judicial Retirement System for a period of five or more years may, upon application of the member, be transferred from this Retirement System to the Consolidated Judicial Retirement System. In order to effect the transfer of a member's creditable service from the Local Governmental Employees' Retirement System to the Consolidated Judicial Retirement System, there shall be transferred from the Local Governmental Employees' Retirement System to the Consolidated Judicial Retirement System the sum of (i) the accumulated contributions of the member credited in the annuity savings fund and (ii) the amount of reserve held in the Local Governmental Employees' Retirement System as a result of previous contributions by the employer on behalf of the transferring member. (1939, c. 390, s. 14; 1971, c. 325, s. 20; 1973, c. 242, s. 11; 1999-237, s. 28.24(a).)

§ 128-35. Obligations of pension accumulation fund.

The maintenance of annuity reserves and pension reserves as provided for, and regular interest creditable to the various funds as provided in G.S. 128-30, and the payment of all pensions, annuities, retirement allowances, refunds and other benefits granted under the provisions of this Article, are hereby made obligations of the pension accumulation fund. All income, interest and dividends derived from deposits and investments authorized by this Article shall be used for the payment of said obligations of the said fund. (1939, c. 390, s. 15.)

§ 128-36. Local laws unaffected; when benefits begin to accrue.

Nothing in this Article shall have the effect of repealing any public-local or private act creating or authorizing the creation of any officers' or employees' retirement system in any county, city or town or prohibiting the enactment of any public-local or private act creating or authorizing the creation of any officers' or employees' retirement system in any county, city, or town. No payment on account of any benefit granted under the provisions of G.S. 128-27, subsections (a) to (d) inclusive, shall become effective or begin to accrue until the end of one year following the date the System is established nor shall any compulsory retirement be made during that period. The provisions of this Article shall apply only to those counties, cities or towns whose governing authorities voluntarily elect to be bound by same. (1939, c. 390, s. 16; 1941, c. 357, s. 9B; 1945, c. 526, s. 7A.)

§ 128-36.1: Repealed by Session Laws 1977, c. 318.

§ 128-37. Membership of employees of district health departments or public health authorities.

Under such rules and regulations as the Board of Trustees shall establish and promulgate, the boards of county commissioners of any group of counties composing a district health department, or the governing board of any public health authority, or the board of county commissioners of any county as to county boards of health, or the governing authorities of any county and/or city as to city-county boards of health, may elect that employees of such health departments may be members of the North Carolina Local Governmental Employees' Retirement System to the extent of that part of their compensation paid by the various counties composing said district health department. (1949, c. 1012; 1951, c. 700; 1997-502, s. 4.)

§ 128-37.1. Membership of employees of county social services department.

Under such rules and regulations as the Board of Trustees shall establish and promulgate, the board of county commissioners of any county may elect that employees of the county social services department may be members of the North Carolina Local Governmental Employees' Retirement System; provided, that such membership may be elected jointly with such county health department employees as provided under G.S. 128-37. (1959, c. 1179; 1969, c. 982.)

§ 128-38. Reservation of power to change.

The General Assembly reserves the right at any time and from time to time, and if deemed necessary or appropriate by said General Assembly in order to coordinate with any changes in the benefit and other provisions of the Social Security Act made after January 1, 1955, to modify or amend in whole or in part any or all of the provisions of the North Carolina Local Governmental Employees' Retirement System. (1955, c. 1153, s. 9.)

§ 128-38.1. Termination or partial termination; discontinuance of contributions.

In the event of the termination or partial termination of the Retirement System or in the event of complete discontinuance of contributions under the Retirement System, the rights of all affected members to benefits accrued to the date of such termination, partial termination, or discontinuance, to the extent funded as of such date, or the amounts credited to the members' accounts, shall be nonforfeitable and fully vested. (1987, c. 177, s. 1(a), (b).)

§ 128-38.2. Internal Revenue Code compliance.

(a)   Notwithstanding any other provisions of law to the contrary, compensation for any calendar year after 1988 in which employee or employer contributions are made and for which annual compensation is used for computing any benefit under this Article shall not exceed the higher of two hundred thousand dollars ($200,000) or the amount determined by the Commissioner of Internal Revenue as the limitation for calendar years after 1989; provided the imposition of the limitation shall not reduce a member's benefit below the amount determined as of December 31, 1988.

Effective January 1, 1996, the annual compensation of a member taken into account for determining all benefits provided under this Article shall not exceed one hundred fifty thousand dollars ($150,000), as adjusted pursuant to section 401(a)(17)(B) of the Internal Revenue Code and any regulations issued under the Code. However, with respect to a person who became a member of the Retirement System prior to January 1, 1996, the imposition of this limitation on compensation shall not reduce the amount of compensation which may be taken into account for determining the benefits of that member under this Article

41

below the amount of compensation which would have been recognized under the provisions of this Article in effect on July 1, 1993.

Effective January 1, 2002, the annual compensation of a person, who became a member of the Retirement System on or after January 1, 1996, taken into account for determining all benefits accruing under this Article for any plan year after December 31, 2001, shall not exceed two hundred thousand dollars ($200,000) or the amount otherwise set by the Internal Revenue Code or determined by the Commissioner of Internal Revenue as the limitation for calendar years after 2002.

All the provisions in this subsection have been enacted to make clear that the Plan shall not base contributions or Plan benefits on annual compensation in excess of the limits prescribed by Section 401(a)(17) of the Internal Revenue Code, as adjusted from time to time, subject to certain federal grandfathering rules.

(b)   Notwithstanding any other provisions of law to the contrary, the annual benefit payable on behalf of a member shall, if necessary, be reduced to the extent required by Section 415(b) and with respect to calendar years commencing prior to January 1, 2000, Section 415(e) of the Internal Revenue Code, as adjusted by the Secretary of the Treasury or his delegate pursuant to Section 415(d) of the Code. If a member is a participant under any qualified defined contributions plan that is required to be taken into account for the purposes of the limitation contained in Section 415 of the Internal Revenue Code, the annual benefit payable under this Article shall be reduced to the extent required by Section 415(e) prior to making any reduction under the defined contribution plan provided by the employer. However, with respect to a member who has benefits accrued under this Article but whose benefit had not commenced as of December 31, 1999, the combined plan limitation contained in Section 415(e) of the Internal Revenue Code shall not be applied to such member for calendar years commencing on or after January 1, 2000.

(c)   On and after September 8, 2009, and for all Plan years to which the minimum distribution rules of the Internal Revenue Code are applicable, with respect to any member who has terminated employment, the Plan shall comply with federal income tax minimum distribution rules by applying a reasonable and good faith interpretation to Section 401(a)(9) of the Internal Revenue Code.

(d)   This subsection applies to distributions and rollovers from the Plan. The Plan does not have mandatory distributions within the meaning of Section

42

401(a)(31) of the Internal Revenue Code. With respect to distributions from the Plan and notwithstanding any other provision of the Plan to the contrary that would otherwise limit a distributee's election under this Article, a distributee (including, after December 31, 2006, a non-spouse beneficiary if that non-spouse beneficiary elects a direct rollover only to an inherited traditional or Roth IRA as permitted under applicable federal law) may elect, at the time and in the manner prescribed by the Plan administrator, to have any portion of an eligible rollover distribution paid directly to an eligible retirement plan specified by the distributee in a direct rollover. As used in this subsection, an "eligible retirement plan" means an individual retirement account described in Section 408(a) of the Code, an individual retirement annuity described in Section 408(b) of the Code, an annuity plan described in Section 403(a) of the Code, on and after January 1, 2009, a Roth IRA, or a qualified trust described in Section 401(a) of the Code, that accepts the distributee's eligible rollover distribution. Effective on and after January 1, 2002, an eligible retirement plan also means an annuity contract described in Section 403(b) of the Code and an eligible plan under Section 457(b) of the Code that is maintained by a state, political subdivision of a state, or any agency or instrumentality of a state or political subdivision of a state and which agrees to separately account for amounts transferred into that plan from this Plan. As used in this subsection, a "direct rollover" is a payment by the Plan to the eligible retirement plan specified by the distributee. Provided, an eligible rollover distribution is any distribution of all or any portion of the balance to the credit of the distributee, except that an eligible rollover distribution shall not include: any distribution that is one of a series of substantially equal periodic payments (not less frequently than annually) made for the life (or life expectancy) of the distributee or the joint lives (or joint life expectancies) of the distributee and the distributee's designated beneficiary, or for a specified period of 10 years or more; any distribution to the extent such distribution is required under section 401(a)(9) of the Code; and the portion of any distribution that is not includible in gross income (determined without regard to the exclusion for net realized appreciation with respect to employer securities). Effective as of January 1, 2002, and notwithstanding the exclusion of any after-tax portion from such a rollover distribution in the preceding sentence, a portion of a distribution shall not fail to be an eligible rollover distribution merely because the portion consists of after-tax employee contributions which are not includible in gross income. That portion may be transferred, pursuant to applicable federal law, to an individual retirement account or annuity described in Section 408(a) or (b) of the Code, to a qualified defined benefit plan, or to a qualified defined contribution plan described in Section 401(a), 403(a), or 403(b) of the Code that agrees to separately account for amounts so transferred, including separately accounting for the portion of such distribution which is includible in gross income

43

and the portion of such distribution which is not so includible. The definition of eligible retirement plan shall also apply in the case of a distribution to surviving spouse, or to a spouse or former spouse who is the alternate payee under a qualified domestic relations order, as defined in Section 414(p) of the Internal Revenue Code, or a court-ordered equitable distribution of marital property, as provided under G.S. 50-20.1. Effective on and after January 1, 2007, notwithstanding any other provision of this subsection, a nonspouse beneficiary of a deceased member may elect, at the time and in the manner prescribed by the administrator of the Board of Trustees of this Retirement System, to directly roll over any portion of the beneficiary's distribution from the Retirement System; however, such rollover shall conform with the provisions of section 402(c)(11) of the Code. (1989, c. 276, s. 2; 1993, c. 531, s. 4; 1995, c. 361, s. 3; 2002-71, s. 4; 2009-66, s. 1(d); 2012-130, s. 4(b).)

§ 128-38.3. Deduction for payments allowed.

(a)   Any beneficiary who is a member of a domiciled employees' or retirees' association that has at least 2,000 members, the majority of whom are active or retired employees of employers as defined in G.S. 128-21(11), may authorize, in writing, the periodic deduction from the beneficiary's retirement benefits a designated lump sum to be paid to the employees' or retirees' association. The authorization shall remain in effect until revoked by the beneficiary. A plan of deductions pursuant to this section shall become void if the employees' or retirees' association engages in collective bargaining with the State, any political subdivision of the State, or any local school administrative unit.

(b)   Any beneficiary eligible for coverage under the State Health Plan may also authorize, in writing, the monthly deduction from the beneficiary's retirement benefits of a designated lump sum to be paid to the State Health Plan for any dependent whom the beneficiary wishes to cover under the State Health Plan. In the event that the beneficiary's own State Health Plan coverage is contributory, in whole or in part, the beneficiary may also authorize a designated lump sum to be paid to the State Health Plan on behalf of the beneficiary. In addition, a beneficiary may similarly authorize the deduction for supplemental voluntary insurance benefits, provided that the deduction is authorized by the Department of State Treasurer and is payable to a company with which the Department of State Treasurer has or had an exclusive contractual relationship. Any such authorization shall remain in effect until revoked by the beneficiary. (2001-424, s. 32.31; 2002-126, s. 6.4(b); 2012-178, s. 4(b).)

44

§ 128-38.4. Forfeiture of retirement benefits for certain felonies committed while serving as elected government official.

(a)   Except as provided in G.S. 128-26(w), the Board of Trustees shall not pay any retirement benefits or allowances, except for a return of member contributions plus interest, to any member who is convicted of any felony under the federal laws listed in subsection (b) of this section or the laws of this State listed in subsection (c) of this section if all of the following apply:

(1)   The federal or State offense is committed while serving as an elected government official.

(2)   The conduct on which the federal or State offense is based is directly related to the member's service as an elected government official.

(b)   The federal offenses covered by this section are as follows:

(1)   A felony violation of 18 U.S.C. § 201 (Bribery of public officials and witnesses), 18 U.S.C. § 286 (Conspiracy to defraud the Government with respect to claims), 18 U.S.C. § 287 (False, fictitious or fraudulent claims), 18 U.S.C. § 371 (Conspiracy to commit offense or to defraud United States), 18 U.S.C. § 597 (Expenditures to influence voting), 18 U.S.C. § 599 (Promise of appointment by candidate), 18 U.S.C. § 606 (Intimidation to secure political contributions), 18 U.S.C. § 641 (Public money, property, or records), 18 U.S.C. § 666 (Embezzlement and theft), 18 U.S.C. § 1001 (Statements or entries generally), 18 U.S.C. § 1341 (Frauds and swindles), 18 U.S.C. § 1343 (Fraud by wire, radio, or television), 18 U.S.C. § 1503 (Influencing or injuring officer or juror generally), 18 U.S.C. § 1951 (Interference with commerce by threats or violence), 18 U.S.C. § 1952 (Interstate and foreign travel or transportation in aid of racketeering enterprises), 18 U.S.C. § 1956 (Laundering of monetary instruments), 18 U.S.C. § 1962 (Prohibited activities), or section 7201 of the Internal Revenue Code (Attempt to evade or defeat tax).

(2)   Reserved for future codification purposes.

(c)   The offenses under the laws of this State covered by this section are as follows:

(1)   A felony violation of Article 29, 30, or 30A of Chapter 14 of the General Statutes (Relating to bribery, obstructing justice, and secret listening) or G.S. 14-228 (Buying and selling offices), or Part 1 of Article 14 of Chapter 120 of the

45

General Statutes (Code of Legislative Ethics), Article 20 or 22 of Chapter 163 of the General Statutes (Relating to absentee ballots, corrupt practices and other offenses against the elective franchise, and regulating of contributions and expenditures in political campaigns).

(2)   Perjury or false information as follows:

a.   Perjury committed under G.S. 14-209 in falsely denying the commission of an act that constitutes an offense within the purview of an offense listed in subdivision (1) of subsection (c) of this section.

b.   Subornation of perjury committed under G.S. 14-210 in connection with the false denial of another as specified by subdivision (2) of this subsection.

c.   Perjury under Article 22A of Chapter 163 of the General Statutes.

(d)   All monies forfeited under this section shall be remitted to the Civil Penalty and Forfeiture Fund. (2007-179, s. 2(a).)

§ 128-38.4A. Forfeiture of retirement benefits for certain felonies related to employment or holding office.

(a)   Except as provided in G.S. 128-26(x), the Board of Trustees shall not pay any retirement benefits or allowances, except for a return of member contributions plus interest, to any member who is convicted of any felony under federal law or the laws of this State if all of the following apply:

(1)   The offense is committed while the member is in service.

(2)   The conduct resulting in the member's conviction is directly related to the member's office or employment.

(b)   Subdivision (2) of subsection (a) of this section shall apply to felony convictions where the court finds under G.S. 15A-1340.16(d)(9) or other applicable State or federal procedure that the member's conduct is directly related to the member's office or employment.

(c)   If a member or former member whose benefits under the System were forfeited under this section, except for the return of member contributions plus

46

interest, subsequently receives an unconditional pardon of innocence, or the conviction is vacated or set aside for any reason, then the member or former member may seek a reversal of the benefit forfeiture by presenting sufficient evidence to the State Treasurer. If the State Treasurer determines a reversal of the benefit forfeiture is appropriate, then all benefits will be restored upon repayment of all accumulated contributions plus interest. Repayment of all accumulated contributions that have been received by the individual under the forfeiture provisions of this section must be made in a total lump-sum payment with interest compounded annually at a rate of six and one-half percent (6.5%) for each calendar year from the year of forfeiture to the year of repayment. An individual receiving a reversal of benefit forfeiture must receive reinstatement of the service credit forfeited. (2012-193, s. 3.)

§ 128-38.5. Improper receipt of decedent's retirement allowance.

A person is guilty of a Class 1 misdemeanor if the person, with the intent to defraud, receives money as a result of cashing, depositing, or receiving a direct deposit of a decedent's retirement allowance and the person (i) knows that he or she is not entitled to the decedent's retirement allowance, (ii) receives the benefit at least two months after the date of the retiree's or beneficiary's death, and (iii) does not attempt to inform this Retirement System of the retiree's or beneficiary's death. (2011-232, s. 10(b); 2013-288, s. 9(c).)

§ 128-38.6. Employee protection and remedies against unlawful retaliation for furnishing information to the Retirement Systems Division.

(a)   In the absence of fraud or malice, no person who furnishes information to the staff of the Retirement Systems Division relating to the investigation of possible violations of retirement law shall be liable for damages in a civil action for any oral or written statement made or any other action that is necessary to supply such information to the Division.

(b)   Any employee of a participating local employer who is discharged, demoted, suspended, threatened, harassed, or in any other manner discriminated against in the terms and conditions of employment by the employee's employer because of lawful acts done by the employee in furtherance of the Retirement Systems Division's receipt of information

47

concerning possible violations of retirement law, including cooperation with the Division's investigation of possible violations, shall be entitled to all relief necessary to make the employee whole. Relief shall include reinstatement with the same seniority status as the employee would have had but for the discrimination or retaliation by the employing unit, two times the amount of back pay, interest on the back pay, and compensation for any special damages sustained as a result of the discrimination or retaliation, including litigation costs and reasonable attorneys' fees. An employee may bring an action in superior court for the relief provided in this section. (2012-185, s. 1.)

§ 128-38.7: Reserved for future codification purposes.

§ 128-38.8: Reserved for future codification purposes.

§ 128-38.9: Reserved for future codification purposes.

§ 128-38.10. Qualified Excess Benefit Arrangement.

(a)   The following words and phrases as used in this section, unless a different meaning is plainly required by the context, have the following meanings:

(1)   "Board of Trustees" means the Board of Trustees established by G.S. 128-28.

(2)   "Internal Revenue Code" means the Internal Revenue Code of 1986, as amended from time to time.

(3)   "Payee" means a retired member, or the survivor beneficiary of a member or retired member.

(4)   "Qualified Excess Benefit Arrangement" means the qualified excess benefit arrangement under section 415(m) of the Internal Revenue Code established under this Article.

(5)   "Retirement System" means the North Carolina Local Governmental Employees' Retirement System.

(b)   The Qualified Excess Benefit Arrangement (QEBA) is established effective January 1, 2014, and placed under the management of the Board of

48

Trustees. The purpose of the QEBA is solely to provide the part of a retirement allowance or benefit that would otherwise have been payable by the North Carolina Local Governmental Employees' Retirement System except for the limitations under section 415(b) of the Internal Revenue Code. The QEBA, as set forth in this section, is intended to constitute a qualified governmental excess benefit arrangement under section 415(m) of the Internal Revenue Code.

(c)   Eligibility to Participate in the QEBA. - Effective as of January 1, 2014, a payee shall participate in the QEBA for any calendar year, or portion of the calendar year, during which he or she receives a retirement allowance or benefit payment on and after January 1, 2014, from the North Carolina Local Governmental Employees' Retirement System that is reduced due to the application of the maximum benefit provisions of section 415(b) of the Internal Revenue Code. For purposes of the QEBA, a payee is a retired member or survivor beneficiary of a member or retired member who is receiving monthly retirement benefit payments from a Retirement System.

(d)   Supplemental Benefit Payable Under the QEBA. - Effective January 1, 2014, a payee shall receive each month, commencing on and after January 1, 2014, a monthly supplemental benefit equal to the difference between the amount of that payee's monthly retirement benefit paid under the North Carolina Local Governmental Employees' Retirement System on and after January 1, 2014, and the amount that would have been payable to that payee from the North Carolina Local Governmental Employees' Retirement System in that month if not for the reduction due to the application of section 415(b) of the Internal Revenue Code. That supplemental benefit shall be computed and payable under the same terms, at the same time, and to the same person as the related benefit payable under the Retirement System. A payee cannot elect to defer the receipt of all or any part of the supplemental payments due under the QEBA. The supplemental benefit paid under this section shall be taxable under North Carolina law in the same manner as the benefit paid under the North Carolina Local Governmental Employees' Retirement System.

(e)   Funding of the QEBA. - The QEBA shall be unfunded within the meaning of federal tax laws. No payee contributions or deferrals, direct or indirect, by election or otherwise shall be made or allowed. The Board of Trustees, upon the recommendation of the actuary engaged by the Board of Trustees, shall determine the employer contributions required to pay the benefits due under the QEBA for each fiscal year. The required contributions shall be paid by all participating employers. The required contributions shall be deposited in a separate fund from the fund into which regular employer contributions are deposited for the underlying Retirement System. The benefit liability for the QEBA shall be determined each fiscal year and assets shall not be accumulated to pay benefits in future fiscal years.

(f)   Treatment of Unused Assets. - Any assets of the QEBA plan not used to pay benefits in the current fiscal year shall be used for payment of the administrative expenses of the QEBA for the current or future fiscal years or shall be paid to the Retirement System as an additional employer contribution.

(g)   Assets Subject to Claims of Creditors. - A payee, or a payee's beneficiary or heirs, shall have no right to, and shall have no property interest in, any assets held to support the liabilities created under this section. To the extent that any person acquires the right to receive benefits under the QEBA, that right shall be no greater than the right of any unsecured general creditor of the State of North Carolina or such other applicable employer under this section.

(h)   Administration. - The QEBA shall be administered by the Board of Trustees, which shall compile and maintain all records necessary or appropriate for administration. The Board of Trustees shall have full discretionary authority to interpret, construe, and implement the QEBA and to adopt such rules and regulations as may be necessary or desirable to implement the provisions of the QEBA in accordance with section 415(m) of the Internal Revenue Code.

(i)   No Assignment. - Except for the application of the provisions of G.S. 110-136 and G.S. 110-136.3, et seq., or in connection with a court-ordered equitable distribution under G.S. 50-20, any supplemental benefit under this section shall be exempt from levy and sale, garnishment, attachment, or any other process, and shall be unassignable except as specifically otherwise provided in this section.

(j)   Reservation of Power to Change. - The General Assembly reserves the right at any time and, from time to time, to modify or amend, in whole or in part, any or all of the provisions of the QEBA. No member of the Retirement System and no beneficiary of such a member shall be deemed to have acquired any vested right to a supplemental payment under this section.

(k)   Sunset of Eligibility to Participate in the QEBA. - No member of the North Carolina Local Governmental Employees' Retirement System retiring on or after January 1, 2015, shall be eligible to participate in the QEBA, and the Retirement System shall not pay any new retiree more retirement benefits than allowed under the limitations of section 415(b) of the Internal Revenue Code. (2013-405, s. 3(b).)

Article 4.

Leaves of Absence.

§ 128-39. Leaves of absence for State officials for protracted illness or other reason.

Any elective or appointive State official may obtain leave of absence from the official's duties for protracted illness or other reason satisfactory to the Governor, for such period as the Governor may designate. The leave shall be obtained only upon application by the official and with the consent of the Governor. The official shall receive no salary during the period of leave unless the leave of absence is granted by reason of protracted illness, in which event the granting of a leave of absence shall not deprive the official of the benefits of cumulative sick leave to which the official may be entitled under rules and regulations adopted pursuant to G.S. 143-37 or to which he may otherwise be entitled by law. The period of leave may be extended upon application to and with the approval of the Governor if the reason for the original leave still exists, and it may be shortened if the reason shall unexpectedly terminate: Provided, that no leave or extension thereof shall operate to extend the term of office of any official beyond the period for which the official was elected or appointed. If, by reason of the length of the period of absence or the nature of the duties of the official, the Governor deems it necessary, the Governor may appoint any citizen of the State, without regard to residence or district, as a temporary replacement for the period of the official's leave of absence. This appointee shall have all the authority, duties, perquisites, and emoluments of the official temporarily replaced. The appointee shall possess all the qualifications required by law for holding the office for which the temporary replacement official is appointed. (1941, c. 121, s. 1; 2007-432, s. 1.)

§ 128-39.1. Leaves of absence for State officials for military or naval service.

(a)   Any elective or appointive State official may obtain leave of absence from the official's duties when the official enters active duty in the Armed Forces of the United States or the North Carolina National Guard as a result of being voluntarily or involuntarily activated, drafted, or otherwise called to duty. The official shall receive no salary during the period of leave. No vacancy is created by a State official obtaining a leave of absence under this section.

(b)   If the official will be on active duty for a period of at least 30 days, a leave of absence may be obtained, and a temporary replacement for the official may be appointed in the following manner:

(1)   If the official is not a member of the General Assembly:

a.   Leave of absence shall be obtained by filing a copy of the official's active duty orders with the Office of the Governor.

b.   G.S. 128-39 shall provide the procedure for selecting a temporary replacement official.

(2)   If the official is a member of the General Assembly:

a.   Leave of absence shall be obtained by filing a copy of the official's active duty orders with the clerk of the house of the General Assembly of which the official is a member.

b.   The Governor shall select a person to serve as the temporary replacement representative or senator. If the appropriate party executive committee recommends an eligible person within 14 days of the occurrence of the vacancy, the appointment shall be made under the same procedure as provided by G.S. 163-11. If a recommendation is not made on a timely basis, the Governor may appoint any person who is both:

1.   A resident of the legislative district represented by the legislator being temporarily replaced.

2.   A member of the same political party as the legislator being temporarily replaced.

In any case, the person appointed must be eligible to serve under Section 6 of Article II of the North Carolina Constitution if a senator or Section 7 of Article II of the North Carolina Constitution if a representative.

(c)   If the official will be on active duty for a period of less than 30 days, a temporary replacement official shall not be appointed, even if a leave of absence is obtained.

(d)   The Governor shall appoint the temporary replacement to begin service on the date specified in writing by the official being temporarily replaced as the date the official will enter active military service, or as soon as practicable thereafter. A temporary replacement official shall have all the authority, duties, perquisites, and emoluments of the official temporarily replaced.

(e)   The term of the temporary replacement official appointed under this section shall terminate as soon as any of the following occurs:

(1)   On the third day after the last day of active duty status of the official who is temporarily replaced.

(2)   The clerk of the appropriate house of the General Assembly receives written notice from the official who is temporarily replaced that the official is ready and able to resume the duties of his or her office.

(3)   The term of office of the official who is temporarily replaced expires. (2007-432, s. 2; 2011-183, s. 98.)

§ 128-40. Leaves of absence for county officials for protracted illness or other reason.

Any elective or appointive county official may obtain leave of absence from the official's duties for protracted illness or other reason satisfactory to the board of county commissioners of his county, for such period as the board of county commissioners may designate. The leave shall be obtained only upon application by the official and with the consent of the board of county commissioners. The official shall receive no salary during the period of leave unless the leave of absence is granted by reason of protracted illness, in which event the granting of a leave of absence shall not deprive the official of the benefits of any sick leave to which the official may be entitled by law. The period of leave may be extended upon application to and with the approval of the board of county commissioners if the reason for the original leave still exists, and it may be shortened if the reason shall unexpectedly terminate: Provided, that no leave or extension thereof shall operate to extend the term of office of any official beyond the period for which the official was elected or appointed. If, by reason of the length of the period of absence or the nature of the duties of the official, the board of county commissioners deems it necessary, the board may appoint any qualified citizen of the county as a temporary replacement for the period of the official's leave of absence. This appointee shall have all the authority, duties, perquisites, and emoluments of the official temporarily replaced. The appointee shall possess all the qualifications required by law for holding the office for which the temporary replacement official is appointed. (1941, c. 121, s. 2; 2007-432, s. 3.)

§ 128-41. Leaves of absence for municipal officials for protracted illness or other reason.

Any elective or appointive municipal official may obtain leave of absence from the official's duties for protracted illness or other reason satisfactory to the governing body of the municipality, for such period as the governing body may designate. The leave shall be obtained only upon application by the official and with the consent of the governing body. The official shall receive no salary during the period of leave unless the leave of absence is granted by reason of protracted illness, in which event the granting of a leave of absence shall not deprive the official of the benefits of any sick leave to which the official may be entitled by law. The period of leave may be extended upon application to and with the approval of the governing body of the municipality if the reason for the original leave still exists, and it may be shortened if the reason shall unexpectedly terminate: Provided, that no leave or extension thereof shall operate to extend the term of office of any official beyond the period for which the official was elected or appointed. If, by reason of the length of the period of absence or the nature of the duties of the official, the governing body deems it necessary, it may appoint any qualified citizen of the municipality as a temporary replacement for the period of the official's leave of absence. This appointee shall have all the authority, duties, perquisites, and emoluments of the official temporarily replaced. The appointee shall possess all the qualifications required by law for holding the office for which the temporary replacement official is appointed. (1941, c. 121, s. 3; 2007-432, s. 4.)

§ 128-42. Leaves of absence for county or municipal officials for military or naval service.

(a)   Any elective or appointive county or municipal official may obtain leave of absence from the official's duties when the official enters active duty in the Armed Forces of the United States or the North Carolina National Guard as a result of being voluntarily or involuntarily activated, drafted, or otherwise called to duty. The official shall receive no salary during the period of leave. No vacancy is created by a county or municipal official obtaining a leave of absence under this section.

(b)   If the official will be on active duty for a period of at least 30 days, a leave of absence may be obtained, and a temporary replacement for the official may be appointed in the following manner:

(1)   Leave of absence shall be obtained by placing a copy of the official's active duty orders with the clerk.

(2)   G.S. 128-41 shall govern the procedure for selecting a temporary replacement official if the official being temporarily replaced is a municipal official; otherwise, G.S. 128-40 shall govern.

(c)   If the official will be on active duty for a period of less than 30 days, a temporary replacement official shall not be appointed, even if a leave of absence is obtained.

(d)   The appropriate authority under G.S. 128-40 or G.S. 128-41 shall appoint the temporary replacement to begin service on the date specified in writing by the official being temporarily replaced as the date the official will enter active military service, or as soon as practicable thereafter. A temporary replacement official shall have all the authority, duties, perquisites, and emoluments of the official temporarily replaced. The appointee shall possess all the qualifications required by law for holding the office for which the temporary replacement official is appointed.

(e)   The term of the temporary replacement official appointed under this section shall terminate as soon as any of the following occurs:

(1)   On the third day after the last day of active duty status of the official who is temporarily replaced.

55

(2)   The clerk receives written notice from the official who is temporarily replaced that the official is ready and able to resume the duties of his or her office.

(3)   The term of office of the official who is temporarily replaced expires.

(f)   As used in this section, the term "clerk" means the city clerk as defined in G.S. 160A-171 if the official being temporarily replaced is a municipal official and means the clerk to the board of county commissioners as defined in G.S. 153A-1(2) if the official being temporarily replaced is a county official. (2007-432, s. 5; 2011-183, s. 99.)

Chapter 129.

Public Buildings and Grounds.

Article 1.

General Services Division.

§§ 129-1 through 129-3. Repealed by Session Laws 1971, c. 1097, s. 5.

§ 129-4. Transferred to G.S. 143-340 by Session Laws 1971, c. 1097, s. 2.

§ 129-5. Transferred to G.S. 143-341 by Session Laws 1971, c. 1097, s. 3.

§§ 129-6 through 129-9. Transferred to G.S. 143-345.1 to 143-345.4 by Session Laws 1971, c. 1097, s. 4.

§§ 129-10 through 129-11: Repealed by Session Laws 1971, c. 1097, s. 5.

Article 2.

Building Program.

§ 129-12: Transferred to G.S. 143-345.5 by Session Laws 1971, c. 1097, s. 4.

Article 2A.

State Legislative Building.

§ 129-12.1. Official name.

The building constructed under the direction of the State Legislative Building Commission in Raleigh, and which is used to house the legislative branch of the State government is officially designated as the State Legislative Building, and all references in publications issued by the State of North Carolina or any agency, department or institution thereof shall refer to the building as the State Legislative Building. (1963, c. 8.)

Article 3.

State Legislative Building Commission.

§§ 129-13 through 129-17. Repealed by Session Laws 1973, c. 99, s. 3.

Article 3.1.

Legislative Building Governing Commission.

§§ 129-17.1 through 129-17.5. Repealed by Session Laws 1973, c. 99, s. 4.

Article 4.

Heritage Square and Commission.

§§ 129-18 through 129-25. Repealed by Session Laws 1965, c. 1002, s. 1

Article 5.

State Capital Planning Commission.

§§ 129-26 to 129-30. Expired.

Article 6.

North Carolina Capital Planning Commission.

§§ 129-31 through 129-39. Repealed by Session Laws 1975, c. 879, s. 12.

Article 7.

North Carolina Capital Building Authority.

§ 129-40 through 129-49: Repealed by Session Laws 1987, c. 71, s. 2.

Article 8.

State Construction Finance Authority.

§§ 129-50 through 129-70. Repealed by Session Laws 1975, c. 879, s. 46.

Chapter 130.

Public Health.

§§ 130-1 through 130-285: Repealed.

Chapter 130A.

Public Health.

Article 1.

Definitions, General Provisions and Remedies.

Part 1. General Provisions.

§ 130A-1. Title.

This Chapter shall be known as the Public Health Law of North Carolina. (1983, c. 891, s. 2.)

§ 130A-1.1. Mission and essential services.

(a)   The General Assembly recognizes that unified purpose and direction of the public health system is necessary to ensure that all citizens in the State have equal access to essential public health services. The General Assembly declares that the mission of the public health system is to promote and contribute to the highest level of health possible for the people of North Carolina by:

(1)   Preventing health risks and disease;

(2)   Identifying and reducing health risks in the community;

(3)   Detecting, investigating, and preventing the spread of disease;

(4)   Promoting healthy lifestyles;

(5)   Promoting a safe and healthful environment;

(6)   Promoting the availability and accessibility of quality health care services through the private sector; and

(7)   Providing quality health care services when not otherwise available.

(b)   A local health department shall ensure that the following 10 essential public health services are available and accessible to the population in each county served by the local health department:

(1)   Monitoring health status to identify community health problems.

(2)   Diagnosing and investigating health hazards in the community.

(3)   Informing, educating, and empowering people about health issues.

(4)   Mobilizing community partnerships to identify and solve health problems.

(5)   Developing policies and plans that support individual and community health efforts.

(6)   Enforcing laws and regulations that protect health and ensure safety.

(7)   Linking people to needed personal health care services and ensuring the provision of health care when otherwise unavailable.

(8)   Ensuring a competent public health workforce and personal health care workforce.

(9)   Evaluating effectiveness, accessibility, and quality of personal and population-based health services.

(10)   Conducting research.

(c)   The General Assembly recognizes that there are health-related services currently provided by State and local government and the private sector that are important to maintaining a healthy social and ecological environment but that are not included on the list of essential public health services required under this section. Omission of these services from the list of essential public health services shall not be construed as an intent to prohibit or decrease their availability. Rather, such omission means only that the omitted services may be more appropriately assured by government agencies or private entities other than the public health system.

(d)   The list of essential public health services required by this section shall not be construed to limit or restrict the powers and duties of the Commission for Public Health or the Departments of Environment and Natural Resources and Health and Human Services as otherwise conferred by State law. (1991, c. 299, s. 1; 1997-443, s. 11A.54; 2007-182, s. 2; 2009-442, s. 1; 2012-126, s. 4; 2012-194, s. 62.)

§ 130A-2. Definitions.

The following definitions shall apply throughout this Chapter unless otherwise specified:

(1)   "Accreditation board" or "Board" means the Local Health Department Accreditation Board.

(1a)   "Commission" means the Commission for Public Health.

(1b)   "Communicable condition" means the state of being infected with a communicable agent but without symptoms.

(1c)   "Communicable disease" means an illness due to an infectious agent or its toxic products which is transmitted directly or indirectly to a person from an infected person or animal through the agency of an intermediate animal, host, or vector, or through the inanimate environment.

(2)   "Department" means the Department of Health and Human Services.

(3)   "Imminent hazard" means a situation that is likely to cause an immediate threat to human life, an immediate threat of serious physical injury, an immediate threat of serious adverse health effects, or a serious risk of irreparable damage to the environment if no immediate action is taken.

(3a)   "Isolation authority" means the authority to issue an order to limit the freedom of movement or action of persons or animals that are infected or reasonably suspected to be infected with a communicable disease or communicable condition for the period of communicability to prevent the direct or indirect conveyance of the infectious agent from the person or animal to other persons or animals who are susceptible or who may spread the agent to others.

(4)   "Local board of health" means a district board of health or a public health authority board or a county board of health.

(5)   "Local health department" means a district health department or a public health authority or a county health department.

(6)   "Local health director" means the administrative head of a local health department appointed pursuant to this Chapter.

61

(6a)   "Outbreak" means an occurrence of a case or cases of a disease in a locale in excess of the usual number of cases of the disease.

(7)   "Person" means an individual, corporation, company, association, partnership, unit of local government or other legal entity.

(7a)   "Quarantine authority" means the authority to issue an order to limit the freedom of movement or action of persons or animals which have been exposed to or are reasonably suspected of having been exposed to a communicable disease or communicable condition for a period of time as may be necessary to prevent the spread of that disease. Quarantine authority also means the authority to issue an order to limit access by any person or animal to an area or facility that may be contaminated with an infectious agent. The term also means the authority to issue an order to limit the freedom of movement or action of persons who have not received immunizations against a communicable disease when the State Health Director or a local health director determines that the immunizations are required to control an outbreak of that disease.

(8)   "Secretary" means the Secretary of Health and Human Services.

(9)   "Unit of local government" means a county, city, consolidated city-county, sanitary district or other local political subdivision, authority or agency of local government.

(10)   "Vital records" means birth, death, fetal death, marriage, annulment and divorce records registered under the provisions of Article 4 of this Chapter. (1957, c. 1357, s. 1; 1963, c. 492, ss. 5, 6; 1967, c. 343, s. 2; c. 1257, s. 1; 1973, c. 476, s. 128; 1975, c. 751, s. 1; 1981, c. 130, s. 1; c. 340, ss. 1-4; 1983, c. 891, s. 2; 1989, c. 727, s. 141; 1989 (Reg. Sess., 1990), c. 1004, s. 19(b); 1991, c. 631, s. 1; 1997-443, s. 11A.55; 1997-502, s. 2(a), (b); 2002-179, s. 4; 2004-80, s. 1; 2005-369, s. 1(a); 2007-182, s. 2.)

§ 130A-3. Appointment of the State Health Director.

The Secretary shall appoint the State Health Director. The State Health Director shall be a physician licensed to practice medicine in this State. The State Health Director shall perform duties and exercise authority assigned by the Secretary. (1983, c. 891, s. 2.)

§ 130A-4. Administration.

(a)   Except as provided in subsection (c) of this section, the Secretary shall administer and enforce the provisions of this Chapter and the rules of the Commission. A local health director shall administer the programs of the local health department and enforce the rules of the local board of health.

(b)   When requested by the Secretary, a local health department shall enforce the rules of the Commission under the supervision of the Department. The local health department shall utilize local staff authorized by the Department to enforce the specific rules.

(c)   The Secretary of Environment and Natural Resources shall administer and enforce the provisions of Articles 9 and 10 of this Chapter and the rules of the Commission.

(d)   When requested by the Secretary of Environment and Natural Resources, a local health department shall enforce the rules of the Commission and the rules adopted by the Environmental Management Commission pursuant to G.S. 87-87 under the supervision of the Department of Environment and Natural Resources. The local health department shall utilize local staff authorized by the Department of Environment and Natural Resources to enforce the specific rules. (1983, c. 891, s. 2; 1995, c. 123, s. 2; 1997-443, s. 11A.56; 2001-474, s. 18; 2006-202, s. 5; 2006-255, s. 13.1; 2011-145, s. 13.3(pp).)

§ 130A-4.1. State funds for maternal and child health care/nonsupplanting.

(a)   The Department shall ensure that local health departments do not reduce county appropriations for maternal and child health services provided by the local health departments because they have received State appropriations for this purpose.

(b)   All income earned by local health departments for maternal and child health programs supported in whole or in part from State or federal funds, received from the Department, shall be budgeted and expended by local health departments to further the objectives of the program that generated the income. (1991, c. 689, s. 170; 1997-443, s. 11A.57.)

§ 130A-4.2. State funds for health promotion/nonsupplanting.

The Department shall ensure that local health departments do not reduce county appropriations for health promotion services provided by the local health departments because they have received State appropriations for this purpose. (1991, c. 689, s. 171; 1997-443, s. 11A.58.)

§ 130A-5. Duties of the Secretary.

The Secretary shall have the authority:

(1)   To enforce the State health laws and the rules of the Commission;

(2)   To investigate the causes of epidemics and of infectious, communicable and other diseases affecting the public health in order to control and prevent these diseases; to provide, under the rules of the Commission, for the prevention, detection, reporting and control of communicable, infectious or any other diseases or health hazards considered harmful to the public health;

(3)   To develop and carry out reasonable health programs that may be necessary for the protection and promotion of the public health and the control of diseases. The Commission is authorized to adopt rules to carry out these programs;

(4)   To make sanitary and health investigations and inspections;

(5)   To investigate occupational health hazards and occupational diseases and to make recommendations for the elimination of the hazards and diseases. The Secretary shall work with the Industrial Commission and shall file sufficient reports with the Industrial Commission to enable it to carry out all of the provisions of the Workers' Compensation Act with respect to occupational disease.

(6)   To receive donations of money, securities, equipment, supplies, realty or any other property of any kind or description which shall be used by the Department for the purpose of carrying out its public health programs;

64

(7)   To acquire by purchase, devise or otherwise in the name of the Department equipment, supplies and other property, real or personal, necessary to carry out the public health programs;

(8)   To use the official seal of the Department. Copies of documents in the possession of the Department may be authenticated with the seal of the Department, attested by the signature or a facsimile of the signature of the Secretary, and when authenticated shall have the same evidentiary value as the originals;

(9)   To disseminate information to the general public on all matters pertaining to public health; to purchase, print, publish, and distribute free, or at cost, documents, reports, bulletins and health informational materials. Money collected from the distribution of these materials shall remain in the Department to be used to replace the materials;

(10)   To be the health advisor of the State and to advise State officials in regard to the location, sanitary construction and health management of all State institutions; to direct the attention of the State to health matters which affect the industries, property, health and lives of the people of the State; to inspect at least annually State institutions and facilities; to make a report as to the health conditions of these institutions or facilities with suggestions and recommendations to the appropriate State agencies. It shall be the duty of the persons in immediate charge of these institutions or facilities to furnish all assistance necessary for a thorough inspection;

(11)   To establish a schedule of fees based on income to be paid by a recipient for services provided by Migrant Health Clinics and Development Evaluation Centers;

(12)   To establish fees for the sale of specimen containers, vaccines and other biologicals. The fees shall not exceed the actual cost of such items, plus transportation costs;

(13)   To establish a fee to cover costs of responding to requests by employers for industrial hygiene consultation services and occupational consultation services. The fee shall not exceed two hundred dollars ($200.00) per on site inspection; and

65

(14)   To establish a fee for companion animal certificate of examination forms to be distributed, upon request, by the Department to licensed veterinarians. The fee shall not exceed the cost of the form and shipping costs.

(15)   To establish a fee not to exceed the cost of analyzing clinical Pap smear specimens sent to the State Laboratory by local health departments and State-owned facilities and for reporting the results of the analysis. This fee shall be in addition to the charge for the Pap smear test kit.

(16)   To charge a fee of up to fifty-five dollars ($55.00) for analyzing private well-water samples sent to the State Laboratory of Public Health by local health departments. The fee shall be imposed only for analyzing samples from newly constructed wells. The fee shall be computed annually by the Director of the State Laboratory of Public Health by analyzing the previous year's testing at the State Laboratory of Public Health, and applying the amount of the total cost of the private well-water testing, minus State appropriations that support this effort. The fee includes the charge for the private well-water panel test kit. (1957, c. 1357, s. 1; 1961, c. 51, s. 4; c. 833, s. 14; 1969, c. 982; 1973, c. 476, ss. 128, 138; 1979, c. 714, s. 2; 1981, c. 562, s. 4; 1983, c. 891, s. 2; 1985, c. 470, s. 1; 1991, c. 227, s. 1; 1993 (Reg. Sess., 1994), c. 715, s. 1; 2003-284, s. 34.13(a); 2006-66, s. 10.20(a); 2007-115, s. 2.)

§ 130A-5.1. State health standards.

(a)   The Secretary shall adopt measurable standards and goals for community health against which the State's actions to improve the health status of its citizens will be measured. The Secretary shall report annually to the General Assembly upon its convening or reconvening and to the Governor on all of the following:

(1)   How the State compares to national health measurements and established State goals for each standard. Comparisons shall be reported using disaggregated data for health standards.

(2)   Steps taken by State and non-State entities to meet established goals.

(3)   Additional steps proposed or planned to be taken to achieve established goals.

(b)   The Secretary may coordinate and contract with other entities to assist in the establishment of standards and preparation of the report. The Secretary may use resources available to implement this section. (2000-67, s. 11.)

§ 130A-6. Delegation of authority.

Whenever authority is granted by this Chapter upon a public official, the authority may be delegated to another person authorized by the public official. (1983, c. 891, s. 2.)

§ 130A-7. Grants-in-aid.

The State is authorized to accept, allocate and expend any grants-in-aid for public health purposes which may be made available to the State by the federal government. This Chapter is to be liberally construed in order that the State and its citizens may benefit fully from these grants-in-aid. The Commission is authorized to adopt rules, not inconsistent with the laws of this State, as required by the federal government for receipt of federal funds. Any federal funds received are to be deposited with the State Treasurer and are to be appropriated by the General Assembly for the public health purposes specified. (1957, c. 1357, s. 1; 1983, c. 891, s. 2.)

§ 130A-8. Counties to recover indirect costs on certain federal public health or mental health grants.

(a)   The Department shall include in its request for federal funds applicable to public health or mental health grants from the federal government to the State or any of its agencies, indirect costs incurred by counties acting as subgrantees under the grants or otherwise providing services to the Department with regard to the grants to the full extent permitted by OMB Circular A-87 or its successor. The Department shall allow counties to claim and recover their indirect costs on these grants to the full extent permitted by the Circular.

(b)   This section shall not apply to those federal public health or mental health grants which are formula grants to the State or which are otherwise

67

limited as to the maximum amounts receivable on a statewide basis. (1977, c. 876, ss. 1, 2; 1983, c. 891, s. 2.)

§ 130A-9. Standards.

The Commission is authorized to establish reasonable standards governing the nature and scope of public health services rendered by local health departments. (1957, c. 1357, s. 1; 1973, c. 110; 1975, c. 83; 1979, c. 504, s. 15; 1983, c. 891, s. 2.)

§ 130A-10. Advisory Committees.

The Secretary is authorized to establish and appoint as many special advisory committees as may be necessary to advise and confer with the Department concerning the public health. Members of any special advisory committee shall serve without compensation but may be allowed travel and subsistence expenses in accordance with G.S. 138-6. (1957, c. 1357, s. 1; 1975, c. 281; 1983, c. 891, s. 2.)

§ 130A-11. Residencies in public health.

The Department shall establish a residency program designed to attract dentists into the field of public health and to train them in the specialty of public health practice. The program shall include practical experience in public health principles and practices. (1975, c. 945, s. 1; 1983, c. 891, s. 2; 1991, c. 342, s. 6.)

§ 130A-12. Confidentiality of records.

All records containing privileged patient medical information, information protected under 45 Code of Federal Regulations Parts 160 and 164, and information collected under the authority of Part 4 of Article 5 of this Chapter that are in the possession of the Department of Health and Human Services or local health departments shall be confidential and shall not be public records pursuant to G.S. 132-1. Notwithstanding G.S. 8-53, the information contained in the records may be disclosed for purposes of treatment, payment, research, or health care operations to the extent that disclosure is permitted under 45 Code of Federal Regulations §§ 164.506 and 164.512(i). For purposes of this section, the terms "treatment," "payment," "research," and "health care operations" have the meanings given those terms in 45 Code of Federal Regulations § 164.501. (1985, c. 470, s. 2; 1991 (Reg. Sess., 1992), c. 890, s. 9; 1995, c. 428, s. 1.1; 2004-80, s. 4; 2006-255, s. 13.2; 2011-145, s. 13.3(qq); 2011-314, s. 3.)

§ 130A-13. Application for eligibility for Department medical payment program constitutes assignment to the State of right to third party benefits.

(a)   Notwithstanding any other provisions of law, by applying for financial eligibility for any Department medical payment program administered under this Chapter, the recipient patient or responsible party for the recipient patient shall be deemed to have made an assignment to the State of the right to third party benefits, contractual or otherwise, to which he may be entitled to the extent of the amount of the Department's payment on behalf of the recipient patient. Any attorney retained by the recipient patient shall be compensated for his services in accordance with the following schedule and in the following order of priority from any amount of such third party benefits obtained on behalf of the recipient by settlement, with judgment against, or otherwise from a third party:

(1)   First to the payment of any court costs taxed by the judgment;

(2)   Second to the payment of the fee of the attorney representing the beneficiary making the settlement or obtaining the judgment, but this fee shall not exceed one-third of the amount obtained or recovered to which the right of subrogation applies;

(3)   Third to the payment of the amount of assistance received by the beneficiary as prorated with other claims against the amount obtained or received from the third party to which the right of subrogation applies, but the amount shall not exceed one-third of the amount obtained or recovered to which the right of subrogation applies; and

(4)   Fourth to the payment of any amount remaining to the beneficiary or his personal representative.

The United States and the State of North Carolina shall be entitled to shares in each net recovery under this section. Their shares shall be promptly paid under this section and their proportionate parts of such sum shall be determined in accordance with the matching formulas in use during the period for which assistance was paid to the recipient.

(b)   The Department shall establish a third party resources collection unit that is adequate to ensure collection of third party resources.

(c)   The Commission may adopt rules necessary to implement this section.

(d)   Notwithstanding any other law to the contrary, in all actions brought by the State pursuant to subsection (a) of this section to obtain reimbursement for payments for medical services, liability shall be determined on the basis of the same laws and standards, including bases for liability and applicable defenses, as would be applicable if the action were brought by the individual on whose behalf the medical services were rendered. (1989, c. 483, s. 1; 1995, c. 508, s. 1.)

§ 130A-14. Department may assist private nonprofit foundations.

(a)   The Secretary may allow employees of the Department to assist any private nonprofit foundation that works directly with services or programs of the Department and whose sole purpose is to support the services and programs of the Department, and may provide other appropriate services to any such foundation. No employee of the Department may work with a foundation for more than 20 hours in any one month. Chapter 150B of the General Statutes does not apply to any assistance or services provided to a private nonprofit foundation pursuant to this section.

(b)   The board of directors of any private nonprofit foundation that receives assistance or services pursuant to this section shall secure and pay for the services of the Department of State Auditor or shall employ a certified public accountant to conduct an annual audit of the financial accounts of the foundation. The board of directors of the foundation shall transmit a copy of the annual financial audit report to the Secretary. (1991, c. 761, s. 37.3; 1993, c. 553, s. 40.1)

§ 130A-15. Access to information.

(a)   Health care providers and persons in charge of health care facilities or laboratories shall, upon request and proper identification, permit the State Health Director to examine, review, and obtain a copy of records containing privileged medical information or information protected under the Health Information Portability and Accountability Act (HIPAA) medical privacy rule, 45 C.F.R. Parts 160 and 164, that the State Health Director deems are necessary to prevent, control, or investigate a disease or health hazard that may present a clear danger to the public health.

(b)   Privileged medical information or protected health information received by the State Health Director pursuant to this section shall be confidential and is not a public record under G.S. 132-1. The information shall not be released, except when the release is made pursuant to any other provision of law, to another federal, state, or local public health agency for the purpose of preventing or controlling a disease or public health hazard or to a court or law enforcement official or law enforcement officer for the purpose of enforcing the provisions of this Chapter or for the purpose of investigating a disease or public health hazard.

(c)   A person who permits examination, review, or copying of records or who provides copies of the records pursuant to subsection (a) of this section is immune from any civil or criminal liability that might otherwise be incurred or imposed. (2007-115, s. 1.)

§ 130A-16. Collection and reporting of race and ethnicity data.

All medical care providers required by the provisions of this Chapter to report to the Division of Public Health shall collect and document patient self-reported race and ethnicity data and shall include such data in their reports to the Division. (2008-119, s. 1.)

Part 2. Remedies.

§ 130A-17. Right of entry.

71

(a)   The Secretary and a local health director shall have the right of entry upon the premises of any place where entry is necessary to enforce the provisions of this Chapter or the rules adopted by the Commission or a local board of health. If consent for entry is not obtained, an administrative search and inspection warrant shall be obtained pursuant to G.S. 15-27.2. However, if an imminent hazard exists, no warrant is required for entry upon the premises.

(b)   The Secretary of Environment and Natural Resources and a local health director shall have the same rights enumerated in subsection (a) of this section to enforce the provisions of Articles 9 and 10 of this Chapter. (1983, c. 891, s. 2; 1997-443, s. 11A.60; 2001-474, s. 19; 2006-255, s. 13.3; 2011-145, s. 13.3(rr).)

§ 130A-18. Injunction.

(a)   If a person shall violate any provision of this Chapter, the rules adopted by the Commission or rules adopted by a local board of health, or a condition or term of a permit or order issued under this Chapter, the Secretary or a local health director may institute an action for injunctive relief, irrespective of all other remedies at law, in the superior court of the county where the violation occurred or where a defendant resides.

(b)   The Secretary of Environment and Natural Resources and a local health director shall have the same rights enumerated in subsection (a) of this section to enforce the provisions of Articles 9 and 10 of this Chapter. (1983, c. 891, s. 2; 1997-443, s. 11A.61; 2001-474, s. 20; 2006-255, s. 13.4; 2007-550, s. 2(a); 2011-145, s. 13.3(ss).)

§ 130A-19. Abatement of public health nuisance.

(a)   If the Secretary or a local health director determines that a public health nuisance exists, the Secretary or a local health director may issue an order of abatement directing the owner, lessee, operator or other person in control of the property to take any action necessary to abate the public health nuisance. If the person refuses to comply with the order, the Secretary or the local health director may institute an action in the superior court of the county where the public health nuisance exists to enforce the order. The action shall be calendared for trial within 60 days after service of the complaint upon the defendant. The court may order the owner to abate the nuisance or direct the Secretary or the local health director to abate the nuisance. If the Secretary or the local health director is ordered to abate the nuisance, the Department or the local health department shall have a lien on the property for the costs of the abatement of the nuisance in the nature of a mechanic's and materialmen's lien as provided in Chapter 44A of the General Statutes and the lien may be enforced as provided therein.

(b)   The Secretary of Environment and Natural Resources and a local health director shall have the same rights enumerated in subsection (a) of this section to enforce the provisions of Articles 9 and 10 of this Chapter. (1893, c. 214, s. 22; Rev., ss. 3446, 4450; 1911, c. 62, ss. 12, 13; 1913, c. 181, s. 3; C.S., ss. 7071, 7072; 1957, c. 1357, s. 1; 1983, c. 891, s. 2; 1997-443, s. 11A.62; 2006-255, s. 13.5; 2011-145, s. 13.3(tt).)

§ 130A-20. Abatement of an imminent hazard.

(a)   If the Secretary or a local health director determines that an imminent hazard exists, the Secretary or a local health director may order the owner, lessee, operator, or other person in control of the property to abate the imminent hazard or may, after notice to or reasonable attempt to notify the owner, lessee, operator, or other person in control of the property enter upon any property and take any action necessary to abate the imminent hazard. If the Secretary or a local health director abates the imminent hazard, the Department or the local health department shall have a lien on the property of the owner, lessee, operator, or other person in control of the property where the imminent hazard existed for the cost of the abatement of the imminent hazard. The lien may be enforced in accordance with procedures provided in Chapter 44A of the General Statutes. The lien may be defeated by a showing that an imminent hazard did not exist at the time the Secretary or the local health director took the action. The owner, lessee, operator, or any other person against whose property the lien has been filed may defeat the lien by showing that that person was not culpable in the creation of the imminent hazard.

(b)   The Secretary of Environment and Natural Resources and a local health director shall have the same rights enumerated in subsection (a) of this section to enforce the provisions of Articles 9 and 10 of this Chapter. (1893, c. 214, s. 22; Rev., ss. 3446, 4450; 1911, c. 62, ss. 12, 13; 1913, c. 181, s. 3; C.S., ss.

73

7071, 7072; 1957, c. 1357, s. 1; 1983, c. 891, s. 2; 1997-443, s. 11A.63; 2002-179, s. 6; 2006-255, s. 13.6; 2011-145, s. 13.3(uu).)

§ 130A-20.01. Action for the recovery of costs of hazardous materials emergency medical response.

A person who causes the release of a hazardous material that results in the activation of one or more State Medical Assistance Teams (SMATs) or the Epidemiology Section of the Division of Public Health of the Department of Health and Human Services shall be liable for all reasonable costs incurred by each team or the Epidemiology Section that responds to or mitigates the incident. The Secretary of Health and Human Services shall invoice the person liable for the hazardous materials release and, in the event of nonpayment, may institute an action to recover those costs in the superior court of the county in which the release occurred. (2007-107, s. 3.1(b).)

§ 130A-21. Embargo.

(a)   In addition to the authority of the Department of Agriculture and Consumer Services pursuant to G.S. 106-125, the Secretary or a local health director has authority to exercise embargo authority concerning food or drink pursuant to G.S. 106-125(a), (b) and (c) when the food or drink is in an establishment that is subject to regulation by the Department of Health and Human Services pursuant to this Chapter, that is subject to rules adopted by the Commission, or that is the subject of an investigation pursuant to G.S. 130A-144; however, no such action shall be taken in any establishment or part of an establishment that is under inspection or otherwise regulated by the Department of Agriculture and Consumer Services or the United States Department of Agriculture other than the part of the establishment that is subject to regulation by the Department of Health and Human Services pursuant to this Chapter. Any action under this section shall only be taken by, or after consultation with, Department of Health and Human Services regional environmental health specialists, or the Director of the Division of Public Health or the Director's designee, in programs regulating food and drink pursuant to this Chapter or in programs regulating food and drink that are subject to rules adopted by the Commission. Authority under this section shall not be delegated to individual environmental health specialists in local health departments otherwise

74

authorized and carrying out laws and rules pursuant to G.S. 130A-4. When any action is taken pursuant to this section, the Department of Health and Human Services or the local health director shall immediately notify the Department of Agriculture and Consumer Services. For the purposes of this subsection, all duties and procedures in G.S. 106-125 shall be carried out by the Secretary of Health and Human Services or the local health director and shall not be required to be carried out by the Department of Agriculture and Consumer Services. It shall be unlawful for any person to remove or dispose of the food or drink by sale or otherwise without the permission of a Department of Health and Human Services regional environmental health specialist, the Director of the Division of Public Health or the Director's designee, the local health director, or a duly authorized agent of the Department of Agriculture and Consumer Services, or by the court in accordance with the provisions of G.S. 106-125.

(b)   Recodified as G.S. 106-266.36 by Session Laws 2011-145, s. 13.3(s), effective July 1, 2011.

(c)   Recodified as G.S. 113-221.4 by Session Laws 2011-145, s. 13.3(ttt), effective July 1, 2011.

(d)   Nothing in this section is intended to limit the embargo authority of the Department of Agriculture and Consumer Services. The Department of Health and Human Services and the Department of Agriculture and Consumer Services are authorized to enter agreements respecting the duties and responsibilities of each agency in the exercise of their embargo authority.

(e)   For the purpose of this section, a food or drink is adulterated if the food or drink is deemed adulterated under G.S. 106-129; and food or drink is misbranded if it is deemed misbranded under G.S. 106-130. (1983, c. 891, s. 2; 1997-261, s. 109; 1997-443, s. 11A.63A; 2006-80, s. 1; 2007-7, s. 1; 2011-145, ss. 13.3(s), (vv), (ww), (ttt).)

§ 130A-22. Administrative penalties.

(a)   The Secretary of Environment and Natural Resources may impose an administrative penalty on a person who violates Article 9 of this Chapter, rules adopted by the Commission pursuant to Article 9, or any term or condition of a permit or order issued under Article 9. Each day of a continuing violation shall constitute a separate violation. The penalty shall not exceed fifteen thousand dollars ($15,000) per day in the case of a violation involving nonhazardous waste. The penalty shall not exceed thirty-two thousand five hundred dollars ($32,500) per day in the case of a first violation involving hazardous waste as defined in G.S. 130A-290 or involving the disposal of medical waste as defined in G.S. 130A-290 in or upon water in a manner that results in medical waste entering waters or lands of the State; and shall not exceed fifty thousand dollars ($50,000) per day for a second or further violation involving the disposal of medical waste as defined in G.S. 130A-290 in or upon water in a manner that results in medical waste entering waters or lands of the State. The penalty shall not exceed thirty-two thousand five hundred dollars ($32,500) per day for a violation involving a voluntary remedial action implemented pursuant to G.S. 130A-310.9(c) or a violation of the rules adopted pursuant to G.S. 130A-310.12(b). The penalty shall not exceed one hundred dollars ($100.00) for a first violation; two hundred dollars ($200.00) for a second violation within any 12-month period; and five hundred dollars ($500.00) for each additional violation within any 12-month period for any violation of Part 2G of Article 9 of this Chapter. For violations of Part 7 of Article 9 of this Chapter and G.S. 130A-309.10(m): (i) a warning shall be issued for a first violation; (ii) the penalty shall not exceed two hundred dollars ($200.00) for a second violation; and (iii) the penalty shall not exceed five hundred dollars ($500.00) for subsequent violations. If a person fails to pay a civil penalty within 60 days after the final agency decision or court order has been served on the violator, the Secretary of Environment and Natural Resources shall request the Attorney General to institute a civil action in the superior court of any county in which the violator resides or has his or its principal place of business to recover the amount of the assessment. Such civil actions must be filed within three years of the date the final agency decision or court order was served on the violator.

(a1)   Part 5 of Article 21A of Chapter 143 of the General Statutes shall apply to the determination of civil liability or penalty pursuant to subsection (a) of this section.

(b)   The Secretary of Environment and Natural Resources may impose an administrative penalty on a person who violates G.S. 130A-325. Each day of a continuing violation shall constitute a separate violation. The penalty shall not exceed twenty-five thousand dollars ($25,000) for each day the violation continues.

(b1)   The Secretary may impose an administrative penalty on a person who violates Article 19 of this Chapter or a rule adopted pursuant to that Article. Except as provided in subsection (b2) of this section, the penalty shall not exceed one thousand dollars ($1,000) per day per violation. Until the Department has notified the person of the violation, a continuing violation shall be treated as one violation. Each day thereafter of a continuing violation shall be treated as a separate violation.

In determining the amount of a penalty under this subsection or subsection (b2) of this section, the Secretary shall consider all of the following factors:

(1)   The degree and extent of harm to the natural resources of the State, to the public health, or to private property resulting from the violation.

(2)   The duration and gravity of the violation.

(3)   The effect on air quality.

(4)   The cost of rectifying the damage.

(5)   The amount of money the violator saved by noncompliance.

(6)   The prior record of the violator in complying or failing to comply with Article 19 of this Chapter or a rule adopted pursuant to that Article.

(7)   The cost to the State of the enforcement procedures.

(8)   If applicable, the size of the renovation and demolition involved in the violation.

(b2)   The penalty for violations of the asbestos NESHAP for demolition and renovation, as defined in G.S. 130A-444, shall not exceed ten thousand dollars ($10,000) per day per violation. Until the Department has provided the person with written notification of the violation of the asbestos NESHAP for demolition and renovation that describes the violation, recommends a general course of action, and establishes a time frame in which to correct the violations, a continuing violation shall be treated as one violation. Each day thereafter of a continuing violation shall be treated as a separate violation. A violation of the asbestos NESHAP for demolition and renovation is not considered to continue during the period a person who has received the notice of violation is following the general course of action and complying with the time frame set forth in the notice of violation.

77

(b3)   The Secretary may impose an administrative penalty on a person who violates Article 19A or 19B of this Chapter or any rules adopted pursuant to Article 19A or 19B of this Chapter. Each day of a continuing violation is a separate violation. The penalty shall not exceed five thousand dollars ($5,000) for each day the violation continues for Article 19A of this Chapter. The penalty shall not exceed five thousand dollars ($5,000) for each day the violation continues for Article 19B of this Chapter. The penalty authorized by this section does not apply to a person who is not required to be certified under Article 19A or 19B.

(c)   The Secretary may impose an administrative penalty on a person who willfully violates Article 11 of this Chapter, rules adopted by the Commission pursuant to Article 11 or any condition imposed upon a permit issued under Article 11. An administrative penalty may not be imposed upon a person who establishes that neither the site nor the system may be improved or a new system installed so as to comply with Article 11 of this Chapter. Each day of a continuing violation shall constitute a separate violation. The penalty shall not exceed fifty dollars ($50.00) per day in the case of a wastewater collection, treatment and disposal system with a design daily flow of no more than 480 gallons or in the case of any system serving a single one-family dwelling. The penalty shall not exceed three hundred dollars ($300.00) per day in the case of a wastewater collection, treatment and disposal system with a design daily flow of more than 480 gallons which does not serve a single one-family dwelling.

(c1)   The Secretary may impose a monetary penalty on a vendor who violates rules adopted by the Commission pursuant to Article 13 of this Chapter when the Secretary determines that disqualification would result in hardship to participants in the Women, Infants, and Children (WIC) program. The penalty shall be calculated using the following formula: multiply five percent (5%) times the average dollar amount of the vendor's monthly redemptions of WIC food instruments for the 12-month period immediately preceding disqualification, then multiply that product by the number of months of the disqualification period determined by the Secretary.

(d)   In determining the amount of the penalty in subsections (a), (b) and (c), the Secretary and the Secretary of Environment and Natural Resources shall consider all of the following factors:

(1)   Type of violation.

(2)   Type of waste involved.

78

(3)   Duration of the violation.

(4)   Cause (whether resulting from a negligent, reckless, or intentional act or omission).

(5)   Potential effect on public health and the environment.

(6)   Effectiveness of responsive measures taken by the violator.

(7)   Damage to private property.

(8)   The degree and extent of harm caused by the violation.

(9)   Cost of rectifying any damage.

(10)   The amount of money the violator saved by noncompliance.

(11)   The violator's previous record in complying or not complying with the provisions of Article 9 of this Chapter, Article 11 of this Chapter, or G.S. 130A-325, and any regulations adopted thereunder, as applicable to the violation in question.

(e)   A person contesting a penalty shall, by filing a petition pursuant to G.S. 150B-23(a) not later than 30 days after receipt by the petitioner of the document which constitutes agency action, be entitled to an administrative hearing and judicial review in accordance with Chapter 150B of the General Statutes, the Administrative Procedure Act.

(f)   The Commission shall adopt rules concerning the imposition of administrative penalties under this section.

(g)   The Secretary or the Secretary of Environment and Natural Resources may bring a civil action in the superior court of the county where the violation occurred or where the defendant resides to recover the amount of an administrative penalty authorized under this section whenever a person:

(1)   Who has not requested an administrative hearing in accordance with subsection (e) of this section fails to pay the penalty within 60 days after being notified of the penalty; or

(2)   Who has requested an administrative hearing fails to pay the penalty within 60 days after service of a written copy of the final agency decision.

(h)   A local health director may impose an administrative penalty on any person who willfully violates the wastewater collection, treatment, and disposal rules of the local board of health adopted pursuant to G.S. 130A-335(c) or who willfully violates a condition imposed upon a permit issued under the approved local rules. An administrative penalty may not be imposed upon a person who establishes that neither the site nor the system may be improved or a new system installed so as to comply with Article 11 of this Chapter. The local health director shall establish and recover the amount of the administrative penalty in accordance with subsections (d) and (g). Each day of a continuing violation shall constitute a separate violation. The penalty shall not exceed fifty dollars ($50.00) per day in the case of a wastewater collection, treatment and disposal system with a design daily flow of no more than 480 gallons or in the case of any system serving a single one-family dwelling.

The penalty shall not exceed three hundred dollars ($300.00) per day in the case of a wastewater collection, treatment and disposal system with a design daily flow of more than 480 gallons which does not serve a single one-family dwelling. A person contesting a penalty imposed under this subsection shall be entitled to an administrative hearing and judicial review in accordance with G.S. 130A-24. A local board of health shall adopt rules concerning the imposition of administrative penalties under this subsection.

(h1)   A local health director may take the following actions and may impose the following administrative penalty on a person who manages, operates, or controls a public place or place of employment and fails to comply with the provisions of Part 1C of Article 23 of this Chapter or with rules adopted thereunder or with local ordinances, rules, laws, or policies adopted pursuant to Part 2 of Article 23 of this Chapter:

(1)   First violation. - Provide the person in violation with written notice of the person's first violation and notification of action to be taken in the event of subsequent violations.

(2)   Second violation. - Provide the person in violation with written notice of the person's second violation and notification of administrative penalties to be imposed for subsequent violations.

(3)   Subsequent violations. - Impose on the person in violation an administrative penalty of not more than two hundred dollars ($200.00) for the third and subsequent violations.

Each day on which a violation of this Article or rules adopted pursuant to this Article occurs may be considered a separate and distinct violation. Notwithstanding G.S. 130A-25, a violation of Article 23 of this Chapter shall not be punishable as a criminal violation.

(i)   The clear proceeds of penalties assessed pursuant to this section shall be remitted to the Civil Penalty and Forfeiture Fund in accordance with G.S. 115C-457.2.

(j)   The Secretary of Environment and Natural Resources may also assess the reasonable costs of any investigation, inspection, or monitoring associated with the assessment of the civil penalty against any person who is assessed a civil penalty under this section. (1983, c. 891, s. 2; 1987, c. 269, s. 2; c. 656; c. 704, s. 1; c. 827, s. 247; 1989, c. 742, s. 4; 1991, c. 691, s. 1; c. 725, s. 8; 1991 (Reg. Sess., 1992), c. 944, s. 11; 1993 (Reg. Sess., 1994), c. 686, s. 1; 1995, c. 504, s. 8; 1997-443, s. 11A.64; 1997-523, s. 2; 1998-215, s. 54(a); 2001-474, s. 21; 2002-154, s. 1; 2007-550, ss. 3(a), 4(a); 2009-27, s. 2; 2009-163, s. 2; 2009-488, s. 2; 2010-180, s. 14(c); 2011-145, s. 13.3(xx); 2013-378, s. 7; 2013-413, s. 49.)

§ 130A-23. Suspension and revocation of permits and program participation.

(a)   The Secretary may suspend or revoke a permit issued under this Chapter upon a finding that a violation of the applicable provisions of this Chapter, the rules of the Commission or a condition imposed upon the permit has occurred. A permit may also be suspended or revoked upon a finding that its issuance was based upon incorrect or inadequate information that materially affected the decision to issue the permit.

(b)   The Secretary may suspend or revoke a person's participation in a program administered under this Chapter upon a finding that a violation of the applicable provisions of this Chapter or the rules of the Commission has occurred. Program participation may also be suspended or revoked upon a finding that participation was based upon incorrect or inadequate information that materially affected the decision to grant program participation.

81

(c)   A person shall be given notice that there has been a tentative decision to suspend or revoke the permit or program participation and that an administrative hearing will be held in accordance with Chapter 150B of the General Statutes, the Administrative Procedure Act, at which time the person may challenge the tentative decision.

(d)   A permit shall be suspended or revoked immediately if a violation of the Chapter, the rules or a condition imposed upon the permit presents an imminent hazard. An operation permit issued pursuant to G.S. 130A-281 shall be immediately suspended for failure of a public swimming pool to maintain minimum water quality or safety standards or design and construction standards pertaining to the abatement of suction hazards which result in an unsafe condition. A permit issued pursuant to G.S. 130A-248 shall be revoked immediately for failure of an establishment to maintain a minimum grade of C. The Secretary of Environment and Natural Resources shall immediately give notice of the suspension or revocation and the right of the permit holder or program participant to appeal the suspension or revocation under G.S. 150B-23.

(e)   The Secretary of Environment and Natural Resources shall have all of the applicable rights enumerated in this section to enforce the provisions of Articles 9 and 10 of this Chapter. (1983, c. 891, s. 2; 1987, c. 827, s. 1; c. 438, s. 3; 1993, c. 211, s. 2; 1993 (Reg. Sess., 1994), c. 732, s. 2; 1995, c. 123, s. 15; 1997-443, s. 11A.65; 2011-145, s. 13.3(yy).)

§ 130A-24. Appeals procedure.

(a)   Appeals concerning the enforcement of rules adopted by the Commission, concerning the suspension and revocation of permits and program participation by the Secretary and concerning the imposition of administrative penalties by the Secretary shall be governed by Chapter 150B of the General Statutes, the Administrative Procedure Act.

(a1)   Any person appealing an action taken by the Department pursuant to this Chapter or rules of the Commission shall file a petition for a contested case with the Office of Administrative Hearings as provided in G.S. 150B-23(a). The petition shall be filed not later than 30 days after notice of the action which confers the right of appeal unless a federal statute or regulation provides for a different time limitation. The time limitation imposed under this subsection shall commence when notice of the agency decision is given to all persons aggrieved. Such notice shall be provided to all persons known to the agency by personal delivery or by the placing of notice in an official depository of the United States Postal Service addressed to the person at the latest address provided to the agency by the person.

(b)   Appeals concerning the enforcement of rules adopted by the local board of health and concerning the imposition of administrative penalties by a local health director shall be conducted in accordance with this subsection and subsections (c) and (d) of this section. The aggrieved person shall give written notice of appeal to the local health director within 30 days of the challenged action. The notice shall contain the name and address of the aggrieved person, a description of the challenged action and a statement of the reasons why the challenged action is incorrect. Upon filing of the notice, the local health director shall, within five working days, transmit to the local board of health the notice of appeal and the papers and materials upon which the challenged action was taken.

(c)   The local board of health shall hold a hearing within 15 days of the receipt of the notice of appeal. The board shall give the person not less than 10 days' notice of the date, time and place of the hearing. On appeal, the board shall have authority to affirm, modify or reverse the challenged action. The local board of health shall issue a written decision based on the evidence presented at the hearing. The decision shall contain a concise statement of the reasons for the decision.

(d)   A person who wishes to contest a decision of the local board of health under subsection (b) of this section shall have a right of appeal to the district court having jurisdiction within 30 days after the date of the decision by the board. The scope of review in district court shall be the same as in G.S. 150B-51.

(e)   The appeals procedures enumerated in this section shall apply to appeals concerning the enforcement of rules, the imposition of administrative penalties, or any other action taken by the Department of Environment and Natural Resources pursuant to Articles 8, 9, 10, 11, and 12 of this Chapter. (1983, c. 891, s. 2; 1987, c. 482; c. 827, s. 248; 1993, c. 211, s. 1; 1997-443, s. 11A.66; 1998-217, s. 33.)

§ 130A-25. Misdemeanor.

(a)   Except as otherwise provided, a person who violates a provision of this Chapter or the rules adopted by the Commission or a local board of health shall be guilty of a misdemeanor.

(b)   A person convicted under this section for violation of G.S. 130A-144(f) or G.S. 130A-145 shall not be sentenced under Article 81B of Chapter 15A of the General Statutes but shall instead be sentenced to a term of imprisonment of no more than two years and shall serve any prison sentence in McCain Hospital, Section of Prisons of the Division of Adult Correction, McCain, North Carolina; the North Carolina Correctional Center for Women, Section of Prisons of the Division of Adult Correction, Raleigh, North Carolina; or any other confinement facility designated for this purpose by the Secretary of Public Safety after consultation with the State Health Director. The Secretary of Public Safety shall consult with the State Health Director concerning the medical management of these persons.

(c)   Notwithstanding G.S. 148-4.1, G.S. 148-13, or any other contrary provision of law, a person imprisoned for violation of G.S. 130A-144(f) or G.S. 130A-145 shall not be released prior to the completion of the person's term of imprisonment unless and until a determination has been made by the District Court that release of the person would not create a danger to the public health. This determination shall be made only after the medical consultant of the confinement facility and the State Health Director, in consultation with the local health director of the person's county of residence, have made recommendations to the Court.

(d)   A violation of Part 7 of Article 9 of this Chapter or G.S. 130A-309.10(m) shall be punishable as a Class 3 misdemeanor. (1983, c. 891, s. 2; 1987, c. 782, s. 19; 1991, c. 187, s. 1; 1993, c. 539, s. 946; 1994, Ex. Sess., c. 24, s. 14(c); 1993 (Reg. Sess., 1994), c. 767, s. 18; 2010-180, s. 14(d); 2011-145, s. 19.1(h), (i), (j).)

§ 130A-26: Repealed by Session Laws 1995, c. 311, s. 1.

§ 130A-26.1. Criminal violation of Article 9.

(a)   The definition of "person" set out in G.S. 130A-290 shall apply to this section. In addition, for purposes of this section, the term "person" shall also include any responsible corporate or public officer or employee.

(b)   No proceeding shall be brought or continued under this section for or on account of a violation by any person who has previously been convicted of a federal violation based upon the same set of facts.

(c)   In proving the defendant's possession of actual knowledge, circumstantial evidence may be used, including evidence that the defendant took affirmative steps to shield himself from relevant information. Consistent with the principles of common law, the subjective mental state of defendants may be inferred from their conduct.

(d)   For the purposes of the felony provisions of this section, a person's state of mind shall not be found "knowingly and willfully" or "knowingly" if the conduct that is the subject of the prosecution is the result of any of the following occurrences or circumstances:

(1)   A natural disaster or other act of God which could not have been prevented or avoided by the exercise of due care or foresight.

(2)   An act of third parties other than agents, employees, contractors, or subcontractors of the defendant.

(3)   An act done in reliance on the written advice or emergency on-site direction of an employee of the Department of Environment and Natural Resources. In emergencies, oral advice may be relied upon if written confirmation is delivered to the employee as soon as practicable after receiving and relying on the advice.

(4)   An act causing no significant harm to the environment or risk to the public health, safety, or welfare and done in compliance with other conflicting environmental requirements or other constraints imposed in writing by environmental agencies or officials after written notice is delivered to all relevant agencies that the conflict exists and will cause a violation of the identified standard.

(5)   Violations of permit limitations causing no significant harm to the environment or risk to the public health, safety, or welfare for which no enforcement action or civil penalty could have been imposed under any written civil enforcement guidelines in use by the Department of Environment and Natural Resources at the time, including but not limited to, guidelines for the pretreatment permit civil penalties. This subdivision shall not be construed to

require the Department of Environment and Natural Resources to develop or use written civil enforcement guidelines.

(e)   All general defenses, affirmative defenses, and bars to prosecution that may apply with respect to other criminal offenses under State criminal offenses may apply to prosecutions brought under this section or other criminal statutes that refer to this section and shall be determined by the courts of this State according to the principles of common law as they may be applied in the light of reason and experience. Concepts of justification and excuse applicable under this section may be developed in the light of reason and experience.

(f)   Any person who knowingly and willfully does any of the following shall be guilty of a Class I felony, which may include a fine not to exceed one hundred thousand dollars ($100,000) per day of violation, provided that this fine shall not exceed a cumulative total of five hundred thousand dollars ($500,000) for each period of 30 days during which a violation continues:

(1)   Transports or causes to be transported any hazardous waste identified or listed under G.S. 130A-294(c) to a facility which does not have a permit or interim status under G.S. 130A-294(c) or 42 U.S.C. § 6921, et seq.

(2)   Transports or causes to be transported such hazardous waste with the intent of delivery to a facility without a permit.

(3)   Treats, stores, or disposes of such hazardous waste without a permit or interim status under G.S. 130A-294(c) or 42 U.S.C. § 6921, et seq., or in knowing violation of any material condition or requirement or such permit or applicable interim status rules.

(g)   Any person who knowingly and willfully does any of the following shall be guilty of a Class I felony, which may include a fine not to exceed one hundred thousand dollars ($100,000) per day of violation, provided that the fine shall not exceed a cumulative total of five hundred thousand dollars ($500,000) for each period of 30 days during which a violation continues:

(1)   Transports or causes to be transported hazardous waste without a manifest as required under G.S. 130A-294(c).

(2)   Transports hazardous waste without a United States Environmental Protection Agency identification number as required by rules promulgated under G.S. 130A-294(c).

86

(3)   Omits material information or makes any false material statement or representation in any application, label, manifest, record, report, permit, or other document filed, maintained, or used for purposes of compliance with rules promulgated under G.S. 130A-294(c).

(4)   Generates, stores, treats, transports, disposes of, exports, or otherwise handles any hazardous waste or any used oil burned for energy recovery and who knowingly destroys, alters, conceals, or fails to file any record, application, manifest, report, or other document required to be maintained or filed for purposes of compliance with rules promulgated under G.S. 130A-294(c).

(5)   Provides false information or fails to provide information relevant to a decision by the Department as to whether or not to enter into a brownfields agreement under Part 5 of Article 9 of this Chapter.

(6)   Provides false information or fails to provide information required by a brownfields agreement under Part 5 of Article 9 of this Chapter.

(7)   Provides false information relevant to a decision by the Department pursuant to:

a.   G.S. 130A-308(b).

b.   G.S. 130A-310.7(c).

c.   G.S. 143-215.3(f).

d.   G.S. 143-215.84(e).

(h)   For the purposes of subsections (f) and (g) of this section, the phrase "knowingly and willfully" shall mean intentionally and consciously as the courts of this State, according to the principles of common law interpret the phrase in the light of reason and experience.

(i)   (1)   Any person who knowingly transports, treats, stores, disposes of, or exports any hazardous waste or used oil regulated under G.S. 130A-294(c) in violation of subsection (f) or (g) of this section, who knows at the time that he thereby places another person in imminent danger of death or personal bodily injury shall be guilty of a Class C felony which may include a fine not to exceed two hundred fifty thousand dollars ($250,000) per day of violation,

87

provided that this fine shall not exceed a cumulative total of one million dollars ($1,000,000) for each period of 30 days during which a violation continues.

(2)   For the purposes of this subsection, a person's state of mind is knowing with respect to:

a.   His conduct, if he is aware of the nature of his conduct;

b.   An existing circumstance, if he is aware or believes that the circumstance exists; or

c.   A result of his conduct, if he is aware or believes that his conduct is substantially certain to cause danger of death or serious bodily injury.

(3)   Under this subsection, in determining whether a defendant who is a natural person knew that his conduct placed another person in imminent danger of death or serious bodily injury:

a.   The person is responsible only for actual awareness or actual belief that he possessed; and

b.   Knowledge possessed by a person other than the defendant but not by the defendant himself may not be attributed to the defendant.

(4)   It is an affirmative defense to a prosecution under this subsection that the conduct charged was conduct consented to by the person endangered and that the danger and conduct charged were reasonably foreseeable hazards of an occupation, a business, or a profession; or of medical treatment or medical or scientific experimentation conducted by professionally approved methods and such other person had been made aware of the risks involved prior to giving consent. The defendant may establish an affirmative defense under this subdivision by a preponderance of the evidence.

(j)   Any person convicted of an offense under subsection (f), (g), or (h) of this section following a previous conviction under this section shall be subject to a fine, or imprisonment, or both, not exceeding twice the amount of the fine, or twice the term of imprisonment provided in the subsection under which the second or subsequent conviction occurs. (1989 (Reg. Sess., 1990), c. 1045, s. 9; 1993, c. 539, ss. 1303-1305; 1994, Ex. Sess., c. 24, s. 14(c); 1997-357, s. 3; 1997-443, s. 11A.67.)

§ 130A-26.2. Penalty for false reporting under Article 9.

Any person who knowingly makes any false statement, representation, or certification in any application, record, report, plan, or other document filed or required to be maintained under Article 9 of this Chapter or rules adopted under Article 9 of this Chapter; or who knowingly makes a false statement of a material fact in a rule-making proceeding or contested case under Article 9 of this Chapter; or who falsifies, tampers with, or knowingly renders inaccurate any recording or monitoring device or method required to be operated or maintained under Article 9 of this Chapter or rules adopted under Article 9 of this Chapter is guilty of a Class 2 misdemeanor. The maximum fine that may be imposed for an offense under this section is ten thousand dollars ($10,000). (1993 (Reg. Sess., 1994), c. 598, s. 3.)

§ 130A-26A. Violations of Article 4.

(a)   A person who commits any of the following acts shall be guilty of a Class 1 misdemeanor:

(1)   Willfully and knowingly makes any false statement in a certificate, record, or report required by Article 4 of this Chapter;

(2)   Removes or permits the removal of a dead body of a human being without authorization provided in Article 4 of this Chapter;

(3)   Refuses or fails to furnish correctly any information in the person's possession or furnishes false information affecting a certificate or record required by Article 4 of this Chapter;

(4)   Fails, neglects, or refuses to perform any act or duty required by Article 4 of this Chapter or by the instructions of the State Registrar prepared under authority of the Article.

(5)   Charges a fee for performing any act or duty required by Article 4 of this Chapter or by the State Registrar pursuant to Article 4 of this Chapter, other than fees specifically authorized by law.

(b)   A person who commits any of the following acts shall be guilty of a Class I felony:

(1)   Willfully and knowingly makes any false statement in an application for a certified copy of a vital record, or who willfully and knowingly supplies false information intending that the information be used in the obtaining of any copy of a vital record;

(2)   Without lawful authority and with the intent to deceive makes, counterfeits, alters, amends, or mutilates a certificate, record, or report required by Article 4 of this Chapter or a certified copy of the certificate, record, or report;

(3)   Willfully and knowingly obtains, possesses, sells, furnishes, uses, or attempts to use for any purpose of deception, a certificate, record, or report required by Article 4 of this Chapter or a certified copy of the certificate, record, or report, which is counterfeited, altered, amended, or mutilated, or which is false in whole or in part or which relates to the birth of another person, whether living or deceased;

(4)   When employed by the Vital Records Section of the Department or designated under Article 4 of this Chapter, willfully and knowingly furnishes or processes a certificate of birth, death, marriage, or divorce, or certified copy of a certificate of birth, death, marriage, or divorce with the knowledge or intention that it be used for the purposes of deception;

(5)   Without lawful authority possesses a certificate, record, or report required by Article 4 of this Chapter or a certified copy of the certificate, record, or report knowing that it was stolen or otherwise unlawfully obtained;

(6)   Willfully alters, except as provided by G.S. 130A-118, or falsifies a certificate or record required by Article 4 of this Chapter; or willfully alters, falsifies, or changes a photocopy, certified copy, extract copy, or any document containing information obtained from an original or copy of a certificate or record required by Article 4 of this Chapter; or willfully makes, creates, or uses any altered, falsified or changed record, reproduction, copy or document for the purpose of attempting to prove or establish for any purpose whatsoever any matter purported to be shown on it;

(7)   Without lawful authority, manufactures or possesses the seal of: (i) the Vital Records Section, (ii) a county register of deeds, or (iii) a county health department, or without lawful authority, manufactures or possesses a reproduction or a counterfeit copy of the seal;

90

(8)   Without lawful authority prepares or issues any certificate which purports to be an official certified copy of a vital record;

(9)   Without lawful authority, manufactures or possesses Vital Records Section, county register of deeds, or county health department vital records forms or safety paper used to certify births, deaths, marriages, and divorces, or reproductions or counterfeit copies of the forms or safety paper; or

(10)   Willfully and knowingly furnishes a certificate of birth or certified copy of a record of birth with the intention that it be used by an unauthorized person or for an unauthorized purpose. (1995, c. 311, s. 2.)

§ 130A-27. Recovery of money.

The Secretary or the Secretary of Environment and Natural Resources may institute an action in the county where the action arose or the county where the defendant resides to recover any money, other property or interest in property or the monetary value of goods or services provided or paid for by the Department or the Secretary of Environment and Natural Resources which are wrongfully paid or transferred to a person under a program administered by the Department or the Secretary of Environment and Natural Resources pursuant to this Chapter. (1983, c. 891, s. 2; 1997-443, s. 11A.68.)

§ 130A-28. Forfeiture of gain.

In the case of a violation of this Chapter or the rules adopted by the Commission, money or other property or interest in property so acquired shall be forfeited to the State unless ownership by an innocent person may be established. An action may be instituted by the Attorney General or a district attorney pursuant to G.S. 1-532. (1983, c. 891, s. 2.)

Article 1A.

Commission for Public Health.

§ 130A-29. Commission for Public Health - Creation, powers and duties.

(a)   The Commission for Public Health is created with the authority and duty to adopt rules to protect and promote the public health.

(b)   The Commission is authorized to adopt rules necessary to implement the public health programs administered by the Department as provided in this Chapter.

(c)   The Commission shall adopt rules:

(1)   Repealed by Session Laws 1983 (Regular Session, 1984), c. 1022, s. 5.

(2)   Establishing standards for approving sewage-treatment devices and holding tanks for marine toilets as provided in G.S. 75A-6(o).

(3)   Establishing specifications for sanitary privies for schools where water-carried sewage facilities are unavailable as provided in G.S. 115C-522.

(4)   Establishing requirements for the sanitation of local confinement facilities as provided in Part 2 of Article 10 of Chapter 153A of the General Statutes.

(5)   Repealed by Session Laws 1989 (Regular Session, 1990), c. 1075, s. 1.

(5a)   Establishing eligibility standards for participation in Department reimbursement programs.

(6)   Requiring proper treatment and disposal of sewage and other waste from chemical and portable toilets.

(7)   Establishing statewide health outcome objectives and delivery standards.

(8)   Establishing permit requirements for the sanitation of premises, utensils, equipment, and procedures to be used by a person engaged in tattooing, as provided in Part 11 of Article 8 of this Chapter.

(9) Implementing immunization requirements for adult care homes as provided in G.S. 131D-9 and for nursing homes as provided in G.S. 131E-113.

(10) Pertaining to the biological agents registry in accordance with G.S. 130A-479.

(11) For matters within its jurisdiction that allow for and regulate horizontal drilling and hydraulic fracturing for the purpose of oil and gas exploration and development.

(d) The Commission is authorized to create:

(1) Metropolitan water districts as provided in G.S. 162A-33;

(2) Sanitary districts as provided in Part 2 of Article 2 of this Chapter; and

(3) Mosquito control districts as provided in Part 2 of Article 12 of this Chapter.

(e) Rules adopted by the Commission shall be enforced by the Department. (1973, c. 476, s. 123; 1975, c. 19, s. 57; c. 694, s. 6; 1979, c. 41, s. 1; 1981, c. 614, s. 9; 1983, c. 891, s. 15; 1983 (Reg. Sess., 1984), c. 1022, s. 5; 1989, c. 727, ss. 175, 176; 1989 (Reg. Sess., 1990), c. 1004, s. 50; c. 1075, s. 1; 1991, c. 548, s. 2; 1993, c. 321, s. 274; 1993 (Reg. Sess., 1994), c. 670, s. 3; 2000-112, s. 6; 2001-469, s. 2; 2002-179, s. 2(b); 2007-182, s. 2; 2012-143, s. 2(i).)

§ 130A-30. Commission for Public Health - Members; selection; quorum; compensation.

(a) The Commission for Public Health shall consist of 13 members, four of whom shall be elected by the North Carolina Medical Society and nine of whom shall be appointed by the Governor.

(b) One of the members appointed by the Governor shall be a licensed pharmacist, one a registered engineer experienced in sanitary engineering or a soil scientist, one a licensed veterinarian, one a licensed optometrist, one a licensed dentist, and one a registered nurse. The initial members of the Commission shall be the members of the State Board of Health who shall serve for a period equal to the remainder of their current terms on the State Board of

Health, three of whose appointments expire May 1, 1973, and two of whose appointments expire May 1, 1975. At the end of the respective terms of office of initial members of the Commission, their successors shall be appointed for terms of four years and until their successors are appointed and qualify. Any appointment to fill a vacancy on the Commission created by the resignation, dismissal, death, or disability of a member shall be for the balance of the unexpired term.

(c)   The North Carolina Medical Society shall have the right to remove any member elected by it for misfeasance, malfeasance, or nonfeasance, and the Governor shall have the right to remove any member appointed by him for misfeasance, malfeasance, or nonfeasance in accordance with the provisions of G.S. 143B-13. Vacancies on said Commission among the membership elected by the North Carolina Medical Society shall be filled by the executive committee of the Medical Society until the next meeting of the Medical Society, when the Medical Society shall fill the vacancy for the unexpired term. Vacancies on said Commission among the membership appointed by the Governor shall be filled by the Governor for the unexpired term.

(d)   A majority of the members of the Commission shall constitute a quorum for the transaction of business.

(e)   The members of the Commission shall receive per diem and necessary traveling and subsistence expenses in accordance with the provisions of G.S. 138-5. (1973, c. 476, s. 124; c. 1367, ss. 1, 2; 1981, c. 553; 1989, c. 727, ss. 175, 177; 1989 (Reg. Sess., 1990), c. 1004, s. 51; 1995, c. 507, s. 26.8(d); 2007-182, s. 2.)

§ 130A-31. Commission for Public Health - Officers.

The Commission for Public Health shall have a chairman and a vice-chairman. The chairman shall be designated by the Governor from among the members of the Commission to serve as chairman at his pleasure. The vice-chairman shall be elected by and from the members of the Commission and shall serve for a term of two years or until the expiration of his regularly appointed term. (1973, c. 476, s. 125; 1989, c. 727, s. 175; 2007-182, s. 2.)

§ 130A-32. Commission for Public Health - Election meetings.

The meeting of the Commission for Public Health for the election of vice-chairman shall be at the first regular meeting after the joint session of the Commission for Public Health and the North Carolina Medical Society at the annual meeting of the North Carolina Medical Society each odd-numbered year. (1973, c. 476, s. 126; 1989, c. 727, s. 175; 2007-182, s. 2.)

§ 130A-33. Commission for Public Health - Regular and special meetings.

Each year there shall be four regular meetings of the Commission for Public Health, one of which shall be held conjointly with a general session of the annual meeting of the North Carolina Medical Society. The State Health Director shall submit an annual report on public health at this meeting. The other three meetings shall be at such times and places as the chairman of the Commission shall designate. Special meetings of the Commission may be called by the chairman, or by a majority of the members of the Commission. (1973, c. 476, s. 127; 1989, c. 727, ss. 175, 178; 1993, c. 513, s. 6; 2007-182, s. 2.)

§ 130A-33.1: Reserved for future codification purposes.

§ 130A-33.2: Reserved for future codification purposes.

§ 130A-33.3: Reserved for future codification purposes.

§ 130A-33.4: Reserved for future codification purposes.

§ 130A-33.5: Reserved for future codification purposes.

§ 130A-33.6: Reserved for future codification purposes.

§ 130A-33.7: Reserved for future codification purposes.

§ 130A-33.8: Reserved for future codification purposes.

§ 130A-33.9: Reserved for future codification purposes.

§ 130A-33.10: Reserved for future codification purposes.

§ 130A-33.11: Reserved for future codification purposes.

§ 130A-33.12: Reserved for future codification purposes.

§ 130A-33.13: Reserved for future codification purposes.

§ 130A-33.14: Reserved for future codification purposes.

§ 130A-33.15: Reserved for future codification purposes.

§ 130A-33.16: Reserved for future codification purposes.

§ 130A-33.17: Reserved for future codification purposes.

§ 130A-33.18: Reserved for future codification purposes.

§ 130A-33.19: Reserved for future codification purposes.

§ 130A-33.20: Reserved for future codification purposes.

§ 130A-33.21: Reserved for future codification purposes.

§ 130A-33.22: Reserved for future codification purposes.

§ 130A-33.23: Reserved for future codification purposes.

§ 130A-33.24: Reserved for future codification purposes.

§ 130A-33.25: Reserved for future codification purposes.

§ 130A-33.26: Reserved for future codification purposes.

§ 130A-33.27: Reserved for future codification purposes.

§ 130A-33.28: Reserved for future codification purposes.

§ 130A-33.29: Reserved for future codification purposes.

Article 1B.

Commissions and Councils.

Part 1. Commission of Anatomy.

§ 130A-33.30. Commission of Anatomy - Creation; powers and duties.

There is created the Commission of Anatomy in the Department with the power and duty to adopt rules for the distribution of dead human bodies and parts thereof for the purpose of promoting the study of anatomy in the State of North Carolina. The Commission is authorized to receive dead bodies pursuant to G.S. 130A-412.13 and to be a donee of a body or parts thereof pursuant to Part 3A, Article 16 of Chapter 130A of the General Statutes known as the Revised Uniform Anatomical Gift Act and to distribute such bodies or parts thereof pursuant to the rules adopted by the Commission. (1975, c. 694, s. 2; 1989, c. 727, ss. 182(a), 183; 1989 (Reg. Sess., 1990), c. 1024, s. 29; 1997-443, s. 11A.69; 2007-538, s. 9.)

§ 130A-33.31. Commission of Anatomy - Members; selection; term; chairman; quorum; meetings.

(a)   The Commission of Anatomy shall consist of five members, one representative from the field of mortuary science, and one each from The University of North Carolina School of Medicine, East Carolina University School of Medicine, Duke University School of Medicine, and Bowman Gray School of Medicine. The dean of each school shall make recommendations and the Secretary shall appoint from such recommendations a member to the Commission. The president of the State Board of Funeral Service shall appoint the representative from the field of mortuary science to the Commission. The members shall serve terms of four years except two of the original members shall serve a term of one year, one shall serve a term of two years, one shall serve a term of three years, and one shall serve a term of four years. The Secretary shall determine the terms of the original members.

(b)   Any appointment to fill a vacancy on the Commission created by the resignation, dismissal, death, or disability of a member shall be for the balance of the unexpired term.

(c)   The Secretary shall remove any member of the Commission from office for misfeasance, malfeasance or nonfeasance.

(d)   The Commission shall elect a chair annually from its own membership.

(e)   A majority of the Commission shall constitute a quorum for the transaction of business.

(f)   The Commission shall meet at any time and place within the State at the call of the chair or upon the written request of three members.

(g)   All clerical and other services required by the Commission shall be supplied by the Secretary. (1975, c. 694, s. 2; 1989, c. 727, ss. 182(a), 184; 1995, c. 123, s. 5; 1997-443, s. 11A.70; 2003-420, s. 1.)

§ 130A-33.32. Commission of Anatomy - Reference to former Board of Anatomy in testamentary disposition.

A testamentary disposition of a body or part thereof to the former Board of Anatomy shall be deemed in all respects to be a disposition to the Commission of Anatomy. (1975, c. 694, s. 2; 1989, c. 727, ss. 182(a), 185.)

§ 130A-33.33: Reserved for future codification purposes.

§ 130A-33.34: Reserved for future codification purposes.

§ 130A-33.35: Reserved for future codification purposes.

§ 130A-33.36: Reserved for future codification purposes.

§ 130A-33.37: Reserved for future codification purposes.

§ 130A-33.38: Reserved for future codification purposes.

§ 130A-33.39: Reserved for future codification purposes.

Part 2. Governor's Council on Physical Fitness and Health.

§ 130A-33.40: Repealed by Session Laws 2011-266, s. 1.30(a), effective July 1, 2011.

§ 130A-33.41: Repealed by Session Laws 2011-266, s. 1.30(a), effective July 1, 2011.

§ 130A-33.42. Reserved for future codification purposes.

Part 3. Minority Health Advisory Council.

§ 130A-33.43. Minority Health Advisory Council.

There is established the Minority Health Advisory Council in the Department. The Council shall have the following duties and responsibilities:

(1)   To make recommendations to the Governor and the Secretary aimed at improving the health status of North Carolina's minority populations;

(2)   To identify and examine the limitations and problems associated with existing laws, regulations, programs and services related to the health status of North Carolina's minority populations;

(3)   To examine the financing and access to health services for North Carolina's minority populations;

(4)   To identify and review health promotion and disease prevention strategies relating to the leading causes of death and disability among minority populations; and

(5)   To advise the Governor and the Secretary upon any matter which the Governor or Secretary may refer to it. (1991 (Reg. Sess., 1992), c. 900, s. 166; 1997-443, s. 11A.73.)

§ 130A-33.44. Minority Health Advisory Council - members; selection; quorum; compensation.

(a)   The Minority Health Advisory Council in the Department shall consist of 15 members to be appointed as follows:

(1)   Five members shall be appointed by the Governor. Members appointed by the Governor shall be representatives of the following: health care providers, public health, health related public and private agencies and organizations, community-based organizations, and human services agencies and organizations.

(2)   Five members shall be appointed by the Speaker of the House of Representatives, two of whom shall be members of the House of Representatives, and at least one of whom shall be a public member. The remainder of the Speaker's appointees shall be representative of any of the entities named in subdivision (1) of this subsection.

(3)   Five members shall be appointed by the President Pro Tempore of the Senate, two of whom shall be members of the Senate, and at least one of whom shall be a public member. The remainder of the President Pro Tempore's appointees shall be representative of any of the entities named in subdivision (1) of this subsection.

(4)   Of the members appointed by the Governor, two shall serve initial terms of one year, two shall serve initial terms of two years, and one shall serve an initial term of three years. Thereafter, the Governor's appointees shall serve terms of four years.

(5)   Of the nonlegislative members appointed by the Speaker of the House of Representatives, two shall serve initial terms of two years, and one shall serve an initial term of three years. Thereafter, nonlegislative members appointed by the Speaker of the House of Representatives shall serve terms of four years. Of the nonlegislative members appointed by the President Pro Tempore of the Senate, two shall serve initial terms of two years, and one shall serve an initial term of three years. Thereafter, nonlegislative members appointed by the President Pro Tempore of the Senate shall serve terms of four years. Legislative members of the Council shall serve two-year terms.

(b)   The Chairperson of the Council shall be elected by the Council from among its membership.

100

(c)   The majority of the Council shall constitute a quorum for the transaction of business.

(d)   Members of the Council shall receive per diem and necessary travel and subsistence expenses in accordance with the provisions of G.S. 138-5 or G.S. 138-6, or travel and subsistence expenses in accordance with the provisions of G.S. 120-3.1, as applicable.

(e)   All clerical support and other services required by the Council shall be provided by the Department. (1991 (Reg. Sess., 1992), c. 900, s. 166; 1997-443, s. 11A.74.)

§§ 130A-33.45 through 130A-33.49. Reserved for future codification purposes.

Part 4. Advisory Committee on Cancer Coordination and Control.

§ 130A-33.50. Advisory Committee on Cancer Coordination and Control established; membership, compensation.

(a)   The Advisory Committee on Cancer Coordination and Control is established in the Department.

(b)   The Committee shall have up to 34 members, including the Secretary of the Department or the Secretary's designee. The members of the Committee shall elect a chair and vice-chair from among the Committee membership. The Committee shall meet not more than twice a year at the call of the chair. Six of the members shall be legislators, three of whom shall be appointed by the Speaker of the House of Representatives, and three of whom shall be appointed by the President Pro Tempore of the Senate. Four of the members shall be cancer survivors, two of whom shall be appointed by the Speaker of the House of Representatives, and two of whom shall be appointed by the President Pro Tempore of the Senate. The remainder of the members shall be appointed by the Governor as follows:

(1)   One member from the Department of Environment and Natural Resources;

101

(2)   Three members, one from each of the following: the Department, the Department of Public Instruction, and the North Carolina Community College System;

(3)   Four members representing the cancer control programs at North Carolina medical schools, one from each of the following: the University of North Carolina at Chapel Hill School of Medicine, the Bowman Gray School of Medicine, the Duke University School of Medicine, and the East Carolina University School of Medicine;

(4)   One member who is an oncology nurse representing the North Carolina Nurses Association;

(5)   One member representing the Cancer Committee of the North Carolina Medical Society;

(6)   One member representing the Old North State Medical Society;

(7)   One member representing the American Cancer Society, North Carolina Division, Inc.;

(8)   One member representing the North Carolina Hospital Association;

(9)   One member representing the North Carolina Association of Local Health Directors;

(10)   One member who is a primary care physician licensed to practice medicine in North Carolina;

(11)   One member representing the American College of Surgeons;

(12)   One member representing the North Carolina Oncology Society;

(13)   One member representing the Association of North Carolina Cancer Registrars;

(14)   One member representing the Medical Directors of the North Carolina Association of Health Plans; and

(15)   Up to four additional members at large.

Except for the Secretary, the members shall be appointed for staggered four-year terms and until their successors are appointed and qualify. The Governor may remove any member of the Committee from office in accordance with the provisions of G.S. 143B-13. Members may succeed themselves for one term and may be appointed again after being off the Committee for one term.

(c)   The Speaker of the House of Representatives, the President Pro Tempore of the Senate, and the Governor shall make their appointments to the Committee not later than 30 days after the adjournment of the 1993 Regular Session of the General Assembly. A vacancy on the Committee shall be filled by the original appointing authority, using the criteria set out in this section for the original appointment.

(d)   To the extent that funds are made available, members of the Committee shall receive per diem and necessary travel and subsistence expenses in accordance with G.S. 138-5.

(e)   A majority of the Committee shall constitute a quorum for the transaction of its business.

(f)   The Committee may use funds allocated to it to employ an administrative staff person to assist the Committee in carrying out its duties. The Secretary shall provide clerical and other support staff services needed by the Committee. (1993, c. 321, s. 288; 1997-443, s. 11A.75; 1998-212, s. 12.48(a); 2013-360, s. 12A.10.)

§ 130A-33.51. Advisory Committee on Cancer Coordination and Control; responsibilities.

(a)   The Advisory Committee on Cancer Coordination and Control has the following responsibilities:

(1)   To recommend to the Secretary a plan for the statewide implementation of an interagency comprehensive coordinated cancer control program;

(2)   To identify and examine the limitations and problems associated with existing laws, regulations, programs, and services related to cancer control;

(3)   To examine the financing and access to cancer control services for North Carolina's citizens, and advise the Secretary on a coordinated and efficient use of resources;

(4)   To identify and review health promotion and disease prevention strategies relating to the leading causes of cancer mortality and morbidity;

(5)   To recommend standards for:

a.   Oversight and development of cancer control services;

b.   Development and maintenance of interagency training and technical assistance in the provision of cancer control services;

c.   Program monitoring and data collection;

d.   Statewide evaluation of locally based cancer control programs;

e.   Coordination of funding sources for cancer control programs; and

f.   Procedures for awarding grants to local agencies providing cancer control services.

(b)   The Committee shall submit a written report not later than May 1, 1994, and not later than October 1 of each subsequent year, to the Secretary. The report shall address the progress in implementation of a cancer control program. The report shall include an accounting of funds expended and anticipated funding needs for full implementation of recommended programs. (1993, c. 321, s. 288; 2013-360, s. 12A.9.)

Article 2.

Local Administration.

Part 1. Local Health Departments.

§ 130A-34. Provision of local public health services.

104

(a)   A county shall provide public health services.

(b)   A county shall operate a county health department, establish a consolidated human services agency pursuant to G.S. 153A-77, participate in a district health department, or contract with the State for the provision of public health services. (1901, c. 245, s. 3; Rev., s. 4444; 1911, c. 62, s. 9; C.S., s. 7604; 1931, c. 149; 1941, c. 185; 1945, c. 99; c. 1030, s. 2; 1947, c. 474, s. 3; 1951, c. 92; 1957, c. 1357, s. 1; 1963, c. 359; 1967, c. 1224, s. 1; 1969, c. 719, s. 1; 1971, c. 175, s. 1; 1973, c. 137, s. 1; c. 1151; 1975, c. 272; 1979, c. 621; 1983, c. 891, s. 2; 1995 (Reg. Sess., 1996), c. 690, s. 13.)

§ 130A-34.1. Accreditation of local health departments; board established.

(a)   The Local Health Department Accreditation Board is established within the North Carolina Institute for Public Health. The Board shall be composed of 17 members appointed by the Secretary of the Department of Health and Human Services as follows:

(1)   Four shall be county commissioners recommended by the North Carolina Association of County Commissioners, and four shall be members of a local board of health as recommended by the Association of North Carolina Boards of Health.

(2)   Three local health directors.

(3)   Three staff members from the Division of Public Health, Department of Health and Human Services.

(4)   Repealed by Session Laws 2011-145, s. 13.3(zz), effective July 1, 2011.

(5)   Three at large.

(b)   Members shall serve four-year terms except that initial terms shall be staggered such that three members are appointed for one year, four members are appointed for two years, four members are appointed for three years, and six members are appointed for four years. An appointment to fill a vacancy on the Board created by the resignation, dismissal, ineligibility, death, or disability of any member shall be made for the balance of the unexpired term. The Secretary may remove any member for misfeasance, malfeasance, or nonfeasance. The chair shall be designated by the Secretary and shall designate the times and places at which the Board shall meet. The Board shall meet as often as necessary to carry out its duty to develop and review periodically accreditation standards, to engage in activities necessary to assign accreditation status to local health departments, and to engage in other activities necessary to implement this section.

(c)   Members of the Board who are not officers or employees of the State shall receive reimbursement for travel and subsistence expenses at the rates specified in G.S. 138-5. Members of the Board who are officers or employees of the State shall receive reimbursement for travel and subsistence at the rate set out in G.S. 138-6.

(d)   The Board shall assign an accreditation status to each local health department that applies for initial accreditation, reaccreditation, or relief from conditional accreditation. The Board shall assign the appropriate accreditation status, as follows:

(1)   Accredited, which means that the local health department has satisfied the accreditation standards adopted by the Board and applicable rules adopted by the Commission.

(2)   Conditionally accredited, which means that the local health department has failed to meet one or more accreditation standards and has therefore been granted short-term accreditation subject to conditions specified by the Board.

(3)   Unaccredited, which means that the local health department has continued to fail to meet one or more accreditation standards after a period of conditional accreditation.

(e)   The Commission shall, after reviewing standards developed by and consulting with the Board, adopt rules establishing accreditation standards for local health departments. The accreditation standards shall include at least all of the following:

(1)   An accreditation process that consists of the following components:

a.   A self-assessment conducted by the local health department seeking accreditation.

106

b.   A site visit by a team of experts to clarify, verify, and amplify the information in the self-assessment.

c.   Final action by the Board on the local health department's accreditation status.

(2)   The local health department's capacity to provide the essential public health services, as follows:

a.   Monitoring health status to identify community health problems.

b.   Diagnosing and investigating health hazards in the community.

c.   Informing, educating, and empowering people about health issues.

d.   Mobilizing community partnerships to identify and solve health problems.

e.   Developing policies and plans that support individual and community health efforts.

f.   Enforcing laws and regulations that protect health and ensure safety.

g.   Linking people to needed personal health care services and assuring the provision of health care when otherwise unavailable.

h.   Assuring a competent public health workforce and personal health care workforce.

i.   Evaluating effectiveness, accessibility, and quality of personal and population-based health services.

j.   Conducting research.

(3)   The local health department's facilities and administration.

(4)   The local health department's staff competencies and training procedures or programs.

(5)   The local health department's governance and fiscal management; and

(6)   Informal procedures for reviewing Board decisions.

(f)   All local health departments shall obtain and maintain accreditation in accordance with this section. The Board shall implement accreditation over a period of eight years, beginning January 1, 2006. The Board shall establish a schedule specifying when each local health department shall apply for initial accreditation and ensuring that all local health departments have applied for initial accreditation by December 1, 2014.

(g)   The Board shall assign the following accreditation status, as applicable:

(1)   "Accredited" to a local health department that satisfies the accreditation standards. The initial period of accreditation shall expire four calendar years after initial accreditation is granted.

(2)   "Conditionally accredited" to a local health department that, in its initial accreditation application, fails to satisfy the accreditation standards. The period of conditional accreditation shall expire two calendar years after conditional accreditation is granted. The Board shall provide to the local health department a written statement of the conditions that must be satisfied in order for the local health department to be accredited. At any time during the two-year period, the local health department may request that its status be reviewed and changed from "conditionally accredited" to "accredited." If the Board finds that the conditions have been met, the Board shall change the local health department's status to "accredited" with the accreditation period to expire four calendar years after the conditional accreditation was initially granted. If the Board finds that the conditions have not been satisfied, the local health department shall continue under its grant of conditional accreditation. During the conditional accreditation period, the local health department may apply again for accreditation in accordance with rules adopted by the Commission.

(h)   Each accredited local health department shall apply for reaccreditation in accordance with rules adopted by the Commission.

(i)   When the Board assigns the status "unaccredited" to a local health department, the Board shall send written notification of that status to the local health department and to the Secretary.

(j)   The Commission shall adopt rules to implement this section. (2005-369, s. 1(b); 2011-145, s. 13.3(zz).)

§ 130A-34.2. Billing of Medicaid.

(a)   Local health departments, district health departments, and consolidated human services agencies shall have the following two options to bill public health program services to Medicaid:

(1)   Submit claim data to HIS and manage 837/835 billing files within HIS.

(2)   Submit claim data to any approved Medicaid clearinghouse and manage 837/835 billing files within that system.

(b)   The Division of Public Health may require local health departments, district health departments, and consolidated human services agencies, regardless of how those entities choose to bill public health program services to Medicaid, to submit aggregate data to the Division of Public Health. These data shall be provided in a format specified by the Division of Public Health.

(c)   Local health departments, district health departments, and consolidated human services agencies shall make available encounter-level data for the Division of Public Health as necessary to comply with federal grant reporting requirements. These data shall be provided in a format specified by the Division of Public Health. However, local health departments shall not be required to use Common Name Data System (CNDS) for any purpose.

(d)   Local health departments, district health departments, and consolidated human services agencies that bill services through a Medicaid clearinghouse shall be entitled to the same reimbursement rates negotiated for agencies classified as public health entities and the same Medicaid cost settlement reimbursement as those agencies that bill services through HIS.

(e)   The Division of Public Health shall provide aggregate data requirements for the purposes of Medicaid cost study reimbursement on behalf of the local health departments, district health departments, and consolidated human services agencies that choose to bill services through a Medicaid clearinghouse. Those local health departments, district health departments, and consolidated human services agencies shall submit to the Division of Public Health the data required for the purposes of Medicaid cost study reimbursement and shall retain responsibility to supply the Division of Medical Assistance and/or Centers for Medicare and Medicaid Services (CMS) documentation to support audit processes and procedures to confirm and validate cost study reimbursement data, as defined by CMS cost find regulations.

109

(f)   As used in this section, unless otherwise specified, the following definitions apply:

(1)   "Aggregate data" means high-level reports about services provided by local health departments, district health departments, and consolidated human services agencies, such as the number of patients meeting particular criteria served by a health department or consolidated human service agency or the count of and dollars received for each particular service being performed by a health department or consolidated human service agency, by funding source program and appropriate service code and that comply with appropriate State and federal regulations.

(2)   "Encounter-level data" means patient-identified data specific to each medical encounter used to bill medical services.

(3)   "Health Information System" or "HIS" means the system operated by the North Carolina Division of Public Health and used by local health departments to record information about services the local health departments provide.

(4)   "Public health program services" means services normally provided by a local health department under agreements with the North Carolina Division of Public Health or the North Carolina Division of Medical Assistance. (2011-90, s. 1.)

§ 130A-34.3. Incentive program for public health improvement.

(a)   In order to promote efficiency and effectiveness of the public health delivery system, the Department shall establish a Public Health Improvement Incentive Program. The Program shall provide monetary incentives for the creation and expansion of multicounty local health departments serving a population of not less than 75,000.

(b)   The Commission shall adopt rules to implement the Public Health Improvement Incentive Program. (2012-126, s. 3.)

§ 130A-34.4. Strengthening local public health infrastructure.

(a)   By July 1, 2014, in order for a local health department to be eligible to receive State and federal public health funding from the Division of Public Health, the following criteria shall be met:

(1)   A local health department shall obtain and maintain accreditation pursuant to G.S. 130A-34.1.

(2)   The county or counties comprising the local health department shall maintain operating appropriations to local health departments from local ad valorem tax receipts at levels equal to amounts appropriated in State fiscal year 2010-2011.

(b)   The criteria established in subsection (a) of this section shall be in addition to any other funding criteria established by State or federal law. (2012-126, s. 3.)

§ 130A-35. County board of health; appointment; terms.

(a)   A county board of health shall be the policy-making, rule-making and adjudicatory body for a county health department.

(b)   The members of a county board of health shall be appointed by the county board of commissioners. The board shall be composed of 11 members. The composition of the board shall reasonably reflect the population makeup of the county and shall include: one physician licensed to practice medicine in this State, one licensed dentist, one licensed optometrist, one licensed veterinarian, one registered nurse, one licensed pharmacist, one county commissioner, one professional engineer, and three representatives of the general public. Except as otherwise provided in this section, all members shall be residents of the county. If there is not a licensed physician, a licensed dentist, a licensed veterinarian, a registered nurse, a licensed pharmacist, or a professional engineer available for appointment, an additional representative of the general public shall be appointed. If however, one of the designated professions has only one person residing in the county, the county commissioners shall have the option of appointing that person or a member of the general public. In the event a licensed optometrist who is a resident of the county is not available for appointment, then the county commissioners shall have the option of appointing either a licensed optometrist who is a resident of another county or a member of the general public.

111

(c)   Except as provided in this subsection, members of a county board of health shall serve three-year terms. No member may serve more than three consecutive three-year terms unless the member is the only person residing in the county who represents one of the professions designated in subsection (b) of this section. The county commissioner member shall serve only as long as the member is a county commissioner. When a representative of the general public is appointed due to the unavailability of a licensed physician, a licensed dentist, a resident licensed optometrist or a nonresident licensed optometrist as authorized by subsection (b) of this section, a licensed veterinarian, a registered nurse, a licensed pharmacist, or a professional engineer, that member shall serve only until a licensed physician, a licensed dentist, a licensed resident or nonresident optometrist, a licensed veterinarian, a registered nurse, a licensed pharmacist, or a professional engineer becomes available for appointment. In order to establish a uniform staggered term structure for the board, a member may be appointed for less than a three-year term.

(d)   Vacancies shall be filled for any unexpired portion of a term.

(e)   A chairperson shall be elected annually by a county board of health. The local health director shall serve as secretary to the board.

(f)   A majority of the members shall constitute a quorum.

(g)   A member may be removed from office by the county board of commissioners for:

(1)   Commission of a felony or other crime involving moral turpitude;

(2)   Violation of a State law governing conflict of interest;

(3)   Violation of a written policy adopted by the county board of commissioners;

(4)   Habitual failure to attend meetings;

(5)   Conduct that tends to bring the office into disrepute; or

(6)   Failure to maintain qualifications for appointment required under subsection (b) of this section.

A board member may be removed only after the member has been given written notice of the basis for removal and has had the opportunity to respond.

(h)   A member may receive a per diem in an amount established by the county board of commissioners. Reimbursement for subsistence and travel shall be in accordance with a policy set by the county board of commissioners.

(i)   The board shall meet at least quarterly. The chairperson or three of the members may call a special meeting. (1901, c. 245, s. 3; Rev., s. 4444; 1911, c. 62, s. 9; C.S., s. 7604; 1931, c. 149; 1941, c. 185; 1945, c. 99; c. 1030, s. 2; 1947, c. 474, s. 3; 1951, c. 92; 1957, c. 1357, s. 1; 1963, c. 359; 1967, c. 1224, s. 1; 1969, c. 719, s. 1; 1971, c. 175, s. 1; c. 940, s. 1; 1973, c. 137, s. 1; c. 1151; 1975, c. 272; 1979, c. 621; 1981, c. 104; 1983, c. 891, s. 2; 1985, c. 418, s. 1; 1987, c. 84, s. 1; 1989, c. 764, s. 2; 1995, c. 264, s. 1; 2009-447, s. 1.)

§ 130A-36. Creation of district health department.

(a)   A district health department including more than one county may be formed in lieu of county health departments upon agreement of the county boards of commissioners and local boards of health having jurisdiction over each of the counties involved. A county may join a district health department upon agreement of the boards of commissioners and local boards of health having jurisdiction over each of the counties involved. A district health department shall be a public authority as defined in G.S. 159-7(b)(10).

(b)   Upon creation of or addition to a district health department, the existing rules of the former board or boards of health shall continue in effect until amended or repealed by the district board of health. (1957, c. 1357, s. 1; 1969, c. 719, s. 2; 1971, c. 175, s. 2; 1973, c. 143, ss. 1-4; c. 476, s. 128; 1975, c. 396, s. 1; 1981, c. 238; c. 408; 1983, c. 891, s. 2.)

§ 130A-37. District board of health.

(a)   A district board of health shall be the policy-making, rule-making and adjudicatory body for a district health department and shall be composed of 15 members; provided, a district board of health may be increased up to a maximum number of 18 members by agreement of the boards of county

113

commissioners in all counties that comprise the district. The agreement shall be evidenced by concurrent resolutions adopted by the affected boards of county commissioners.

(b)   The county board of commissioners of each county in the district shall appoint one county commissioner to the district board of health. The county commissioner members of the district board of health shall appoint the other members of the board, including at least one physician licensed to practice medicine in this State, one licensed dentist, one licensed optometrist, one licensed veterinarian, one registered nurse, one licensed pharmacist, and one professional engineer. The composition of the board shall reasonably reflect the population makeup of the entire district and provide equitable district-wide representation. All members shall be residents of the district. If there is not a licensed physician, a licensed dentist, a licensed optometrist, a licensed veterinarian, a registered nurse, a licensed pharmacist, or a professional engineer available for appointment, an additional representative of the general public shall be appointed. If however, one of the designated professions has only one person residing in the district, the county commissioner members shall have the option of appointing that person or a member of the general public.

(c)   Except as provided in this subsection, members of a district board of health shall serve terms of three years. Two of the original members shall serve terms of one year and two of the original members shall serve terms of two years. No member shall serve more than three consecutive three-year terms unless the member is the only person residing in the district who represents one of the professions designated in subsection (b) of this section. County commissioner members shall serve only as long as the member is a county commissioner. When a representative of the general public is appointed due to the unavailability of a licensed physician, a licensed dentist, a licensed optometrist, a licensed veterinarian, a registered nurse, a licensed pharmacist, or a professional engineer that member shall serve only until a licensed physician, a licensed dentist, a licensed optometrist, a licensed veterinarian, a registered nurse, a licensed pharmacist, or a professional engineer becomes available for appointment. The county commissioner members may appoint a member for less than a three-year term to achieve a staggered term structure.

(d)   Whenever a county shall join or withdraw from an existing district health department, the district board of health shall be dissolved and a new board shall be appointed as provided in subsection (c).

(e)   Vacancies shall be filled for any unexpired portion of a term.

114

(f)   A chairperson shall be elected annually by a district board of health. The local health director shall serve as secretary to the board.

(g)   A majority of the members shall constitute a quorum.

(h)   A member may be removed from office by the district board of health for:

(1)   Commission of a felony or other crime involving moral turpitude;

(2)   Violation of a State law governing conflict of interest;

(3)   Violation of a written policy adopted by the county board of commissioners of each county in the district;

(4)   Habitual failure to attend meetings;

(5)   Conduct that tends to bring the office into disrepute; or

(6)   Failure to maintain qualifications for appointment required under subsection (b) of this section.

A board member may be removed only after the member has been given written notice of the basis for removal and has had the opportunity to respond.

(i)   A member may receive a per diem in an amount established by the county commissioner members of the district board of health. Reimbursement for subsistence and travel shall be in accordance with a policy set by the county commissioner members of the district board of health.

(j)   The board shall meet at least quarterly. The chairperson or three of the members may call a special meeting.

(k)   A district board of health is authorized to provide liability insurance for the members of the board and the employees of the district health department. A district board of health is also authorized to contract for the services of an attorney to represent the board, the district health department and its employees, as appropriate. The purchase of liability insurance pursuant to this subsection waives both the district board of health's and the district health department's governmental immunity, to the extent of insurance coverage, for any act or omission occurring in the exercise of a governmental function. By entering into a liability insurance contract with the district board of health, an insurer waives any defense based upon the governmental immunity of the district board of health or the district health department. (1957, c. 1357, s. 1; 1969, c. 719, s. 2; 1971, c. 175, s. 2; c. 940, s. 1; 1973, c. 143, ss. 1-4; c. 476, s. 128; 1975, c. 396, s. 1; 1981, cc. 104, 238, 408; 1983, c. 891, s. 2; 1983 (Reg. Sess., 1984), c. 1077; 1985, c. 418, s. 2; 1987, c. 84, s. 2; 1989, c. 764, s. 3; 1995, c. 264, s. 2.)

§ 130A-38. Dissolution of a district health department.

(a)   Whenever the board of commissioners of each county constituting a district health department determines that the district health department is not operating in the best health interests of the respective counties, they may direct that the district health department be dissolved. In addition, whenever a board of commissioners of a county which is a member of a district health department determines that the district health department is not operating in the best health interests of that county, it may withdraw from the district health department. Dissolution of a district health department or withdrawal from the district health department by a county shall be effective only at the end of the fiscal year in which the action of dissolution or withdrawal transpired.

(b)   Notwithstanding the provisions of subsection (a), no district health department shall be dissolved without prior written notification to the Department.

(c)   Any budgetary surplus available to a district health department at the time of its dissolution shall be distributed to those counties comprising the district on the same pro rata basis that the counties appropriated and contributed funds to the district health department budget during the current fiscal year. Distribution to the counties shall be determined on the basis of an audit of the financial record of the district health department. The district board of health shall select a certified public accountant or an accountant who is subsequently certified by the Local Government Commission to conduct the audit. The audit shall be performed in accordance with G.S. 159-34. The same method of distribution of funds described above shall apply when one or more counties of a district health department withdraw from a district.

(d)   Upon dissolution or withdrawal, all rules adopted by a district board of health shall continue in effect until amended or repealed by the new board or boards of health. (1971, c. 858; 1975, c. 396, s. 2; c. 403; 1983, c. 891, s. 2.)

§ 130A-39. Powers and duties of a local board of health.

(a)   A local board of health shall have the responsibility to protect and promote the public health. The board shall have the authority to adopt rules necessary for that purpose.

(b)   A local board of health may adopt a more stringent rule in an area regulated by the Commission for Public Health or the Environmental Management Commission where, in the opinion of the local board of health, a more stringent rule is required to protect the public health; otherwise, the rules of the Commission for Public Health or the rules of the Environmental Management Commission shall prevail over local board of health rules. However, a local board of health may not adopt a rule concerning the grading, operating, and permitting of food and lodging facilities as listed in Part 6 of Article 8 of this Chapter and as defined in G.S. 130A-247(1), and a local board of health may adopt rules concerning wastewater collection, treatment and disposal systems which are not designed to discharge effluent to the land surface or surface waters only in accordance with G.S. 130A-335(c).

(c)   The rules of a local board of health shall apply to all municipalities within the local board's jurisdiction.

(d)   Not less than 10 days before the adoption, amendment or repeal of any local board of health rule, the proposed rule shall be made available at the office of each county clerk within the board's jurisdiction, and a notice shall be published in a newspaper having general circulation within the area of the board's jurisdiction. The notice shall contain a statement of the substance of the proposed rule or a description of the subjects and issues involved, the proposed effective date of the rule and a statement that copies of the proposed rule are available at the local health department. A local board of health rule shall become effective upon adoption unless a later effective date is specified in the rule.

(e)   Copies of all rules shall be filed with the secretary of the local board of health.

117

(f)   A local board of health may, in its rules, adopt by reference any code, standard, rule or regulation which has been adopted by any agency of this State, another state, any agency of the United States or by a generally recognized association. Copies of any material adopted by reference shall be filed with the rules.

(g)   A local board of health may impose a fee for services to be rendered by a local health department, except where the imposition of a fee is prohibited by statute or where an employee of the local health department is performing the services as an agent of the State. Notwithstanding any other provisions of law, a local board of health may impose cost-related fees for services performed pursuant to Article 11 of this Chapter, "Wastewater Systems," for services performed pursuant to Part 10, Article 8 of this Chapter, "Public Swimming Pools", for services performed pursuant to Part 11, Article 8 of this Chapter, "Tattooing", and for services performed pursuant to G.S. 87-97. Fees shall be based upon a plan recommended by the local health director and approved by the local board of health and the appropriate county board or boards of commissioners. The fees collected under the authority of this subsection are to be deposited to the account of the local health department so that they may be expended for public health purposes in accordance with the provisions of the Local Government Budget and Fiscal Control Act. (1901, c. 245, s. 3; Rev., s. 4444; 1911, c. 62, s. 9; C.S., s. 7065; 1957, c. 1357, s. 1; 1959, c. 1024, s. 1; 1963, c. 1087; 1973, c. 476, s. 128; c. 508; 1977, c. 857, s. 2; 1981, c. 130, s. 2; c. 281; c. 949, s. 4; 1983, c. 891, s. 2; 1985, c. 175, s. 1; 1989, c. 577, s. 2; 1991 (Reg. Sess., 1992), c. 944, s. 10; 1993 (Reg. Sess., 1994), c. 670, s. 2; 1995, c. 507, s. 26.8(c); 2006-202, s. 6; 2007-182, s. 2.)

§ 130A-40. Appointment of local health director.

(a)   A local board of health, after consulting with the appropriate county board or boards of commissioners, shall appoint a local health director. All persons who are appointed to the position of local health director on or after January 1, 1992, must possess minimum education and experience requirements for that position, as follows:

(1)   A medical doctorate; or

(2)   A masters degree in Public Health Administration, and at least one year of employment experience in health programs or health services; or

(3)   A masters degree in a public health discipline other than public health administration, and at least three years of employment experience in health programs or health services; or

(4)   A masters degree in public administration, and at least two years of experience in health programs or health services; or

(5)   A masters degree in a field related to public health, and at least three years of experience in health programs or health services; or

(6)   A bachelors degree in public health administration or public administration and at least three years of experience in health programs or health services.

(b)   Before appointing a person to the position of local health director under subsection (a)(5) of this section, the local board of health shall forward the application and other pertinent materials of such candidate to the State Health Director. If the State Health Director determines that the candidate's masters degree is in a field not related to public health, the State Health Director shall so notify the local board of health in writing within 15 days of the State Health Director's receipt of the application and materials, and such candidate shall be deemed not to meet the education requirements of subsection (a)(5) of this section. If the State Health Director fails to act upon the application within 15 days of receipt of the application and materials from the local board of health, the application shall be deemed approved with respect to the education requirements of subsection (a)(5) of this section, and the local board of health may proceed with appointment process.

(c)   The State Health Director shall review requests of educational institutions to determine whether a particular masters degree offered by the requesting institution is related to public health for the purposes of subsection (a)(5) of this section. The State Health Director shall act upon such requests within 90 days of receipt of the request and pertinent materials from the institution, and shall notify the institution of its determination in writing within the 90-day review period. If the State Health Director determines that an institution's particular masters degree is not related to public health, the State Health Director shall include the reasons therefor in his written determination to the institution.

(d)   When a local board of health fails to appoint a local health director within 60 days of the creation of a vacancy, the State Health Director may appoint a

119

local health director to serve until the local board of health appoints a local health director in accordance with this section. (1957, c. 1357, s. 1; 1973, c. 152; c. 476, s. 128; 1983, c. 891, s. 2; 1983 (Reg. Sess., 1984), c. 1034, s. 75; 1991, c. 612.)

§ 130A-40.1. Pilot program for nurse as health director.

(a)   Notwithstanding G.S. 130A-40, a local board of health, after consulting with the appropriate county board of commissioners, and with the approval of the Secretary of Health and Human Services, may appoint a local health director who meets the following education and experience requirements for that position:

(1)   Graduation from a four-year college or university with a Bachelor of Science in Nursing degree that includes a public health nursing rotation; or

(2)   A candidate with an RN but not a bachelors degree if the candidate has at least 10 years' experience, at least seven years of which must be in an administrative or supervisory role, and of this seven years, at least five years must be at the agency at which the candidate is an applicant for employment as local health director.

(b)   The Secretary of Health and Human Services may approve only one request under subsection (a) of this section, this section being designed as a pilot program concerning alternative qualifications for a local health director. The Secretary of Health and Human Services shall report any approval under this section to the Joint Legislative Oversight Committee on Health and Human Services.

(c)   All bachelors level candidates appointed under this section shall have a total of 10 years' public health experience, at least five years of which must be in a supervisory capacity at the agency at which the candidate is an applicant for employment as a local health director. Bachelor of Science in Nursing candidates with a public health rotation may use this BSN degree as credit for one year's public health experience.

(d)   In addition to possessing the qualifications required in this section, all Bachelor of Science, Bachelor of Arts, or Registered Nurse candidates must complete at least six contact hours of continuing education annually on the

120

subject of local and State government finance, organization, or budgeting. The training must be in a formal setting offered through the State or local government or through an accredited educational institution. This training is in addition to any other required training for local health director or other continuing education required to maintain other professional credentials. If during the course of employment as local health director the employee meets the requirements of this subsection, the additional training requirements of this section are waived. (2003-284, s. 10.33C; 2011-266, s. 1.16(b); 2011-291, s. 2.46; 2012-194, s. 27.)

§ 130A-41. Powers and duties of local health director.

(a)   A local health director shall be the administrative head of the local health department, shall perform public health duties prescribed by and under the supervision of the local board of health and the Department and shall be employed full time in the field of public health.

(b)   A local health director shall have the following powers and duties:

(1)   To administer programs as directed by the local board of health;

(2)   To enforce the rules of the local board of health;

(3)   To investigate the causes of infectious, communicable and other diseases;

(4)   To exercise quarantine authority and isolation authority pursuant to G.S. 130A-145;

(5)   To disseminate public health information and to promote the benefits of good health;

(6)   To advise local officials concerning public health matters;

(7)   To enforce the immunization requirements of Part 2 of Article 6 of this Chapter;

(8)   To examine and investigate cases of venereal disease pursuant to Parts 3 and 4 of Article 6 of this Chapter;

121

(9)   To examine and investigate cases of tuberculosis pursuant to Part 5 of Article 6 of this Chapter;

(10)   To examine, investigate and control rabies pursuant to Part 6 of Article 6 of this Chapter;

(11)   To abate public health nuisances and imminent hazards pursuant to G.S. 130A-19 and G.S. 130A-20;

(12)   To employ and dismiss employees of the local health department in accordance with Chapter 126 of the General Statutes;

(13)   To enter contracts, in accordance with The Local Government Finance Act, G.S. Chapter 159, on behalf of the local health department. Nothing in this paragraph shall be construed to abrogate the authority of the board of county commissioners.

(c)   Authority conferred upon a local health director may be exercised only within the county or counties comprising the local health department. (1957, c. 1357, s. 1; 1973, c. 476, s. 128; 1983, c. 891, s. 2; 1985, c. 175, s. 2; 1999-110, s. 1.)

§ 130A-42. Personnel records of district health departments.

Employee personnel records of a district health department shall have the same protections from disclosure as county employee personnel records under G.S. 153A-98. For the purposes of this section, the local health director shall perform the duties assigned to the county manager pursuant to G.S. 153A-98 and the district board of health shall perform the duties assigned to the county board of commissioners pursuant to G.S. 153A-98. (1983, c. 891, s. 2.)

Part 1A. Consolidated Human Services Agency.

§ 130A-43. Consolidated human services agency; board; director.

(a)   Except as otherwise provided by this section and subject to any limitations that may be imposed by the board of county commissioners under

G.S. 153A-77, a consolidated human services agency created pursuant to G.S. 153A-77 shall have the responsibility to carry out the duties of a local health department and the authority to administer the local public health programs established in this Chapter in the same manner as a local health department.

(b)   In addition to the powers conferred by G.S. 153A-77(d), a consolidated human services board shall have all the powers and duties of a local board of health as provided by G.S. 130A-39, except that the consolidated human services board may not:

(1)   Appoint the human services director.

(2)   Transmit or present the budget for local health programs.

(c)   In addition to the powers conferred by G.S. 153A-77(e), a human services director shall have all the powers and duties of a local health director provided by G.S. 130A-41, except that the human services director may:

(1)   Serve as the executive officer of the consolidated human services agency only to the extent and in the manner authorized by the county manager.

(2)   Appoint staff of the consolidated human services agency only upon the approval of the county manager. (1995 (Reg. Sess., 1996), c. 690, s. 14.)

§ 130A-44. Reserved for future codification purposes.

Part 1B. Public Health Authorities Authorized.

§ 130A-45. Title and purpose.

(a)   This Part shall be known and may be cited as the "Public Health Authorities Act".

(b)   The purpose of this Part is to provide an alternative method for counties to provide public health services. This Part shall not be regarded as repealing any powers now existing under any other law, either general, special, or local.

(c)   It is the policy of the General Assembly that Public Health Authorities should have adequate authority to exercise the powers, rights, duties, functions, privileges, and immunities conferred upon them by law. (1997-502, s. 1.)

§ 130A-45.01. Definitions.

As used in this Part, unless otherwise specified:

(1)   "Authority service area" means the area within the boundaries of the authority as provided for in G.S. 130A-45.4.

(2)   "Board" means a public health authority board created under this Part.

(3)   "County" means the county which is, or is about to be, included in the territorial boundaries of a public health authority when created hereunder.

(4)   "County board of commissioners" means the legislative body charged with governing the county.

(5)   "Department" means the Department of Health and Human Services.

(6)   "Federal government" means the United States of America, or any agency, instrumentality, corporate or otherwise, of the United States of America.

(7)   "Government" means the State and federal governments and any subdivision, agency, or instrumentality, corporate or otherwise, of either of them.

(8)   "Public health authority" means a public body and a body corporate and politic organized under the provisions of this Part.

(9)   "Public health facility" means any one or more buildings, structures, additions, extensions, improvements, or other facilities, whether or not located on the same site or sites, machinery, equipment, furnishings or other real or personal property suitable for providing public health services; and includes, without limitation, local public health departments or centers; public health

124

clinics and outpatient facilities; nursing homes, including skilled nursing facilities and intermediate care facilities, adult care homes for the aged and disabled; public health laboratories; administration buildings, central service and other administrative facilities; communication, computer and other electronic facilities; pharmaceutical facilities; storage space; vehicular parking lots and other such public health facilities, customarily under the jurisdiction of or provided by public health departments, or any combination of the foregoing, with all necessary, convenient or related interests in land, machinery, apparatus, appliances, equipment, furnishings, appurtenances, site preparation, landscaping, and physical amenities.

(10)   "Real property" means lands, lands under water, structures, and any and all easements, franchises and incorporeal hereditaments and every estate and right therein, legal and equitable, including terms for years and liens by way of judgment, mortgage or otherwise.

(11)   "State" means the State of North Carolina. (1997-502, s. 1.)

§ 130A-45.02. Creation of a public health authority.

(a)   A public health authority may be created upon joint resolution of the county board of commissioners and the local board of health that it is in the interest of the public health and welfare to create a public health authority to provide public health services as required under G.S. 130A-34.

(b)   A public health authority including more than one county may be formed upon joint resolution of the county boards of commissioners and local boards of health having jurisdiction over each of the counties involved.

(c)   After the adoption of a resolution creating a public health authority, a public health authority board shall be appointed in accordance with G.S. 130A-45.1.

(d)   A county may join a public health authority upon joint resolution of the boards of commissioners and local boards of health having jurisdiction over each of the counties involved.

125

(e)   A public health authority board shall govern the public health authority. All powers, duties, functions, rights, privileges, or immunities conferred on the public health authority may be exercised by the authority board.

(f)   The public health authority board shall absorb the functions, assets, and liabilities of the county or district boards of health, and that board is dissolved.

(g)   For the purpose of Chapter 159 of the General Statutes, a public health authority is a public authority as defined in G.S. 159-7(b)(10).

(h)   Before adopting a resolution creating a public health authority, the county board of commissioners shall hold a public hearing with notice published at least 10 days before the hearing.

(i)   For the purposes of Article 9 of Chapter 131E of the General Statutes, a public health authority is a person as defined in G.S. 131E-176(19). (1997-502, s. 1; 2001-92, s. 3.)

§ 130A-45.1. Membership of the public health authority board.

(a)   A public health authority board shall be the policy-making, rule-making, and adjudicatory body for a public health authority and shall be composed of no fewer than seven members and no more than nine members; except that in an authority comprising two or more counties, the board shall be composed of no more than 11 members. Boards which intend to pursue federally qualified health center (or look-alike) status may have no fewer than nine and no more than 25 members.

(b)   In a single county authority, the county board of commissioners shall appoint the members of the board; in an authority comprising two or more counties, the chair of the county board of commissioners of each county in the authority shall appoint one county commissioner, or the commissioner's express designee, to the authority board and these members shall jointly appoint the other members of the board.

(c)   The members of the board shall include:

(1)   At least one physician licensed under Chapter 90 of the General Statutes to practice medicine in this State, and at least one dentist licensed

126

under Article 2 of Chapter 90 of the General Statutes to practice dentistry in this State;

(2)   At least one county commissioner or the commissioner's express designee from each county in the authority;

(3)   At least two licensed or registered professionals from any of the following professions: optometry, veterinary science, nursing, pharmacy, engineering, or accounting;

(4)   At least one member from the administrative staff of a hospital serving the authority service area; and

(5)   At least one member from the general public.

(d)   Except as provided in this subsection, members of the board shall serve terms of three years. In order to establish a uniform staggered term structure for the Board, a member may be appointed for less than a three-year term.

(e)   Any member who is a county commissioner serves on the board in an ex officio capacity.

(f)   Whenever a county shall join or withdraw from an existing public health authority, the board shall be dissolved and a new board shall be appointed as provided in subsection (b) of this section.

(g)   Vacancies shall be filled within 120 days for any unexpired portion of a term.

(h)   A chair shall be elected annually by a board. The authority director shall serve as secretary to the board.

(i)   A majority of the members shall constitute a quorum.

(j)   A member may be removed from office by the board for any of the following:

(1)   Commission of a felony or other crime involving moral turpitude.

(2)   Violation of a State law governing conflict of interest.

(3)   Violation of a written policy adopted by the county board of commissioners of each county in the authority.

(4)   Habitual failure to attend meetings.

(5)   Conduct that tends to bring the office into disrepute.

(6)   Failure to maintain qualifications for appointment required under subsection (c) of this section.

A board member may be removed only after the member has been given written notice of the basis for removal and has had the opportunity to respond.

(k)   Board members may receive per diem in an amount established by the county commissioner members of the Public Health Authority Board. Reimbursement for subsistence and travel shall be in accordance with a policy set by the county commissioner members of the Public Health Authority Board.

(l)   The board shall meet at least quarterly. The chair or three of the members may call a special meeting. (1997-502, s. 1; 2005-459, s. 2; 2007-229, s. 1.)

§ 130A-45.2. Dissolution of a public health authority.

(a)   Whenever the board of commissioners of each county constituting a public health authority determines that the authority is not operating in the best health interests of the authority service area, they may direct that the authority be dissolved. In addition, whenever a board of commissioners of a county which is a member of an authority determines that the authority is not operating in the best health interests of that county, it may withdraw from the authority. Dissolution of an authority or withdrawal from the authority by a county shall be effective only at the end of the fiscal year in which the action of dissolution or withdrawal transpired.

(b)   Notwithstanding the provisions of subsection (a) of this section, no public health authority shall be dissolved without prior written notification to the Department.

(c)   Any budgetary surplus available to a public health authority at the time of its dissolution shall be distributed to those counties comprising the authority on the same pro rata basis that the counties appropriated and contributed funds to the authority's budget during the current fiscal year. Distribution to the counties shall be determined on the basis of an audit of the financial record of the authority. The public health authority board shall select a certified public accountant or an accountant who is subsequently certified by the Local Government Commission to conduct the audit. The audit shall be performed in accordance with G.S. 159-34. The same method of distribution of funds described above shall apply when one or more counties of an authorIty wIthdraw from the authority.

(d)   Upon dissolution or withdrawal, all rules adopted by the board continue in effect until amended or repealed by the new authority board or boards of health. (1997-502, s. 1.)

§ 130A-45.3. Powers and duties of authority board.

(a)   A public health authority shall have all the powers necessary or convenient to carry out the purposes of this Part, including the following powers to:

(1)   Protect and promote the public health. The board shall have the authority to adopt rules necessary for that purpose.

(2)   Construct, equip, operate, and maintain public health facilities.

(3)   Use property owned or controlled by the authority.

(4)   Acquire real or personal property, including existing public health facilities, by purchase, grant, gift, devise, lease or, with the permission of the county commissioners, condemnation.

(5)   Establish a fee schedule for services received from public health facilities and make services available regardless of ability to pay.

(6)   Appoint a public health authority director to serve at the pleasure of the authority board.

(7)   Establish a salary plan which shall set the salaries for employees of the area authority.

(8)   To adopt and enforce a professional reimbursement policy which may include the following provisions: (i) require that fees for the provision of services received directly under the supervision of the public health authority shall be paid to the authority, (ii) prohibit employees of the public health authority from providing services on a private basis which require the use of the resources and facilities of the public health authority, and (iii) provide that employees may not accept dual compensation and dual employment unless they have the written permission of the public health authority director.

(9)   Delegate to its agents or employees any powers or duties as it may deem appropriate.

(10)   Employ its own counsel and legal staff.

(11)   Adopt, amend, and repeal bylaws for the conduct of its business.

(12)   Enter into contracts for necessary supplies, equipment, or services for the operation of its business.

(13)   Act as an agent for the federal, State, or local government in connection with the acquisition, construction, operation, or management of a public health facility, or any part thereof.

(14)   Insure the property or the operations of the authority against risks as the authority may deem advisable.

(15)   Sue and be sued.

(16)   Accept donations or money, personal property, or real estate for the benefit of the authority and to take title to the same from any person, firm, corporation, or society.

(17)   Appoint advisory boards, committees, and councils composed of qualified and interested residents of the authority service area to study, interpret, and advise the public health authority board.

(18)   To purchase or finance real or personal property in the manner provided for cities and counties under G.S. 160A-20.

(b)   A public health authority shall have the power to establish and operate health care networks and may contract with or enter into any arrangement with other public health authorities or local health departments of this or other states, federal, or other public agencies, or with any person, private organization, or nonprofit corporation or association for the provision of public health services, including managed health care activities; provided, however, that for the purposes of this subsection only, a public health authority shall be permitted to and shall comply with the requirements of Article 67 of Chapter 58 of the General Statutes to the extent that such requirements apply to the activities undertaken by the public health authority pursuant to this subsection. The public health authority may pay for or contribute its share of the cost of any such contract or arrangement from revenues available for these purposes, including revenues arising from the provision of public health services.

(c)   A public health authority may lease any public health facility, or part, to a nonprofit association on terms and conditions consistent with the purposes of this Part. The authority will determine the length of the lease. No lease executed under this subsection shall be deemed to convey a freehold interest.

(d)   A public health authority shall neither sell nor convey any rights of ownership the county has in any public health facility, including the buildings, land, and equipment associated with the facility, to any corporation or other business entity operated for profit, except that nothing herein shall prohibit the sale of surplus buildings, surplus land, or surplus equipment by an authority to any corporation or other business entity operated for profit. For purposes of this subsection, "surplus" means any building, land, or equipment which is not required for use in the delivery of public health care services by a public health facility at the time of the sale or conveyance of ownership rights.

(e)   A public health authority may lease any public health facility, or part, to any corporation, foreign or domestic, authorized to do business in North Carolina on terms and conditions consistent with the purposes of this Part and with G.S. 160A-272.

(f)   A public health authority may exercise any or all of the powers conferred upon it by this Part, either generally or with respect to any specific public health facility or facilities, through or by designated agents, including any corporation or corporations which are or shall be formed under the laws of this State.

(g)   An authority may contract to insure itself and any of its board members, agents, or employees against liability for wrongful death or negligent or

131

intentional damage to person or property or against absolute liability for damage to person or property caused by an act or omission of the authority or of any of its board members, agents, or employees when acting within the scope of their authority and the course of their employment. The board shall determine what liabilities and what members, agents, and employees shall be covered by any insurance purchased pursuant to this subsection.

Purchase of insurance pursuant to this subsection waives the authority's governmental immunity, to the extent of insurance coverage, for any act or omission occurring in the exercise of a governmental function. Participation in a local government risk pool pursuant to Article 23 of Chapter 58 of the General Statutes shall be deemed to be the purchase of insurance for the purposes of this section. By entering into an insurance contract with the authority, an insurer waives any defense based upon the governmental immunity of the authority.

(h)   If an authority has waived its governmental immunity pursuant to subsection (g) of this section, any person, or in the event of death, their personal representative, sustaining damages as a result of an act or omission of the authority or any of its board members, agents, or employees, occurring in the exercise of a governmental function, may sue the authority for recovery of damages. To the extent of the coverage of insurance purchased pursuant to subsection (g) of this section, governmental immunity may not be a defense to the action. Otherwise, however, the authority has all defenses available to private litigants in any action brought pursuant to this section without restriction, limitation, or other effect, whether the defense arises from common law or by virtue of a statute.

Despite the purchase of insurance as authorized by subsection (g) of this section, the liability of an authority for acts or omissions occurring in the exercise of governmental functions does not attach unless the plaintiff waives the right to have all issues of law or fact relating to insurance in the action determined by a jury. The judge shall hear and determine these issues without resort to a jury, and the jury shall be absent during any motion, argument, testimony, or announcement of findings of fact or conclusions of law relating to these issues unless the defendant requests a jury trial on them. (1997-502, s. 1; 2007-229, s. 2.)

§ 130A-45.4. Appointment of a public health authority director.

132

(a)   A public health authority board, after consulting with the appropriate county board or boards of commissioners, shall appoint a public health authority director.

(b)   All persons who are appointed to the position of public health authority director must possess minimum education and experience requirements for that position, as follows:

(1)   A medical doctorate; or

(2)   A masters degree in Public Health Administration, and at least one year of employment experience in health programs or health services; or

(3)   A masters degree in a public health discipline other than public health administration, and at least three years of employment experience in health programs or health services; or

(4)   A masters degree in public administration, and at least two years of experience in health programs or health services; or

(5)   A masters degree in a field related to public health, and at least three years of experience in health programs or health services; or

(6)   A bachelors degree in public health administration or public administration and at least three years of experience in health programs or health services.

(c)   Before appointing a person to the position of public health authority director under subdivision (a)(5) of this section, the authority board shall forward the application and other pertinent materials of such candidate to the State Health Director. If the State Health Director determines that the candidate's masters degree is in a field not related to public health, the State Health Director shall so notify the authority board in writing within 15 days of the State Health Director's receipt of the application and materials, and such candidate shall be deemed not to meet the education requirements of subdivision (a)(5) of this section. If the State Health Director fails to act upon the application within 15 days of receipt of the application and materials from the authority board, the application shall be deemed approved with respect to the education requirements of subdivision (a)(5) of this section, and the authority board may proceed with the appointment process.

133

(d)   The State Health Director shall review requests of educational institutions to determine whether a particular masters degree offered by the requesting institution is related to public health for the purposes of subdivision (a)(5) of this section. The State Health Director shall act upon such requests within 90 days of receipt of the request and pertinent materials from the institution, and shall notify the institution of its determination in writing within the 90-day review period. If the State Health Director determines that an institution's particular masters degree is not related to public health, the State Health Director shall include the reasons therefor in his written determination to the institution.

(e)   When an authority board fails to appoint a public health authority director within 60 days of the creation of a vacancy, the State Health Director may appoint an authority director to serve until the authority board appoints an authority director in accordance with this section. (1997-502, s. 1.)

§ 130A-45.5. Powers and duties of a public health authority director.

(a)   The public health authority director is an employee of the authority board and shall serve at the pleasure of the authority board.

(b)   An authority health director shall perform public health duties prescribed by and under the supervision of the public health authority board and the Department and shall be employed full time in the field of public health.

(c)   An authority health director shall have the following powers and duties:

(1)   To administer programs as directed by the public health authority board;

(2)   To enforce the rules of the public health authority board;

(3)   To investigate the causes of infectious, communicable, and other diseases;

(4)   To exercise quarantine authority and isolation authority pursuant to G.S. 130A-145;

(5)   To disseminate public health information and to promote the benefits of good health;

134

(6)   To advise local officials concerning public health matters;

(7)   To enforce the immunization requirements of Part 2 of Article 7 of this Chapter;

(8)   To examine and investigate cases of venereal disease pursuant to Parts 3 and 4 of Article 6 of this Chapter;

(9)   To examine and investigate cases of tuberculosis pursuant to Part 5 of Article 6 of this Chapter;

(10)   To examine, investigate, and control rabies pursuant to Part 6 of Article 6 of this Chapter;

(11)   To abate public health nuisances and imminent hazards pursuant to G.S. 130A-19 and G.S. 130A-20; and

(12)   To employ, discipline, and dismiss employees of the public health authority.

(d)   Authority conferred upon a public health authority director may be exercised only within the county or counties comprising the public health authority. (1997-502, s. 1.)

§ 130A-45.6. Boundaries of the authority.

A public health authority may provide or contract to provide public health services and to acquire, construct, establish, enlarge, improve, maintain, own, or operate, and contract for the operation of any public health facilities outside the territorial limits, within reasonable limitation, of the county or counties creating the authority, but in no case shall a public health authority be held liable for damages to those outside the territorial limits of the county or counties creating the authority for failure to provide any public health service. (1997-502, s. 1.)

§ 130A-45.7. Medical review committee.

135

(a)   A member of a duly appointed medical review committee who acts without malice or fraud shall not be subject to liability for damages in any civil action on account of any act, statement, or proceeding undertaken, made, or performed within the scope of the functions of the committee.

(b)   The proceedings of a medical review committee, the records and materials it produces and the materials it considers shall be confidential and not considered public records within the meaning of G.S. 132-1, "Public records" defined, and shall not be subject to discovery or introduction into evidence in any civil action against a public health authority or a provider of professional health services which results from matters which are the subject of evaluation and review by the committee. No person who was in attendance at a meeting of the committee shall be required to testify in any civil action as to any evidence or other matters produced or presented during the proceedings of the committee or as to any findings, recommendations, evaluations, opinions, or other actions of the committee or its members. However, information, documents, or records otherwise available are not immune from discovery or use in a civil action merely because they were presented during proceedings of the committee. A member of the committee or a person who testifies before the committee may testify in a civil action but cannot be asked about his testimony before the committee or any opinions formed as a result of the committee hearings. (1997-502, s. 1.)

§ 130A-45.8. Confidentiality of patient information.

(a)   Medical records compiled and maintained by public health authorities in connection with the admission, treatment, and discharge of individual patients are not public records as defined by Chapter 132 of the General Statutes.

(b)   Charges, accounts, credit histories, and other personal financial records compiled and maintained by public health authorities in connection with the admission, treatment, and discharge of individual patients are not public records as defined by Chapter 132 of the General Statutes. (1997-502, s. 1.)

§ 130A-45.9. Confidentiality of personnel information.

136

(a)   Except as provided in subsection (b) of this section, the personnel files of employees or former employees and the files of applicants for employment maintained by a public health authority are not public records as defined by Chapter 132 of the General Statutes.

(b)   The following information with respect to each employee of a public health authority is a matter of public record: name; age; date of original employment or appointment; beginning and ending dates, position title, position descriptions, and total compensation of current and former positions; the terms of any contract by which the employee is employed whether written or oral, past and current, to the extent that the authority has the written contract or a record of the oral contract in its possession, and date of the most recent promotion, demotion, transfer, suspension, separation, or other change in position classification. In addition, the following information with respect to each licensed medical provider employed by or having privileges to practice in a public health facility shall be a matter of public record: educational history and qualifications, date and jurisdiction or original and current licensure; and information relating to medical board certifications or other qualifications of medical specialists. For the purposes of this subsection, the term "total compensation" includes pay, benefits, incentives, bonuses, and deferred and all other forms of compensation paid by the employing entity.

(c)   Information regarding the qualifications, competence, performance, character, fitness, or conditions of appointment of an independent contractor who provides health care services under a contract with a public health authority is not a public record as defined by Chapter 132 of the General Statutes. Information regarding a hearing or investigation of a complaint, charge, or grievance by or against an independent contractor who provides health care services under a contract with a public health authority is not a public record as defined by Chapter 132 of the General Statutes. Final action making an appointment or discharge or removal by a public health authority having final authority for the appointment or discharge or removal shall be taken in an open meeting, unless otherwise exempted by law. The following information with respect to each independent contractor of health care services of a public health authority is a matter of public record: name; age; date of original contract; beginning and ending dates; position title; position descriptions; and total compensation of current and former positions; and the date of the most recent promotion, demotion, transfer, suspension, separation, or other change in position classification. (1997-502, s. 1; 2007-508, s. 5.)

§ 130A-45.10. Confidentiality of credentialing information.

Information acquired by a public health authority or by persons acting for or on behalf of a public health authority in connection with the credentialing and peer review of persons having or applying for privileges to practice in a public health facility is confidential and is not a public record under Chapter 132 of the General Statutes; provided that information otherwise available to the public shall not become confidential merely because it was acquired by the authority or by persons acting for or on behalf of the authority. (1997-502, s. 1.)

§ 130A-45.11. Confidentiality of competitive health care information.

Information relating to competitive health care activities by or on behalf of public health authorities shall be confidential and not a public record under Chapter 132 of the General Statutes; provided that any contract entered into by or on behalf of a public health authority shall be a public record unless otherwise exempted by law. (1997-502, s. 1.)

§ 130A-45.12. Personnel.

Employees under the supervision of the public health authority director are employees of the public health authority and shall be exempt from Chapter 126 of the General Statutes, unless otherwise provided in this Part. (2001-92, s. 1.)

§ 130A-45.13. Authority to contract directly with private providers to operate billing system for county Medicaid claims.

A public health authority board may contract directly with private vendors to operate the authority's Medicaid billing system as an alternative to the State-operated health services information system. The contract may provide for the private vendor to bill directly the State Medicaid billing system (MMIS), thereby bypassing the State health services information system (HSIS). The public health authority shall issue a "request for proposal" to solicit private vendor bids for contracts authorized under this section. Information systems authorized under this section shall be consistent with and interface with relevant statewide

138

public health data systems to address State cost containment and service reporting needs. (2005-459, s. 1.)

§ 130A-46. Reserved for future codification purposes.

Part 2. Sanitary Districts.

§ 130A-47. Creation by Commission.

(a)   For the purpose of preserving and promoting the public health and welfare, the Commission may create sanitary districts without regard for county, township or municipal lines. However, no municipal corporation or any part of the territory in a municipal corporation shall be included in a sanitary district except at the request of the governing board of the municipal corporation. If the municipal corporation has not levied any tax nor performed any official act nor held any elections within a period of four years preceding the date of the petition for the sanitary district, a request of the governing board shall not be required.

(b)   For the purposes of this Part, the term "Department" means the Department of Environment and Natural Resources, and the term "Secretary" means the Secretary of Environment and Natural Resources. (1927, c. 100, s. 1; 1955, c. 1307; 1957, c. 1357, s. 1; 1973, c. 476, s. 128; 1983, c. 891, s. 2; 2007-187, s. 1.)

§ 130A-48. Procedure for incorporating district.

A sanitary district shall be incorporated as follows. Either fifty-one percent (51%) or more of the resident freeholders within a proposed sanitary district or fifty-one percent (51%) or more of the freeholders within a proposed sanitary district, whether or not the freeholders are residents of the proposed sanitary district, may petition the county board of commissioners of the county in which all or the largest portion of the land of the proposed district is located. This petition shall set forth the boundaries of the proposed sanitary district and the objectives of the proposed district. For the purposes of this Part, the term "freeholder" shall mean a person holding a deed to a tract of land within the district or proposed district, and also shall mean a person who has entered into a contract to purchase a tract of land within the district or proposed district, is making

139

payments pursuant to a contract and will receive a deed upon completion of the contractual payments. The contracting purchaser, rather than the contracting seller, shall be deemed to be the freeholder. The county tax office shall be responsible for checking the freeholder status of those persons signing the petition. That office shall also be responsible for confirming the location of the property owned by those persons. Upon receipt of the petition, the county board of commissioners, through its chairperson, shall notify the Department and the chairperson of the county board of commissioners of any other county or counties in which any portion of the proposed district lies of the receipt of the petition. The chairperson shall request that the Department hold a joint public hearing with the county commissioners of all the counties in which a portion of the district lies concerning the creation of the proposed sanitary district. The Secretary and the chairperson of the county board of commissioners shall name a time and place within the proposed district to hold the public hearing. The chairperson of the county board of commissioners shall give prior notice of the hearing by posting a notice at the courthouse door of the county and also by publication at least once a week for four successive weeks in a newspaper published in the county. In the event the hearing is to be before a joint meeting of the county boards of commissioners of more than one county, or in the event the land to be affected lies in more than one county, publication and notice shall be made in each of the affected counties. In the event that all matters pertaining to the creation of this sanitary district cannot be concluded at the hearing, the hearing may be continued at a time and place within the proposed district named by the Department. (1927, c. 100, ss. 2-4; 1951, c. 178, s. 1; 1957, c. 1357, s. 1; 1959, c. 1189, s. 1; 1965, c. 135; 1967, c. 24, s. 21; 1973, c. 476, s. 128; 1975, c. 536; 1983, c. 891, s. 2; 2002-159, s. 55(f).)

§ 130A-49. Declaration that district exists; status of industrial villages within boundaries of district.

(a)   If, after the required public hearing, the Commission and the county commissioners determine that a district shall be created for the purposes stated in the petition, the Commission shall adopt a resolution defining the boundaries of the district and declaring the territory within the boundaries to be a sanitary district. The Commission may make minor deviation in defining the boundaries from those prescribed in the petition when it determines the change to be in the interest of the public health.

(b)   The owner or controller of an industrial plant may make application requesting that the plant or the plant and its contiguous village be included within or excluded from the sanitary district. The application shall be filed with the Commission on or before the date of the public hearing. If an application is properly filed, the Commission shall include or exclude the industrial plant and contiguous village in accordance with the application.

(c)   Each district when created shall be identified by a name or number assigned by the Commission. (1927, c. 100, s. 5; 1957, c. 1357, s. 1; 1973, c. 476, s. 128; 1983, c. 891, s. 2.)

§ 130A-49.5. Ethics.

(a)   The governing board shall adopt a resolution or policy containing a code of ethics, as required by G.S. 160A-86.

(b)   All members of the governing board, whether elected or appointed, shall receive the ethics education required by G.S. 160A-87. (2009-403, s. 6.)

§ 130A-50. Election and terms of office of sanitary district boards.

(a)   The Department shall send a copy of the resolution creating the sanitary district to the board or boards of county commissioners of the county or counties in which all or part of the district is located. The Department shall file or cause to be filed with the county board or boards of elections in the same county or counties a map of the district. With the map it shall include supporting documents. That map and documents shall be filed within 10 business days after the creation of the district and amended within 10 days after any change to the boundaries of the district. The board or boards of commissioners shall hold a meeting or joint meeting for the purpose of electing the members of the sanitary district board.

(b)   The sanitary district board shall be composed of either three or five members as the county commissioners in their discretion shall determine. The members first appointed shall serve as the governing body of the sanitary district until the next regular election for municipal and special district officers as provided in G.S. 163-279, which occurs more than 90 days after their appointment. At that election, their successors shall be elected. The terms of the members shall be for two years or four years and may be staggered as determined by the county board of commissioners so that some members are elected at each biennial election. The members of the sanitary district board shall be residents of the district. The county board of commissioners shall notify the county board of elections of any decision made under this subsection.

If the sanitary district board consists of three members, the county commissioners may at any time increase the sanitary district board to five members. The increase shall become effective with respect to any election where the filing period for candidacy opens at least 30 days after approval of the expansion to five members. The effective date of the expansion is the organizational meeting of the sanitary district board after the election.

The county commissioners may provide for staggering terms of an existing sanitary district board whose members serve two-year terms by providing for some of the members to be elected at the next election to be for four-year terms. The change shall become effective with respect to any election where the filing period for candidacy opens at least 30 days after approval of the staggering of terms.

The sanitary district board may provide for staggering its terms if its members serve unstaggered four-year terms by providing for some of the members to be elected at the next election for two-year terms. The change shall become effective with respect to any election where the filing period for candidacy opens at least 30 days after approval of the staggering of terms.

The county commissioners may provide for changing a sanitary district board from two-year terms to unstaggered four-year terms. This may be done either by providing that at the next election, all members shall be elected for four-year terms, or by extending the terms of existing members from two years to four years. The change shall become effective with respect to any election where the filing period for candidacy opens at least 30 days after approval of the change of length of terms.

(b1)   If a sanitary district:

1.   Does not share territory with any city as defined by G.S. 160A-1(2), and

2.   The sanitary district is in more than one county,

the boards of county commissioners in all counties with territory in the sanitary district may set the sanitary district elections to be held on the same date as

142

general elections in even-numbered years under G.S. 163-1 and may extend the terms of any sanitary district board members who are in office at the ratification of this act until the next even-year general election can been [be] held and successors qualified.

(b2)   If a sanitary district:

(1)   Is located entirely within a county which has no incorporated city as defined by G.S. 160A-1(2) located within that county; and

(2)   Has a sanitary district board whose members serve four-year terms which are not staggered and which next expire in 1991,

the board of commissioners of that county may, by resolution adopted prior to December 31, 1989, set the sanitary district election to be held on the same date as general elections in even-numbered years under G.S. 163-1. Such resolution shall extend the terms of office of the then serving members of the sanitary district board by one year, so that they will expire on the first Monday in December following the 1992 general election. Other than as provided by this subsection, sanitary district elections shall continue to be conducted in accordance with this Article and Chapter 163 of the General Statutes.

(c)   The election shall be nonpartisan and decided by simple plurality as provided in G.S. 163-292 and shall be held and conducted by the county board of elections in accordance with the applicable provisions of Articles 23 and 24 of Chapter 163 of the General Statutes. If the district is in more than one county, then the county board of elections of the county including the largest part of the district shall conduct the election for the entire district with the assistance and full cooperation of the boards of elections in the other counties.

(d)   The board of elections shall certify the results of the election to the clerk of superior court. The clerk of superior court shall take and file the oaths of office of the board members elected.

(e)   The elected members of the board shall take the oath of office on the first Monday in December following their election and shall serve for the term elected and until their successors are elected and qualified. (1927, c. 100, s. 6; 1943, c. 602; 1953, c. 798; 1955, c. 1073; 1957, c. 1357, s. 1; 1963, c. 644; 1973, c. 476, s. 128; 1981, c. 186, s. 1; 1983, c. 891, s. 2; 1987, c. 22, s. 1; 1989, c. 310; 1993 (Reg. Sess., 1994), c. 736, s. 1.1; 1997-117, s. 1; 2007-391, s. 15.)

§ 130A-51. City governing body acting as sanitary district board.

(a)   When the General Assembly incorporates a city or town that includes within its territory fifty percent (50%) or more of the territory of a sanitary district, the governing body of the city or town shall become ex officio the governing board of the sanitary district if the General Assembly provides for this action in the incorporation act and if the existing sanitary district board adopts a final resolution pursuant to this section. The resolution may be adopted at any time within the period beginning on the day the incorporation act becomes law and ending 270 days after that date.

(b)   To begin the process leading to the city or town board becoming ex officio the sanitary district board, the board of the sanitary district shall first adopt a preliminary resolution finding that the interests of the citizens of the sanitary district and of the city or town will be best served if both units of local government are governed by a single governing body. This resolution shall also set the time and place for a public hearing on the preliminary resolution.

(c)   Upon adoption of this preliminary resolution, the chairperson of the sanitary district board shall publish a notice of the public hearing once at least 10 days before the hearing in a newspaper of general circulation within the sanitary district. This notice shall set forth the time and place of the hearing and shall briefly describe its purpose. At the hearing, the board shall hear any citizen of the sanitary district or of the city or town who wishes to speak to the subject of the preliminary resolution.

(d)   Within 30 days after the day of the public hearing, the sanitary district board may adopt a final resolution finding that the interests of the citizens of the sanitary district and of the city or town will be best served if both units are governed by a single board. This resolution shall set the date on which the terms of office of the members of the sanitary district board end and that board is dissolved and service by the ex officio board begins. This date may be the effective date of the incorporation of the city or town or any date within one year after the effective date. At that time, the sanitary district board is dissolved and the mayor and members of the governing body of the city or town become ex officio the board of the sanitary district. The mayor shall act ex officio as chairperson of the sanitary district board.

(e)   The chairperson of the sanitary district board that adopts a final resolution shall within 10 days after the day the resolution is adopted, send a copy of the resolution to the mayor and each member of the city or town

144

governing board and to the Department. (1981, c. 201; 1983, c. 891, s. 2; 1995, c. 20, s. 15.)

§ 130A-52. Special election if election not held in November of 1981.

(a) If in a sanitary district, an election of board members was required to be held in November of 1981 under G.S. 130A-50 but was not held, the board of commissioners of the county or counties in which the district is located may by resolution order a special election of all the board members to be held at the same time as the General Election in November of 1982.

(b) The election shall be held under the procedures of Articles 23 and 24 of Chapter 163 of the General Statutes and in accordance with G.S. 130A-50, except that filing shall open at noon on Monday, August 9, 1982, and close at noon on Monday, August 23, 1982.

(c) In the election held under this section, all of the members of the board shall be elected. If the board of commissioners has provided for two-or four-year terms, the members elected in 1982 shall serve until the 1983 or 1985 election, respectively, and then their successors shall be elected for the two-or four-year terms provided by the county board or boards of commissioners.

(d) Any resolution adopted under subsection (a) of this section shall be filed with the Department. (1981 (Reg. Sess., 1982), c. 1271, s. 1; 1983, c. 891, s. 2.)

§ 130A-52.1. Action if 1983 election not held.

If any sanitary district held an election in 1982 under G.S. 130A-52, but failed to hold the 1983 election, then the persons elected in 1982 shall hold office until the terms that were to begin in 1983 have expired. (1983 (Reg. Sess., 1984), c. 1021, s. 1.)

§ 130A-53. Actions validated.

145

Any action of a sanitary district taken prior to July 1, 1984, shall not be invalidated by failure to hold an election for members of the board. (1981 (Reg. Sess., 1982), c. 1271, s. 1; 1983, c. 891, s. 2; 1983 (Reg. Sess., 1984), c. 1021, s. 2.)

§ 130A-54. Vacancy appointments to district boards.

Any vacancy in a sanitary district board shall be filled by the county commissioners until the next election for sanitary district board members. If the district is located in more than one county, the vacancy shall be filled by the county commissioners of the county from which the vacancy occurred. (1935, c. 357, s. 2; 1957, c. 1357, s. 1; 1981, c. 186, s. 2; 1983, c. 891, s. 2.)

§ 130A-55. Corporate powers.

A sanitary district board shall be a body politic and corporate and may sue and be sued in matters relating to the sanitary district. Notwithstanding any limitation in the petition under G.S. 130A-48, but subject to the provisions of G.S. 130A-55(17)e, each sanitary district may exercise all of the powers granted to sanitary districts by this Article. In addition, the sanitary district board shall have the following powers:

(1)   To acquire, construct, maintain and operate sewage collection, treatment and disposal systems of all types, including septic tank systems or other on-site collection, treatment or disposal facilities or systems; water supply systems; water purification or treatment plants and other utilities necessary for the preservation and promotion of the public health and sanitary welfare within the district. The utilities shall be constructed, operated and maintained in accordance with applicable statutes and rules.

(2)   To acquire, construct, maintain and operate sewage collection, treatment and disposal systems of all types, including septic tank systems or other on-site collection or disposal facilities or systems, water supply systems; water purification or treatment plants and other utilities, within and outside the corporate limits of the district, as may be necessary for the preservation of the public health and sanitary welfare outside the corporate limits of the district,

146

within reasonable limitation. The utilities shall be constructed, operated and maintained in accordance with applicable statutes and rules.

a.   The authority granted to a sanitary district by the provisions of this subsection is supplemental to the authority granted to a sanitary district by other provisions of law.

b.   Actions taken by a sanitary district to acquire, construct, maintain and operate sewage collection, treatment and disposal systems of all types; water supply systems; water purification or treatment plants and other utilities within and outside the corporate limits to provide service outside the corporate limits are approved and validated.

c.   This subsection shall apply only in counties with a population of 70,000 or greater, as determined by the most recent decennial federal census.

(3)   To levy taxes on property within the district in order to carry out the powers and duties conferred and imposed on the district by law, and to pay the principal of and interest on bonds and notes of the district.

(4)   To acquire either by purchase, condemnation or otherwise and hold real and personal property, easements, rights-of-way and water rights in the name of the district within or without the corporate limits of the district, necessary or convenient for the construction or maintenance of the works of the district.

(5)   To employ and compensate engineers, counsel and other persons as may be necessary to carry out projects.

(6)   To negotiate and enter into agreements with the owners of existing water supplies, sewage systems or other utilities as may be necessary to carry out the intent of this Part.

(7)   To adopt rules necessary for the proper functioning of the district. However, these rules shall not conflict with rules adopted by the Commission for Public Health, Environmental Management Commission, or the local board of health having jurisdiction over the area. Further, such sanitary district board rules shall be no more restrictive than or conflict with requirements or ordinances of any county having jurisdiction over the area, and, if a conflict should arise, the requirements or ordinances of the county having jurisdiction over the area shall control.

147

(8)   a.   To contract with any person within or outside the corporate limits of the district to supply raw water without charge to the person in return for an agreement to allow the district to discharge sewage in the person's previous water supply. The district may so contract and construct at its expense all improvements necessary or convenient for the delivery of the water when, in the opinion of the sanitary district board and the Department, it will be for the best of the district.

b.   To contract with any person within or outside the corporate limits of the district to supply raw or filtered water and sewer service to the person where the service is available. For service supplied outside the corporate limits of the district, the sanitary district board may fix a different rate from that charged within the corporate limits but shall not be liable for damages for failure to furnish a sufficient supply of water and adequate sewer service.

c.   To contract with any person within or outside the corporate limits of the district for the treatment of the district's sewage in a sewage disposal or treatment plant owned and constructed or to be constructed by that person.

(9)   After adoption of a plan as provided in G.S. 130A-60, the sanitary district board may, in its discretion, alter or modify the plan if the Department determines that the alteration or modification does not constitute a material deviation from the objective of the plan and is in the public health interest of the district. The alteration or modification must be approved by the Department. The sanitary district board may appropriate or reappropriate money of the district for carrying out the altered or modified plan.

(10)   To take action, subject to the approval of the Department, for the prevention and eradication of diseases transmissible by vectors by instituting programs for the eradication of the mosquito.

(11)   To collect and dispose of garbage, waste and other refuse by contract or otherwise.

(12)   To establish a fire department, or to contract for firefighting apparatus and personnel for the protection of life and property within the district.

(13)   To provide or contract for rescue service, ambulance service, rescue squad or other emergency medical services for use in the district. The sanitary district shall be subject to G.S. 153A-250.

(14)   To have privileges and immunities granted to other governmental units in exercise of the governmental functions.

(15)   To use the income of the district, and if necessary, to levy and collect taxes upon all the taxable property within the district sufficient to pay the costs of collecting and disposing of garbage, waste and other refuse, to provide fire protection and rescue services in the district, and to acquire, construct, maintain, operate, and regulate roads and streets within the district. Taxes shall be levied and collected at the same time and in the same manner as taxes for debt service as provided in G.S. 130A-62.

(16)   To adopt rules for the promotion and protection of the public health and for these purposes to possess the following powers:

a.   To require the owners of developed property on which there are situated one or more residential dwelling units or commercial establishments located within the jurisdiction of the district and within a reasonable distance of any waterline or sewer collection line owned, leased as lessee, or operated by the district to connect the property with the waterline, sewer connection line, or both and fix charges for the connections. The power granted by this subdivision may be exercised by a district only to the extent that the service, whether water, sewer, or a combination thereof, to be provided by the district is not then being provided to the improved property by any other political subdivision or by a public utility regulated by the North Carolina Utilities Commission pursuant to Chapter 62 of the General Statutes. In the case of improved property that would qualify for the issuance of a building permit for the construction of one or more residential dwelling units or commercial establishments and where the district has installed water or sewer lines or a combination thereof directly available to the property, the district may require payment of a periodic availability charge, not to exceed the minimum periodic service charge for properties that are connected.

b.   To require any person owning, occupying or controlling improved real property within the district where the water or sewage systems of the district are not immediately available or it is impractical with the systems, to install sanitary toilets, septic tanks and other health equipment or installations in accordance with applicable statutes and rules.

c.   To order a person to abate a public health nuisance of the district. If the person being ordered to abate the nuisance refuses to comply with the order,

149

the sanitary district board may institute an action in the superior court of the county where the public health nuisance exists to enforce the order.

d.   To abolish or regulate and control the use and occupancy of all pigsties and other animal stockyards or pens within the district and for an additional distance of 500 feet beyond the outer boundaries of the district, unless the 500 feet is within the corporate limits of a city or town.

e.   Upon the noncompliance by a person of a rule adopted by the sanitary district board, the board shall notify the person of the rule being violated and the facts constituting the violation. The person shall have a reasonable time to comply with the rule as determined by the local health director of the person's residence. Upon failure to comply within the specified time or within a time extended by the sanitary district board, the person shall be guilty of a Class 1 misdemeanor.

f.   The sanitary district board is authorized to enforce the rules adopted pursuant to this Part by criminal action or civil action, including injunctive relief.

(17)   For the purpose of promoting and protecting the public health, safety and the general welfare of the State, a sanitary district board is authorized to establish as zoning units any portions of the sanitary district not under the control of the United States or this State or any agency or instrumentality of either, in accordance with the following:

a.   No sanitary district board shall designate an area a zoning area until a petition signed by two-thirds of the qualified voters in the area, as shown by the registration books used in the last general election, and with a petition signed by two-thirds of the owners of real property in the area, as shown by the records in the office of the register of deeds for the county, is filed with the sanitary district board. The petition must be accompanied by a map of the proposed zoning area. The board shall hold a public hearing to obtain comment on the proposed creation of the zoning area. A notice of public hearing must be published in a newspaper of general circulation in the county at least two times, and a copy of the notice shall be posted at the county courthouse and in three other public places in the sanitary district.

b.   When a zoning area is established within a sanitary district, the sanitary district board as to the zoning area shall have all rights, privileges, powers and duties granted to municipal corporations under Part 3, Article 19, Chapter 160A of the General Statutes. However, the sanitary district board shall not be

150

required to appoint any zoning commission or board of adjustment. If neither a zoning commission nor board of adjustment is appointed, the sanitary district board shall have all rights.

c.   A sanitary district board may enter into an agreement with any city, town or sanitary district for the establishment of a joint zoning commission.

d.   A sanitary district board is authorized to use the income of the district and levy and collect taxes upon the taxable property within the district necessary to carry out and enforce the rules and provisions of this subsection.

e.   This subsection shall apply only to sanitary districts which adjoin and are contiguous to an incorporated city or town and are located within three miles or less of the boundaries of two other cities or towns.

(18)   To negotiate for and acquire by contract any distribution system located outside the district when the water for the distribution system is furnished by the district. If the distribution system is acquired by a district, the district may continue the operation of the system even though it remains outside the district.

(19)   To accept gifts of real and personal property for the purpose of operating a nonprofit cemetery; to own, operate and maintain cemeteries with the donated property; and to establish perpetual care funds for the cemeteries in the manner provided by G.S. 160A-347.

(20)   To dispose of real or personal property belonging to the district according to the procedures prescribed in Article 12 of Chapter 160A of the General Statutes. For purposes of this subsection, references in Article 12 of Chapter 160A to the "city," the "council," or a specific city official refer, respectively, to the sanitary district, the sanitary district board, and the sanitary district official who most nearly performs the same duties performed by the specified city official. For purposes of this subsection, references in G.S. 160A-266(c) to "one or more city officials" are deemed to refer to one or more sanitary district officials designated by the sanitary district board.

(21)   To acquire, renovate property for or construct a medical clinic to serve the district, and to maintain real and personal property for a medical clinic to serve the district.

(22)   To make special assessments against benefitted property within the corporate limits of the sanitary district and within the area served or to be served

151

by the sanitary district for the purpose of constructing, reconstructing, extending, or otherwise improving water systems or sanitary collection, treatment, and sewage disposal systems, in the same manner that a county may make special assessments under authority of Article 9 of Chapter 153A of the General Statutes, except that the language appearing in G.S. 153A-185 reading as follows: "A county may not assess property within a city pursuant to subdivision (1) or (2) of this section unless the governing board of the city has by resolution approved the project," shall not apply to assessments levied by sanitary districts. For the purposes of this paragraph, references in Article 9 of Chapter 153A of the General Statutes, to the "county," the "board of county commissioners," "the board" or a specific county official or employee are deemed to refer respectively to the sanitary district and to the official or employee of the sanitary district who performs most nearly the same duties performed by the specified county official or employee.

Assessment rolls after being confirmed shall be filed for registration in the office of the Register of Deeds of the county in which the property being assessed is located, and the term "county tax collector" wherever used in G.S. 153A-195 and G.S. 153A-196, shall mean the officer designated by the sanitary district to perform the functions described in said sections of the statute. This subdivision applies only to sanitary districts with a population of 15,000 or over.

(23)   To acquire (by purchase, lease, gift, or otherwise, but not by condemnation), construct, maintain, operate, and regulate roads and streets within the sanitary district which are not State-maintained. Not all of these powers need be exercised.

(24)   Expired.

(25)   To negotiate and enter into agreements with other municipal corporations or sanitary districts for the purpose of developing and implementing an economic development plan. The agreement may provide for the establishment of a special fund, in which monies not expended at the end of a fiscal year shall remain in the fund. The lead agency designated under the agreement shall be responsible for examination of the fund and compliance with sound accounting principles, including the annual independent audit under G.S. 159-34. The audit responsibilities of the other municipal corporations and sanitary districts extend only to the verification of the contribution to the fund created under the agreement. The procedural requirements of G.S. 158-7.1(c) shall apply to actions of a sanitary district under this subdivision as if it were a city. (1927, c. 100, s. 7; 1933, c. 8, ss. 1, 2; 1935, c. 287, ss. 1, 2; 1941, c. 116;

152

1945, c. 651, ss. 1, 2; 1947, c. 476; 1949, c. 880, s. 1; cc. 1130, 1145; 1951, c. 17, s. 1; c. 1035, s. 1; 1957, c. 1357, s. 1; 1961, cc. 669, 865, 1155; 1963, c. 1232; 1965, c. 496, s. 1; 1967, c. 632; c. 637, s. 1; c. 798, s. 2; 1969, cc. 478, 700, 944; 1971, c. 780, s. 29; 1973, c. 476, s. 128; 1979, c. 520, s. 2; c. 619, s. 7; 1981, cc. 629, 655; c. 820, ss. 1-3; c. 898, ss. 1-4; 1981 (Reg. Sess., 1982), c. 1237; 1983, c. 891, s. 2; c. 925, s. 2; 1993, c. 539, s. 948; 1994, Ex. Sess., c. 24, s. 14(c); 1995, c. 422, ss. 1-4; 2001-221, s. 1; 2006-214, s. 1; 2007-182, s. 2; 2011-256, s. 2; 2011-394, s. 22.)

§ 130A-55.1: Repealed by Session Laws 1997, c. 443, s. 11A.2.

§ 130A-56. Election of officers; board compensation.

(a)   Upon election, a sanitary district board shall meet and elect one of its members as chairperson and another member as secretary.

(b)   The board may employ a clerk or other assistants as necessary and may fix duties of and compensation for employees. A sanitary district board may remove employees and fill vacancies.

(c)   The board may fix the compensation and allowances of the chairman and other members of the board by adoption of the annual budget ordinance, payable from the funds of the district, but no increase may become effective earlier than the first meeting of the board following the next election of board members after adoption of the ordinance. Until adoption of an ordinance under this subsection, each member of the board may receive compensation as provided for members of State boards under G.S. 138-5, payable from funds of the district. (1927, c. 100, s. 8; 1957, c. 1357, s. 1; 1967, c. 723; 1977, c. 183; 1983, c. 891, s. 2; 1985, c. 29, ss. 1, 2; 1995, c. 422, s. 5; 2003-185, s. 1.)

§ 130A-57. Power to condemn property.

A sanitary district board may purchase real estate, right-of-way or easement within or outside the corporate limits of the district for improvements authorized by this Part. If a purchase price cannot be agreed upon, the board may condemn the real estate, right-of-way or easement in accordance with Chapter

153

40A of the General Statutes. (1927, c. 100, s. 9; 1933, c. 8, s. 3; 1957, c. 1357, s. 1; 1981, c. 919, s. 13; 1983, c. 891, s. 2.)

§ 130A-58. Construction of systems by corporations or individuals.

When it is inadvisable or impractical for the sanitary district to build a water supply, sewage system or part of either to serve an area within the sanitary district, a corporation or residents within the sanitary district may build and operate a system at its or their own expense. The system shall be constructed and operated under plans and specifications approved by the district board and by the Department. The system shall also be constructed and operated in accordance with applicable rules and statutes. (1927, c. 100, s. 10; 1957, c. 1357, s. 1; 1973, c. 476, s. 128; 1983, c. 891, s. 2.)

§ 130A-59. Reports.

Upon the election of a sanitary district board, the board shall employ engineers licensed by this State to make a report on the problems of the sanitary district. The report shall be prepared and filed with the sanitary district board and shall include the following:

(1)   Comprehensive maps showing the boundaries of the sanitary district and, in a general way, the location of the various parts of the work that is proposed to be done and information as may be useful for a thorough understanding of the proposed undertaking;

(2)   A general description of existing facilities for carrying out the purposes of the district;

(3)   A general description of the various plans which might be adopted for accomplishment of the purposes of the district;

(4)   General plans and specifications for the work;

(5)   General description of property proposed to be acquired or which may be damaged in carrying out the work;

(6)   Comparative detail estimates of cost for the various construction plans; and

(7)   Recommendations. (1927, c. 100, s. 11; 1957, c. 1357, s. 1; 1983, c. 891, s. 2.)

§ 130A-60. Consideration of reports and adoption of a plan.

(a)   A report filed by the engineers pursuant to G.S. 130A-59 shall be given consideration by the sanitary district board and the board shall adopt a plan. Before adopting a plan the board may hold a public hearing for the purpose of considering objections to the plan. Once adopted, the sanitary district board shall submit the plan to the Department. The plan shall not become effective until it is approved by the Department.

(b)   The provisions of this section and of G.S. 130A-58 shall apply when the sanitary district board determines that adoption of the plan requires the issuance of bonds. However, these provisions shall not apply to a proposed purchase of firefighting equipment and apparatus. Failure to observe or comply with these provisions shall not, however, affect the validity of the bonds of a sanitary district. (1927, c. 100, s. 12; 1949, c. 880, s. 1; 1951, c. 17, s. 1; 1957, c. 1357, s. 1; 1973, c. 476, s. 128; 1983, c. 891, s. 2.)

§ 130A-61. Bonds and notes authorized.

A sanitary district is authorized to issue bonds and notes under the Local Government Finance Act. (1927, c. 100, s. 13; 1949, c. 880, s. 1; 1951, c. 17, s. 1; c. 846, s. 1; 1957, c. 1357, s. 1; 1963, c. 1247, s. 1; 1971, c. 780, s. 27; 1983, c. 891, s. 2.)

§ 130A-62. Annual budget; tax levy.

(a)   A sanitary district shall operate under an annual balanced budget adopted in accordance with the Local Government Budget and Fiscal Control Act.

155

(b)   A sanitary district has the option of either collecting its own taxes or having its taxes collected by the county or counties in which it is located. Unless a district takes affirmative action to collect its own taxes, taxes shall be collected by the county.

(c)   For sanitary districts whose taxes are collected by the county, before May 1 of each year, the assessor of each county in which the district is located shall certify to the district board the total assessed value of property in the county subject to taxation by the district. By July 1 or upon adoption of its annual budget ordinance, the district board shall certify to the county board of commissioners the rate of ad valorem tax levied by the district on property in that county. Upon receiving the district's certification of its tax levy, the county commissioners shall compute the district tax for each taxpayer and shall separately state the district tax on the county tax receipts for the fiscal year. The county shall collect the district tax in the same manner that county taxes are collected and shall remit these collections to the district at least monthly. Partial payments shall be proportionately divided between the county and the district. The district budget ordinance may include an appropriation to the county for the cost to the county of computing, billing, and collecting the district tax. The amount of the appropriation shall be agreed upon by the county and the district, but may not exceed five percent (5%) of the district levy. Any agreement shall remain effective until modified by mutual agreement. The amount due the county for collecting the district tax may be deducted by the county from its monthly remittances to the district or may be paid to the county by the district.

(d)   Sanitary districts electing to collect their own taxes shall be deemed cities for the purposes of the Machinery Act, Subchapter II of Chapter 105 of the General Statutes. (1927, c. 100, s. 17; 1935, c. 287, ss. 3, 4; 1949, c. 880, s. 1; 1951, c. 17, s. 1; 1957, c. 1357, s. 1; 1959, c. 994; 1963, c. 1226; 1965, c. 496, s. 3; 1971, c. 780, s. 29; 1983, c. 891, s. 2; 1987, c. 45, s. 1; 1991 (Reg. Sess., 1992), c. 1007, s. 38.)

§ 130A-63. Engineers to provide plans and supervise work; bids.

(a)   The sanitary district board shall retain engineers licensed by this State to provide detailed plans and specifications and to supervise the work undertaken by the district. The work or any portion of the work may be done by the sanitary district board by purchasing the material and letting a contract for the work or by letting a contract for furnishing all the materials and doing the work.

(b)   All contracts for work performed for construction or repair and for the purchase of materials by sanitary districts shall be in accordance with the provisions of Article 8, Chapter 143 of the General Statutes which are applicable to counties and municipal corporations.

(c)   All work done shall be in accordance with the plans and specifications prepared by the engineers in conformity with the plan adopted by the sanitary district board. (1927, c. 100, s. 19; 1957, c. 1357, s. 1; 1977, c. 544, s. 1; 1983, c. 891, s. 2.)

§ 130A-64. Service charges and rates.

A sanitary district board shall apply service charges and rates based upon the exact benefits derived. These service charges and rates shall be sufficient to provide funds for the maintenance, adequate depreciation and operation of the work of the district. If reasonable, the service charges and rates may include an amount sufficient to pay the principal and interest maturing on the outstanding bonds and, to the extent not otherwise provided for, bond anticipation notes of the district. Any surplus from operating revenues shall be set aside as a separate fund to be applied to the payment of interest on or to the retirement of bonds or bond anticipation notes. The sanitary district board may modify and adjust these service charges and rates. (1927, c. 100, s. 20; 1933, c. 8, s. 5; 1957, c. 1357, s. 1; 1965, c. 496, s. 4; 1983, c. 891, s. 2.)

§ 130A-64.1. Notice of new or increased charges and rates; public comment period.

(a)   A sanitary district shall provide notice to interested parties of the imposition of or increase in service charges or rates applicable solely to the construction of development subject to Part 2 of Article 19 of Chapter 160A or Part 2 of Article 18 of Chapter 153A of the General Statutes for any service provided by the sanitary district at least seven days prior to the first meeting where the imposition of or increase in the charges or rates is on the agenda for consideration. The sanitary district shall employ at least two of the following means of communication in order to provide the notice required by this section:

(1)   Notice of the meeting in a prominent location on a Web site managed or maintained by the sanitary district.

(2)   Notice of the meeting in a prominent physical location, including, but not limited to, the district's headquarters or any government building, library, or courthouse located within the sanitary district.

(3)   Notice of the meeting by electronic mail to a list of interested parties that is created by the sanitary district for the purpose of notification as required by this section.

(4)   Notice of the meeting by facsimile to a list of interested parties that is created by the sanitary district for the purpose of notification as required by this section.

(a1)   If a sanitary district does not maintain its own Web site, it may employ the notice option provided by subdivision (1) of subsection (a) of this section by submitting a request to a county or counties in which the district is located to post such notice in a prominent location on a Web site that is maintained by the county or counties. Any sanitary district that elects to provide such notice shall make its request to the county or counties at least 15 days prior to the date of the first meeting where the imposition of or increase in the fees or charges is on the agenda for consideration.

(b)   During the consideration of the imposition of or increase in service charges or rates as provided in subsection (a) of this section, the governing body of the sanitary district shall permit a period of public comment.

(c)   This section shall not apply if the imposition of or increase in service charges or rates is contained in a budget filed in accordance with the requirements of G.S. 159-12. (2009-436, s. 3; 2010-180, s. 11(c).)

§ 130A-65. Liens for sewer service charges in sanitary districts not operating water distribution system; collection of charges; disconnection of sewer lines.

158

In sanitary districts which maintain and operate a sewage system but do not maintain and operate a water distribution system, the charges made for sewer service or for use of sewer service facilities shall be a lien upon the property served. If the charges are not paid within 15 days after they become due and payable, suit may be brought in the name of the sanitary district in the county in which the property served is located, or the property, subject to the lien, may be sold by the sanitary district under the same rules, rights of redemption and savings as are prescribed by law for the sale of land for unpaid ad valorem taxes. A sanitary district is authorized to adopt rules for the use of sewage works and the collection of charges. A sanitary district is authorized in accordance with its rules to enter upon the premises of any person using the sewage works and failing to pay the charges, and to disconnect the sewer line of that person from the district sewer line or disposal plant. A person who connects or reconnects with district sewer line or disposal plant without a permit from the sanitary district shall be guilty of a Class 1 misdemeanor. (1965, c. 920, s. 1; 1983, c. 891, s. 2; 1993, c. 539, s. 949; 1994, Ex. Sess., c. 24, s. 14(c).)

§ 130A-66. Removal of member of board.

A petition with the signatures of twenty-five percent (25%) or more of the voters within a sanitary district which requests the removal from office of one or more members of a sanitary district board for malfeasance or nonfeasance in office may be filed with the board of commissioners of the county in which all or the greater portion of the voters of a sanitary district are located. Upon receipt of the petition, the county board of commissioners shall meet and adopt a resolution to hold an election on the question of removal. In the event that more than one member of a sanitary district board is subjected to recall in an election, the names of each member of the board subjected to recall shall appear upon separate ballots. If in a recall election, a majority of the votes within the sanitary district are cast for the removal of a member or members of the sanitary district board subject to recall, the member or members shall cease to be a member or members of the sanitary district board. A vacancy shall be immediately filled. The expenses of holding a recall election shall be paid from the funds of the sanitary district. (1927, c. 100, s. 21; 1957, c. 1357, s. 1; 1981, c. 186, s. 3; 1983, c. 891, s. 2.)

§ 130A-67. Rights-of-way granted.

A right-of-way in, along or across a county or State highway, street or property within a sanitary district is granted to a sanitary district in case the board finds it necessary or convenient for carrying out the work of the district. Any work done in, along or across a State highway shall be done in accordance with the rules of the Board of Transportation. (1927, c. 100, s. 22; 1933, c. 172, s. 17; 1957, c. 1357, s. 1; 1973, c. 507, s. 5; 1983, c. 891, s. 2.)

§ 130A-68. Returns of elections.

In all elections provided for in this Part, the board of elections shall file copies of the returns with the county boards of commissioners, sanitary district board and clerk of superior court in which the district is located. (1927, c. 100, s. 23; 1957, c. 1357, s. 1; 1981, c. 186, s. 4; 1983, c. 891, s. 2.)

§ 130A-69. Procedure for extension of district.

(a)   If after a sanitary district has been created or the provisions of this Part have been made applicable to a sanitary district, a petition signed by not less than fifteen percent (15%) of the resident freeholders within any territory contiguous to and adjoining the sanitary district may be presented to the sanitary district board requesting annexation of territory described in the petition. The sanitary district board shall send a copy of the petition to the board of commissioners of the county or counties in which the district is located and to the Department. The sanitary district board shall request that the Department hold a joint public hearing with the sanitary district board on the question of annexation. The Secretary and the chairperson of the sanitary district board shall name a time and place for the public hearing. The chairperson of the sanitary district board shall publish a notice of public hearing once in a newspaper or newspapers published or circulating in the sanitary district and the territory proposed to be annexed. The notice shall be published not less than 15 days prior to the hearing. If after the hearing, the Commission approves the annexation of the territory described in the petition, the Department shall advise the board or boards of commissioners of the approval. The board or boards of commissioners shall order and provide for the holding of a special election in accordance with G.S. 163-287 upon the question of annexation within the territory proposed to be annexed.

(b)   If at or prior to the public hearing, a petition is filed with the sanitary district board signed by not less than fifteen percent (15%) of the freeholders residing in the sanitary district requesting an election be held on the annexation question, the sanitary district board shall send a copy of the petition to the board or boards of commissioners who shall order and provide for the submission of the question to the voters within the sanitary district. This election may be held on the same day as the election in the territory proposed to be annexed, and both elections and registrations may be held pursuant to a single notice. A majority of the votes cast is necessary for a territory to be annexed to a sanitary district.

(c)   The election shall be held by the county board or boards of elections in accordance with G.S. 163-287 after the board or boards of commissioners orders the election. The cost of the election shall be paid by the sanitary district. Registration in the area proposed for annexation shall be under the same procedure as G.S. 163-288.2.

(d)   Notice of the election shall be given as required by G.S. 163-33(8) and shall include a statement that the boundary lines of the territory to be annexed and the boundary lines of the sanitary district have been prepared by the district board and may be examined. The notice shall also state that if a majority of the those voting in the election favor annexation, then the territory annexed shall be subject to all debts of the sanitary district.

(e)   The ballot shall be substantially as follows:

" FOR annexation to the ____ Sanitary District

   AGAINST annexation to the ____ Sanitary District."

The board or boards of elections shall certify the results of the election to the sanitary district board and the board or boards of commissioners of the county or counties in which the district is located.

(f)   Notwithstanding any other provisions of this section, if a petition for extension of the boundaries of a sanitary district is signed by not less than fifty-one percent (51%) of the resident freeholders within the territory proposed to be annexed, it shall not be necessary to hold an election provided for by this section on the question of the extension of the boundaries of the sanitary district.

161

(g)   Notwithstanding any other provisions of this section, if a petition for extension of the boundaries of a sanitary district is signed by the owners of all the real property within the territory proposed to be annexed, it shall not be necessary to hold any election or any hearings provided for by this section on the question of the extension of the boundaries of the sanitary district.

(h)   No right of action or defense founded upon the invalidity of the election shall be asserted, nor shall the validity of the election be open to question in any court on any ground unless the action or proceeding is commenced within 30 days after the certification of the results by the board or boards of elections.

(i)   When additional territory has been annexed to a sanitary district and the proposition of issuing bonds of the sanitary district after the annexation has been approved by the voters at an election held within one year subsequent to annexation, fifty-one percent (51%) or more of the resident freeholders within the annexed territory may petition the sanitary district board for the removal and exclusion of the territory from the sanitary district. No petition may be filed after bonds of the sanitary district have been approved in an election held at any time after annexation. If the sanitary district board approves the petition, it shall send a copy to the Department requesting that the petition be granted and shall send additional copies to the county board or boards of commissioners. A public hearing shall be conducted under the same procedure provided for the annexation of additional territory. If the Commission deems it advisable to comply with the request of the petition, the Commission shall adopt a resolution to that effect and shall redefine the boundaries of the sanitary district. (1927, c. 100, s. 24; 1943, c. 543; 1947, c. 463, s. 1; 1951, c. 897, s. 1; 1957, c. 1357, s. 1; 1959, c. 1189, s. 2; 1961, c. 732; 1973, c. 476, s. 128; 1981, c. 186, s. 5; 1983, c. 891, s. 2; 2013-381, s. 10.20.)

§ 130A-70. District and municipality extending boundaries and corporate limits simultaneously.

(a)   When the boundaries of a sanitary district lie entirely within or are coterminous with the corporate limits of a city or town and the sanitary district provides the only public water supply and sewage disposal system for the city or town, the boundaries of the sanitary district and the corporate limits of the city or town may be extended simultaneously as provided in this section.

(b)   Twenty-five percent (25%) or more of the resident freeholders within the territory proposed to be annexed to the sanitary district and to the city or town may petition the sanitary district board and the governing board of the city or town setting forth the boundaries of the area proposed to be annexed and the objects annexation is proposed to accomplish. The petition may also include any area already within the corporate limits of the city or town but not already within the boundaries of the sanitary district. Upon receipt of the petition, the sanitary district board and the governing board of the city or town shall meet jointly and shall hold a public hearing prior to approval of the petition. Notice of the hearing shall be made by posting a notice at the courthouse door of the county or counties and by publishing a notice at least once a week for four consecutive weeks in a newspaper with a circulation in the county or counties. If at or after the public hearing the sanitary district board and the governing board of the city or town, acting jointly, shall each approve the petition, the petition shall be submitted to the Commission for approval. If the Commission approves the petition, the question shall be submitted to a vote of all voters in the area or areas proposed to be annexed voting as a whole. The election shall be held on a date approved by the sanitary district board and by the governing board of the city or town.

(c)   The words "For Extension" and "Against Extension" shall be printed on the ballots for the election. A majority of all the votes cast is necessary for a district and municipality to extend boundaries and corporate limits simultaneously.

(d)   After declaration of the extension, the territory and its citizens and property shall be subject to all debts, ordinances and rules in force in the sanitary district and in the city or town, and shall be entitled to the same privileges and benefits as other parts of the sanitary district and the city or town. The newly annexed territory shall be subject to the sanitary district and the city or town taxes levied for the fiscal year following the date of annexation.

(e)   The costs of holding and conducting the election for annexation pursuant to this section, shall be shared equally by the sanitary district and by the city or town.

(f)   The sanitary district board and the governing board of the city or town acting jointly, may order the board or boards of elections of the county or counties in which the sanitary district and the city or town are located, to call, hold, conduct and certify the result of the election, according to the provisions of Chapter 163 of the General Statutes.

163

(g)   When the boundaries of a sanitary district and the corporate limits of a city or town are extended as provided in this section, and the proposition of issuing bonds of the sanitary district as enlarged has not been approved by the voters at an election held within one year subsequent to the extension, the annexed territory may be removed and excluded from the sanitary district in the manner provided in G.S. 130A-69. If the petition includes areas within the present corporate limits of the city or town but not within the present boundaries of the sanitary district, these areas shall not be removed or excluded from the city or town under the provisions of this section.

(h)   The powers granted by this section shall be supplemental and additional to powers conferred by any other law and shall not be regarded as in derogation to any powers now existing. (1953, c. 977; 1957, c. 1357, s. 1; 1973, c. 476, s. 128; 1981, c. 186, s. 6; 1983, c. 891, s. 2.)

§ 130A-70.1. Satellite annexation in conjunction with municipal annexation in certain sanitary districts.

(a)   This section only applies to a sanitary district where one or more municipalities lie within its boundaries.

(b)   Whenever a municipality which lies within a sanitary district receives a petition for annexation under Part 4 of Article 4A of Chapter 160A of the General Statutes, the municipality may petition the sanitary district for that sanitary district to also annex the same area. In such case, the sanitary district may, by resolution, annex the same area, but the annexation shall only become effective if the territory is annexed by the requesting municipality.

(c)   If G.S. 160A-58.5 allows the municipality to fix and enforce schedules of rents, rates, fees, charges, and penalties in excess of those fixed and enforced within the primary corporate limits, the sanitary district may do likewise as if G.S. 160A-58.5 applied to it.

(d)   If the annexed area contains utility lines constructed or operated by the county and the sanitary district is to assume control, operation, or management of those lines, the sanitary district and county may by contract agree for the sanitary district to assume the pro rata or otherwise mutually agreeable portion of indebtedness incurred by the county for such purpose, or to contractually agree with the county to reimburse the county for any debt service. (2001-301, s. 1.)

§ 130A-71. Procedure for withdrawing from district.

Fifty-one percent (51%) or more of the resident freeholders of a portion of a sanitary district which has no outstanding indebtedness, with the approval of the sanitary district board, may petition the county board of commissioners of the county in which a major portion of the petitioners reside, that the identified portion of the district be removed and excluded from the district. If the county board of commissioners approves the petition, an election shall be held in the entire district on the question of exclusion. A majority of all the votes cast is necessary for a district to be removed and excluded from a sanitary district. The county board of commissioners shall notify the Commission who shall remove and exclude the portion of the district, and redefine the limits accordingly. (1957, c. 1357, s. 1; 1973, c. 476, s. 128; 1983, c. 891, s. 2.)

§ 130A-72. Dissolution of certain sanitary districts.

Fifty-one percent (51%) or more of the resident freeholders of a sanitary district which has no outstanding indebtedness may petition the board of commissioners of the county in which all or the greater portion of the resident freeholders of the district are located to dissolve the district. Upon receipt of the petition, the county board of commissioners shall notify the Department and the chairperson of the county board of commissioners of any other county or counties in which any portion of the district lies, of the receipt of the petition, and shall request that the Department hold a joint public hearing with the county commissioners concerning the dissolution of the district. The Secretary and the chairperson of the county board of commissioners shall name a time and place within the district for the public hearing. The county board of commissioners shall give prior notice of the hearing by posting a notice at the courthouse door of the county or counties and by publication in a newspaper or newspapers with circulation in the county or counties at least once a week for four consecutive weeks. If all matters pertaining to the dissolution of the sanitary district cannot be concluded at the hearing, the hearing may be continued to a time and place determined by the Department. If after the hearing, the Commission and the county board or boards of commissioners deem it advisable to comply with the

165

request of the petition, the Commission shall adopt a resolution to dissolve the sanitary district. The sanitary district board of the dissolved district is authorized to convey all assets, including cash, to any county, municipality, or other governmental unit, or to any public utility company operating or to be operated under the authority of a certificate of public convenience and necessity granted by the North Carolina Utilities Commission in return for the assumption of the obligation to provide water and sewage services to the area served by the district at the time of dissolution. (1943, c. 620; 1951, c. 178, s. 2; 1957, c. 1357, s. 1; 1967, c. 4, s. 1; 1973, c. 476, s. 128; 1983, c. 891, s. 2.)

§ 130A-73. Dissolution of sanitary districts having no outstanding indebtedness and located wholly within or coterminous with corporate limits of city or town.

When the boundaries of a sanitary district which has no outstanding indebtedness are entirely located within or coterminous with the corporate limits of a city or town, fifty-one percent (51%) or more of the resident freeholders within the district may petition the board of commissioners within the county in which all or the greater portion of the resident freeholders of the district are located to dissolve the district. Upon receipt of the petition, the board of commissioners shall notify the Department, the chairperson of the board of commissioners of any other county or counties in which any portion of the district lies and the governing body of the city or town within which the district lies of the receipt of the petition, and shall request that the Department hold a joint public hearing with the board or boards of commissioners and the governing body of the city or town. The Secretary, the chairperson of the board of commissioners of the county in which all or the greater portion of the resident freeholders are located and the presiding officer of the governing body of the city or town shall name a time and place within the boundaries of the district and the city or town for the public hearing. The county board of commissioners shall give notice of the hearing by posting prior notice at the courthouse door of the county or counties and also by publication in a newspaper or newspapers circulating in the district at least once a week for four consecutive weeks. If all matters pertaining to the dissolution of the sanitary district cannot be concluded at the hearing, the hearing may be continued to a time and place determined by the Department. If, after the hearing, the Commission, the county board or boards of commissioners and the governing body of the city or town shall deem it advisable to comply with the request of the petition, the Commission shall adopt a resolution dissolving the district. All taxes levied by the sanitary district which were levied prior to but which are collected after the dissolution shall vest in the city or town. All property held, owned, controlled or used by the sanitary district upon the dissolution or which may later be vested in the sanitary district, and all judgments, liens, rights and causes of actions in favor of the sanitary district shall vest in the city or town. At the dissolution, taxes owed to the sanitary district shall be collected by the city or town. (1963, c. 512, s. 1; 1973, c. 476, s. 128; 1983, c. 891, s. 2.)

§ 130A-73.1. Dissolution of sanitary districts having no outstanding indebtedness and located wholly within or coterminous with corporate limits of city or town.

(a)   When the boundaries of a sanitary district that (i) is located entirely within one county, (ii) has no outstanding indebtedness, (iii) at the time of its creation was not located entirely within or coterminous with the corporate limits of a city or town, (iv) has not provided any water or sewer service for at least five years, (v) did not levy any ad valorem tax in the current year, (vi) has been for at least five years entirely located within or coterminous with the corporate limits of a city or town, and (vii) at the time of the annexation of the area of the district by that city or town, the city or town assumed all assets and liabilities of the district, the board of that district by unanimous vote may petition the board of commissioners of the county in which the district is located to dissolve the district. Upon receipt of the petition, the board of commissioners shall notify the Department and the governing body of the city or town within which the district lies of the receipt of the petition. If the Commission, the county board of commissioners, and the governing body of the city or town shall deem it advisable to comply with the request of the petition, the Commission shall adopt a resolution dissolving the district. All taxes levied by the sanitary district that were levied prior to, but that are collected after, the dissolution shall vest in the city or town. All property held, owned, controlled, or used by the sanitary district upon the dissolution or that may later be vested in the sanitary district, and all judgments, liens, rights, and causes of actions in favor of the sanitary district shall vest in the city or town. At the dissolution, taxes owed to the sanitary district shall be collected by the city or town.

(b)   The procedure for the dissolution of a sanitary district set out in this section is an alternative to the procedure set out in G.S. 130A-73 and any sanitary district to which both that section and this section apply may be dissolved under either section. (1998-123, s. 1.)

§ 130A-74. Validation of creation of districts.

All actions prior to June 6, 1961, taken by the county boards of commissioners[,] by the State Board of Health, by any officer or by any other agency, board or officer of the State in the formation and creation of sanitary districts in the State, and the formation and creation, or the attempted formation and creation of any sanitary districts are in all respects validated. These sanitary districts are declared lawfully formed and created and in all respects legal and valid sanitary districts. (1953, c. 596, s. 1; 1957, c. 1357, s. 1; 1961, c. 667, s. 1; 1983, c. 891, s. 2.)

§ 130A-75. Validation of extension of boundaries of districts.

(a)   All actions prior to April 1, 1957, taken by the State Board of Health, a county board of commissioners, and a sanitary district board for the purpose of extending the boundaries of a sanitary district where the territory which was annexed contained no resident freeholders, and where the owner or owners of the real property annexed requested of the sanitary district board that the territory be annexed to the sanitary district, are validated, notwithstanding any lack of power to perform these acts or proceedings, and notwithstanding any defect or irregularity in the acts or proceedings.

(b)   All actions and proceedings prior to April 1, 1979, taken by the State Board of Health, the Commission, a board of county commissioners and a sanitary district board for the purpose of annexing additional territory to a sanitary district or with respect to the annexation are validated notwithstanding any lack of power to perform these acts or proceedings or any defect or irregularity in any acts or proceedings; these sanitary districts are lawfully extended to include this additional territory. (1959, c. 415, s. 2; 1975, c. 712, s. 1; 1979, 2nd Sess., c. 1079, s. 1; 1983, c. 891, s. 2.)

§ 130A-76. Validation of dissolution of districts.

All actions prior to January 1, 1981, taken by a county board of commissioners, by the State Board of Health or Commission, by an officer or by any other agency, board or officer of the State in the dissolution of a sanitary district and

168

the dissolution or attempted dissolution of a sanitary district are validated. (1953, c. 596, s. 2; 1957, c. 1357, s. 1; 1981, c. 20, ss. 1, 2; 1983, c. 891, s. 2.)

§ 130A-77. Validation of bonds of districts.

All actions and proceedings prior to April 1, 1979, taken, and all elections held in a sanitary district or in a district purporting to be a legal sanitary district by virtue of the purported authority and acts of a county board of commissioners, State Board of Health, Commission, or any other board, officer or agency for the purpose of authorizing, selling or issuing the bonds of the sanitary district, and all bonds at any time issued by or on behalf of a sanitary district, are in all respects validated. These bonds are declared to be the legal and binding obligations of the sanitary district. (1953, c. 596, s. 3; 1957, c. 1357, s. 1; 1979, 2nd Sess., c. 1079, s. 2; 1983, c. 891, s. 2.)

§ 130A-78. Tax levy for validated bonds.

Sanitary districts are authorized to make appropriations and to levy annually a tax on property having a situs in the district under the rules and according to the procedure prescribed in the Machinery Act for the purpose of paying the principal of and interest on bonds validated in G.S. 130A-77. The tax shall be sufficient for this purpose and shall be in addition to all other taxes which may be levied upon the taxable property in the sanitary district. (1945, c. 89, s. 3; 1957, c. 1357, s. 1; 1973, c. 803, s. 17; 1983, c. 891, s. 2.)

§ 130A-79. Validation of appointment or election of members of district boards.

(a)   All actions and proceedings prior to June 6, 1961, taken in the appointment or election of members of a sanitary district board are validated. Members of these boards shall have all the powers and may perform all the duties required or permitted of them to be pursuant to this Part.

(b)   All actions and proceedings prior to May 1, 1959, taken in the appointment or election of members of a sanitary district board and the appointment or election of members are validated. Members of these boards shall have all the powers and may perform all the duties required or permitted of them pursuant to the provisions of this Part. (1953, c. 596, s. 4; 1957, c. 1357, s. 1; 1959, c. 415, s. 1; 1961, c. 667, s. 2; 1983, c. 891, s. 2.)

§ 130A-80. Merger of district with contiguous city or town; election.

A sanitary district may merge with a contiguous city or town in the following manner:

(1)   The sanitary district board and the governing board of the city or town may resolve that it is advisable to call an election within both the sanitary district and the city or town to determine if the sanitary district and the city or town should merge;

(2)   If the sanitary district board and the governing board of the city or town resolve that it is advisable to call for an election, both boards shall adopt a resolution requesting the board of commissioners in the county or counties in which the district and the town or city or any portion is located to hold an election on a date named by the sanitary district board and the governing board of the city or town after consultation with the appropriate board or boards of elections. The election shall be held within the sanitary district and the city or town on the question of merger;

(3)   The county board or boards of commissioners shall request the appropriate board or boards of elections to hold and conduct the election. All voters of the city or town and the sanitary district shall be eligible to vote if the election is called in both areas as authorized in subsection (1);

(4)   Notice of the election shall be given as required in G.S. 163-33(8). The board or boards of elections may use either method of registration set out in G.S. 163-288.2;

(5)   If an election is called as provided in subsection (2), the board or boards of elections shall provide ballots for the election in substantially the following form:

"[ ] FOR merger of the Town of . . . . and the . . . . Sanitary District, if a majority of the registered voters of both the Sanitary District and the Town vote in favor of merger, the combined territories to be known as the Town

170

of . . . . and to assume all of the obligations of the Sanitary District and to receive from the Sanitary District all the property rights of the District; from and after merger residents of the District would enjoy all of the benefits of the municipality and would assume their proportionate share of the obligations of the Town as merged.

[ ] AGAINST merger."

(6)   A majority of all the votes cast by voters of the sanitary district and a majority of all the votes cast by voters of the city or town is necessary for the merger of a sanitary district with the city or town. The merger shall be effective on July 1 following the election. If a majority of the votes cast in either the sanitary district or the city or town vote against the merger, any election on similar propositions of merger may not occur until one year from the date of the last election.

(7)   Upon the merger of a sanitary district and a city or town pursuant to this section, the city or town shall assume all obligations of the sanitary district and the sanitary district shall convey all property rights to the city or town. The vote for merger shall include a vote for the city or town to assume the obligations of the district. The sanitary district shall cease to exist as a political subdivision from and after the effective date of the merger. After the merger, the residents of the sanitary district enjoy all of the benefits of the municipality and shall assume their share of the obligations of the city or town. All taxes levied and collected by the city or town from and after the effective date of the merger shall be levied and collected uniformly in all the territory included in the enlarged municipality; and

(8)   If merger is approved, the governing board of the city or town shall determine the proportion of the district's indebtedness, if any, which was incurred for the construction of water systems and the proportion which was incurred for construction of sewage disposal systems. The governing board shall send a certified copy of the determination to the local government commission in order that the Commission and the governing body of the merged municipality can determine the net debt of the merged municipality as required by G.S. 159-55. (1961, c. 866; 1981, c. 186, s. 7; 1983, c. 891, s. 2; 1987, c. 314, s. 1.)

§ 130A-80.1. Merger of district with coterminous city or town; election.

A sanitary district may merge with a coterminous city or town in the following manner:

(1)   The sanitary district board and the governing board of the city or town may resolve that it is advisable to call an election within the area of the sanitary district and the city or town to determine if the sanitary district and the city or town should merge;

(2)   If the sanitary district board and the governing board of the city or town resolve that it is advisable to call for an election, both boards shall adopt a resolution requesting the board of commissioners in the county or counties in which the district and the town or city or any portion is located to hold an election on a date named by the sanitary district board and the governing board of the city or town after consultation with the appropriate board or boards of elections. The election shall be held within the sanitary district and the city or town on the question of merger;

(3)   The county board or boards of commissioners shall request the appropriate board or boards of elections to hold and conduct the election. All voters of the city or town and the sanitary district shall be eligible to vote;

(4)   Notice of the election shall be given as required in G.S. 163-33(8);

(5)   The board or boards of elections shall provide ballots for the election in substantially the following form:

"[] FOR merger of the Town of . . . . and the . . . . Sanitary District, if a majority of the registered voters vote in favor of merger, the area to be known as the Town of . . . . and to assume all of the obligations of the Sanitary District and to receive from the Sanitary District all the property rights of the District.

[] AGAINST merger."

(6)   A majority of all the votes cast is necessary for the merger of a sanitary district with the city or town. The merger shall be effective on July 1 following the election. If a majority of the votes cast is not in favor of the merger, an election on merger may not occur until one year from the date of the last election.

(7)   Upon the merger of a sanitary district and a city or town pursuant to this section, the city or town shall assume all obligations of the sanitary district and

172

the sanitary district shall convey all property rights to the city or town. The vote for merger shall include a vote for the city or town to assume the obligations of the district. The sanitary district shall cease to exist as a political subdivision from and after the effective date of the merger; and

(8)   If merger is approved, the governing board of the city or town shall determine the proportion of the district's indebtedness, if any, which was incurred for the construction of water systems and the proportion which was incurred for construction of sewage disposal systems. The governing board shall send a certified copy of the determination to the Local Government Commission in order that the Commission and the governing body of the merged municipality can determine the net debt of the merged municipality as required by G.S. 159-55. (1989, c. 194, s. 1.)

§ 130A-80.2. Merger of district with noncoterminous city or town it is contained wholly within; election.

A sanitary district may merge with a city or town which it is contained wholly within, but where the sanitary district and the city or town do not have coterminous boundaries, in the following manner:

(1)   The sanitary district board and the governing board of the city or town may resolve that it is advisable to call an election within both the sanitary district and the city or town to determine if the sanitary district and the city or town should merge;

(2)   If the sanitary district board and the governing board of the city or town resolve that it is advisable to call for an election, both boards shall adopt a resolution requesting the board of commissioners in the county or counties in which the district and the town or city or any portion is located to hold an election on a date named by the sanitary district board and the governing board of the city or town after consultation with the appropriate board or boards of elections. The election shall be held within the sanitary district and the city or town on the question of merger;

(3)   The county board or boards of commissioners shall request the appropriate board or boards of elections to hold and conduct the election. All voters of the city or town and the sanitary district shall be eligible to vote if the election is called in both areas as authorized in subdivision (1);

173

(4)   Notice of the election shall be given as required in G.S. 163-33(8). The board or boards of elections may use either method of registration set out in G.S. 163-288.2;

(5)   If an election is called as provided in subsection (2), the board or boards of elections shall provide ballots for the election in substantially the following form:

"[]   FOR merger of the Town of . . . . and the . . . . Sanitary District, if a majority of the registered voters of both the Sanitary District and the Town vote in favor of merger, the combined territories to be known as the Town of . . . . and to assume all of the obligations of the Sanitary District and to receive from the Sanitary District all the property rights of the District; from and after merger residents of the District would enjoy all of the benefits of the municipality and would assume their proportionate share of the obligations of the Town as merged.

[]   AGAINST merger."

(6)   A majority of all the votes cast by voters of the sanitary district and a majority of all the votes cast by voters of the city or town is necessary for the merger of a sanitary district with the city or town. The merger shall be effective on July 1 following the election. If a majority of the votes cast in either the sanitary district or the city or town vote against the merger, any election on similar propositions of merger may not occur until one year from the date of the last election.

(7)   Upon the merger of a sanitary district and a city or town pursuant to this section, the city or town shall assume all obligations of the sanitary district and the sanitary district shall convey all property rights to the city or town. The vote for merger shall include a vote for the city or town to assume the obligations of the district. The sanitary district shall cease to exist as a political subdivision from and after the effective date of the merger. After the merger, the residents of the sanitary district enjoy all of the benefits of the municipality and shall assume their share of the obligations of the city or town. All taxes levied and collected by the city or town from and after the effective date of the merger shall be levied and collected uniformly in all the territory included in the enlarged municipality; and

(8)   If merger is approved, the governing board of the city or town shall determine the proportion of the district's indebtedness, if any, which was

incurred for the construction of water systems and the proportion which was incurred for construction of sewage disposal systems. The governing board shall send a certified copy of the determination to the Local Government Commission in order that the Commission and the governing body of the merged municipality can determine the net debt of the merged municipality as required by G.S. 159-55. (1989, c. 194, s. 2.)

§ 130A-80.3. Merger of district with contiguous metropolitan water district.

(a)   A sanitary district may merge with a contiguous, but not coterminous, metropolitan water district organized under Article 4 of Chapter 162A of the General Statutes in the following manner, but only if the metropolitan water district has no outstanding indebtedness:

(1)   The sanitary district board and the district board of the metropolitan water district shall resolve that it is advisable for the sanitary district and the metropolitan water district should merge;

(2)   If the sanitary district board and the district board of the metropolitan water district resolve that it is advisable to merge, they shall call a public hearing on the merger. Each of such boards shall hold a public hearing on the question of merger, and advertisement of the public hearing shall be published at least 10 days before the public hearing;

(3)   After the public hearing, if the sanitary district board and the district board of the metropolitan water district by resolution approve the merger, the merger shall be effective on July 1 following the adoption of the resolution;

(4)   Upon the merger of a sanitary district and a metropolitan water district pursuant to this section, the sanitary district shall assume all obligations of the metropolitan water district, and the metropolitan water district shall convey all property rights to the sanitary district. The metropolitan water district shall cease to exist as a political subdivision from and after the effective date of the merger. After the merger, the residents of the metropolitan water district enjoy all of the benefits of the sanitary district and shall assume their share of the obligations of the sanitary district. All taxes levied and collected by the sanitary district from and after the effective date of the merger shall be levied and collected uniformly in all the territory included in the enlarged sanitary district; and

175

(5)   Certified copies of the merger resolutions shall be filed with the Commission for Public Health.

(b)   At the same time as approving the resolution of merger, the district board of the metropolitan water district shall designate by resolution two of its members to serve on an expanded sanitary district board from and after the date of the merger.

(c)   If the sanitary district board serves staggered four-year terms, the resolution shall designate one of those two persons to serve until the organizational meeting after the next election of a sanitary district board, and the other to serve until the organizational meeting after the second succeeding election of a sanitary district board. Successors shall be elected by the qualified voters of the sanitary district for four-year terms.

(d)   If the sanitary district board serves nonstaggered four-year terms, or serves two-year terms, the two persons shall serve until the organizational meeting after the next election of a sanitary district board. Successors shall be elected by the qualified voters of the sanitary district for terms of the same length as other sanitary district board members.

(e)   When a sanitary district and metropolitan water district are merged under this section, the sanitary district board may change the name of the sanitary district. Notice of such name change shall be filed with the Commission for Public Health. (1989, c. 194, s. 3; 2007-182, s. 2.)

§ 130A-81. Incorporation of municipality and simultaneous dissolution of sanitary district, with transfer of assets and liabilities from the district to the municipality.

The General Assembly may incorporate a municipality, which includes within its boundaries or is coterminous with a sanitary district and provide for the simultaneous dissolution of the sanitary district and the transfer of the district's assets and liabilities to the municipality, in the following manner:

(1)   The incorporation act shall define the boundaries of the proposed municipality; shall set the date for and provide for a referendum on the incorporation of the proposed municipality and dissolution of the sanitary district; shall provide for registration of voters in the area of the proposed municipality in

176

accordance with G.S. 163-288.2; shall set a proposed effective date for the incorporation of the municipality and the dissolution of the sanitary district; shall establish the form of government for the proposed municipality and the composition of its governing board, and provide for transitional arrangements for the sanitary district to the municipality; and may include any other matter appropriate to a municipal charter.

(1a)   As an alternate to subdivision (1) of this section, the incorporation act shall define the boundaries of the proposed municipality; shall provide that the incorporation is not subject to referendum; shall set a proposed effective date for the incorporation of the municipality and the dissolution of the sanitary district; shall establish the form of government for the proposed municipality and the composition of its governing board, and provide for transitional arrangements for the sanitary district to the municipality, and may include any other matter appropriate to a municipal charter. If this subdivision is followed instead of subdivision (1), then the municipality shall be incorporated and the sanitary district simultaneously dissolved at 12 noon on the date set for incorporation in the incorporation act, and the provisions of paragraphs a through g of subdivision (5) of this section shall apply.

(2)   The referendum shall be conducted by the board of elections of the county in which the proposed municipality is located. If the proposed municipality is located in more than one county, the board of elections of the county which has the greatest number of residents of the proposed municipality shall conduct the referendum. The board of election shall conduct the referendum in accordance with this section and the provisions of the incorporation act.

(3)   The form of the ballot for a referendum under this section shall be substantially as follows:

"[] FOR incorporation of the Town (City) of . . . . and the simultaneous dissolution of the . . . . Sanitary District, with transfer of the District's assets and liabilities to the Town (City), and assumption of the District's indebtedness by the Town (City).

[] AGAINST incorporation of the Town (City) of . . . . and the simultaneous dissolution of the . . . . Sanitary District, with transfer of the District's assets and liabilities, to the Town (City), and assumption of the District's indebtedness by the Town (City)."

177

(4)   If a majority of those voting in the referendum vote in favor of incorporating the proposed municipality and dissolving the sanitary district, the board of elections shall notify the Department and the Local Government Commission of the date on which the municipality will be incorporated and the sanitary district dissolved and shall state that all assets and liabilities of the sanitary district will be transferred to the municipality and that the municipality will assume the district's indebtedness.

(5)   If a majority of those voting in the referendum vote in favor of incorporating the proposed municipality and dissolving the sanitary district, the municipality shall be incorporated and the sanitary district shall be simultaneously dissolved at 12 noon on the date set for incorporation in the incorporation act. At that time:

a.   The sanitary district shall cease to exist as a body politic and corporate;

b.   All property, real, personal and mixed, belonging to the sanitary district vests in and is the property of the municipality;

c.   All judgments, liens, rights and courses of action in favor of the sanitary district vest in favor of the municipality;

d.   All rentals, taxes, assessments and other funds, charges or fees owed to the sanitary district are owed to and may be collected by the municipality;

e.   Any action, suit, or proceeding pending against, or instituted by the sanitary district shall not be abated by its dissolution, but shall be continued and completed in the same manner as if dissolution had not occurred. The municipality shall be a party to these actions, suits and proceedings in the place of the sanitary district and shall pay any judgment rendered against the sanitary district in any of these actions or proceedings. No new process need be served in any of the actions, suits or proceedings;

f.   All obligations of the sanitary district, including outstanding indebtedness, are assumed by the municipality, and all the obligations and outstanding indebtedness are constituted obligations and indebtedness of the municipality. The full faith and credit of the municipality is deemed to be pledged for the payment of the principal of and interest on all general obligation bonds and bond anticipation notes of the sanitary district, and all the taxable property within the municipality shall remain subject to taxation for these payments; and

178

g.   All rules of the sanitary district shall continue in effect until repealed or amended by the governing body of the municipality.

(6)   The transition between the sanitary district and the municipality shall be provided for in the incorporation act of the municipality. (1971, c. 737, 1973, c. 476, s. 128; 1983, c. 891, s. 2; 1985, c. 375.)

§ 130A-82. Dissolution of sanitary districts; referendum.

(a)   A county board of commissioners in counties having a population in excess of 275,000 may dissolve a sanitary district by holding a referendum on the questions of dissolution and assumption by the county of any outstanding indebtedness of the district. The county board of commissioners may dissolve a sanitary district which has no outstanding indebtedness when the members of the district shall vote in favor of dissolution.

(b)   Before the dissolution of any district shall be approved, a plan for continued operation and provision of all services and functions being performed or rendered by the district shall be adopted and approved by the board of county commissioners.

(c)   No plan shall be adopted unless at the time of its adoption any water system or sanitary sewer system being operated by the district is in compliance with all local, State and federal rules and regulations, and if the system is to be serviced by a municipality, the municipality shall first approve the plan.

(d)   When all actions relating to dissolution of the sanitary district have been completed, the chairperson of the county board of commissioners shall notify the Department. (1973, c. 476, s. 128; c. 951; 1983, c. 891, s. 2.)

§ 130A-83. Merger of two contiguous sanitary districts.

Two contiguous sanitary districts may merge in the following manner:

(1)   The sanitary district board of each sanitary district must first adopt a common proposed plan of merger. The plan shall contain the name of the new

179

or successor sanitary district, designate the members of the merging boards who shall serve as the interim sanitary district board for the new or successor district until the next election required by G.S. 130A-50(b) and 163-279, and any other matters necessary to complete the merger.

(2)   The merger may become effective only if approved by the voters of the two sanitary districts. In order to call an election, both boards shall adopt a resolution calling upon the board of county commissioners in the county or counties in which the districts are located to call for an election on a date named by the sanitary district boards after consultation with the appropriate boards of election. The board or boards of commissioners shall hold an election on the proposed merger of the sanitary districts.

(3)   The county board or boards of commissioners shall request the appropriate board of elections to hold and conduct the elections. All voters of the two sanitary districts shall be eligible to vote.

(4)   Notice of the elections shall be given as required in G.S. 163-33(8). The board of elections may use the method of registration set out in G.S. 163-288.2.

(5)   If an election is called as provided in subsection (2), the board or boards of elections shall provide ballots for the election in substantially the following form:

"[] FOR the merger of the . . . . Sanitary District and the. . . . . . . Sanitary District into a single district to be known as the . . . . Sanitary District, in which all the property, assets, liabilities, obligations, and indebtedness of the two districts become the property, assets, liabilities, obligations, and indebtedness of the . . . . Sanitary District.

[] AGAINST the merger of the . . . . Sanitary District and the. . . . . . . Sanitary District into a single district to be known as the . . . . Sanitary District, in which all the property, assets, liabilities, obligations, and indebtedness of the two districts become the property, assets, liabilities, obligations, and indebtedness of the . . . . Sanitary District."

(6)   If a majority of all the votes cast in each sanitary district vote in favor of the merger, the two sanitary districts shall be merged on July 1 following the election. Should the majority of the votes cast in either sanitary district be against the proposition, the sanitary districts shall not be merged. If a majority of the votes cast in either sanitary district are against the merger, any election on

similar propositions of merger may not occur until one year from the date of the last election.

(7)   Upon the merger of two sanitary districts pursuant to this section and the creation of a new district, the merger becomes effective at 12 noon on the following July 1. At that time:

a.   The two sanitary districts shall cease to exist as bodies politic and corporate, and the new sanitary district exists as a body politic and corporate.

b.   All property, real, personal and mixed, belonging to the sanitary districts vests in and is the property of the new sanitary district.

c.   All judgments, liens, rights of liens and causes of action in favor of either sanitary district vest in the new sanitary district.

d.   All rentals, taxes, assessments and other funds, charges or fees owed to either of the sanitary districts are owed to and may be collected by the new sanitary district.

e.   Any action, suit, or proceeding pending against, or having been instituted by, either of the sanitary districts shall not be abated by its dissolution, but shall be continued and completed in the same manner as if dissolution had not occurred. The new sanitary district shall be a party to all these actions, suits and proceedings in the place of the dissolved sanitary district and shall pay any judgment rendered against either of the sanitary districts in any of these actions or proceedings. No new process need be served in any of the actions, suits or proceedings.

f.   All obligations of either of the sanitary districts, including any outstanding indebtedness, are assumed by the new sanitary district and all the obligations and outstanding indebtedness are constituted obligations and indebtedness of the new sanitary district. The full faith and credit of the new sanitary district is deemed to be pledged for the punctual payment of the principal of and interest on all general obligation bonds and bond anticipation notes of either of the sanitary districts, and all the taxable property within the new sanitary district shall remain subject to taxation for these payments.

g.   All rules of either of the sanitary districts shall continue in effect until repealed or amended by the governing body of the new sanitary district.

181

(8)   Upon the merger of two sanitary districts pursuant to this section when one district is to be dissolved and the other district is to be a successor covering the territory of both, the merger becomes effective at 12 noon on the following July 1. At that time:

a.   One sanitary district shall cease to exist as a body politic and corporate, and the successor sanitary district continues to exist as a body politic and corporate.

b.   All property, real, personal and mixed, belonging to the sanitary districts vests in, and is the property of the successor sanitary district.

c.   All judgments, liens, rights of liens and causes of action in favor of either sanitary district vest in the successor sanitary district.

d.   All rentals, taxes, assessments and other funds, charges or fees owed either of the sanitary districts are owed to and may be collected by the successor sanitary district.

e.   Any action, suit, or proceeding pending against, or instituted by either of the sanitary districts shall not be abated by its dissolution, but shall be continued and completed in the same manner as if dissolution had not occurred. The successor sanitary district shall be a party to all these actions, suits and proceedings in the place of the dissolved sanitary district and shall pay any judgment rendered against the sanitary district in any of these actions or proceedings. No new process need be served in any of the actions, suits or proceedings.

f.   All obligations of either of the sanitary districts, including any outstanding indebtedness, are assumed by the successor sanitary district and all the obligations and outstanding indebtedness are constituted obligations and indebtedness of the successor sanitary district. The full faith and credit of the successor sanitary district is deemed to be pledged for the punctual payment of the principal of and interest on all general obligation bonds and bond anticipation notes of either of the sanitary districts, and all the taxable property within the successor sanitary district shall be and remain subject to taxation for these payments.

g.   All rules of either of the sanitary districts shall continue in effect until repealed or amended by the governing body of the successor sanitary district. (1981, c. 951; 1983, c. 891, s. 2; 1987, c. 314, s. 2.)

182

§ 130A-84. Withdrawal of water.

A sanitary district is empowered to engage in litigation or to join with other parties in litigation opposing the withdrawal of water from a river or other water supply. (1983, c. 891, s. 2.)

§ 130A-85. Further dissolution procedures.

(a)   The County Board of Commissioners may dissolve a Sanitary District located entirely within one county upon the following conditions:

(1)   There are 500 or less resident freeholders residing within the District;

(2)   The District has no outstanding bonded indebtedness;

(3)   The Board of Commissioners agrees to assume and pay any other outstanding legal indebtedness of the District;

(4)   The Board of Commissioners adopts a plan providing for continued operation and provision of all services previously being performed or rendered to the District. No plan shall be adopted unless at the time of its adoption any water and sewer or sanitary system being operated by the District is in compliance with all local, State, and federal rules and regulations; and

(5)   The Board of Commissioners adopts a resolution finding that the interest of the citizens of the Sanitary District and the county will be best served if the operation and the services provided by the District were provided for by the Board of Commissioners.

(a1)   The County Board of Commissioners may dissolve a Sanitary District located entirely within one county and for which no District Board members have been elected within eight years preceding dissolution, upon the following conditions:

(1)   The District has no outstanding legal indebtedness;

(2)   The Board of Commissioners adopts a plan providing for continued operation and provision of all services, if any, previously being performed or rendered to the District. No plan shall be adopted unless at the time of its

183

adoption any water and sewer or sanitary system being operated by the District is in compliance with all local, State, and federal rules and regulations; and

(3)   The Board of Commissioners adopts a resolution finding that the interest of the citizens of the Sanitary District and the county will be best served if the operation and the services provided by the District are provided for by the Board of Commissioners.

When all actions relating to dissolution of the sanitary district have been completed, the chairperson of the County Board of Commissioners shall notify the Department.

(b)   Prior to taking action to dissolve a Sanitary District, the Board of Commissioners shall hold a public hearing concerning dissolution of the District. The County Board of Commissioners shall give notice of the hearing by publication of notice thereof in a newspaper or newspapers with general circulation in the county, once per week for three consecutive weeks. If, after the hearing, the Board of Commissioners deems it advisable to dissolve the District, they shall thereafter adopt the resolution and plan provided for herein.

During the period commencing with the first publication of notice of the public hearing as herein provided, and for a period of 60 days following the public hearing, the Board of Commissioners of the District may not enter into any contracts, incur any indebtedness or pledge, or encumber any of the District's assets except in the ordinary course of business.

(c)   Upon adoption of the resolution provided for herein, all property, real, personal, and mixed, belonging to the District vests in and becomes the property of the county; all judgments, liens, rights of liens and causes of action in favor of the District vests in the county; and all rentals, taxes and assessments and other funds, charges or fees owed to the District may be collected by the county.

(d)   Following dissolution of the District, the county may operate, maintain, and extend the services previously provided for by the District either:

(1)   As a part of county government; or

(2)   As a service district created on or after January 1, 1987, under Article 16 of Chapter 153A of the General Statutes to serve at least the area of the Sanitary District.

184

In lieu thereof, the services may be provided by any authority or district created after January 1, 1987, under this Article, or Articles 1, 4, 5 or 6 of Chapter 162A of the General Statutes to serve at least the area of the District. In such case, the county may convey the property, including all judgments, liens, rights of liens, causes of action, rentals, taxes and assessments mentioned in subsection (c) of this section, to that authority or District. (1987, c. 521; 1991, c. 417.)

§ 130A-86. Reserved for future codification purposes.

§ 130A-87. Reserved for future codification purposes.

Article 3.

State Laboratory of Public Health.

§ 130A-88. Laboratory established.

(a)   A State Laboratory of Public Health is established within the Department. The Department is authorized to make examinations, and provide consultation and technical assistance as the public health may require.

(b)   The Commission shall adopt rules necessary for the operation of the State Laboratory of Public Health. (1905, c. 415; Rev., s. 3057; 1907, cc. 721, 884; 1911, c. 62, s. 36; C.S., s. 7056; 1957, c. 1357, s. 1; 1973, c. 476, s. 128; 1979, c. 788, s. 3; 1983, c. 891, s. 2.)

§ 130A-89. Reserved for future codification purposes.

Article 4.

Vital Statistics.

§ 130A-90. Vital statistics program.

185

The Department shall maintain a Vital Statistics Program which shall operate the only system of vital records registration throughout this State. (1983, c. 891, s. 2.)

§ 130A-91. State Registrar.

The Secretary shall appoint a State Registrar of Vital Statistics. The State Registrar of Vital Statistics shall exercise all the authority conferred by this Article. (1913, c. 109, s. 2; C.S., s. 7088; 1955, c. 951, s. 5; 1957, c. 1357, s. 1; 1969, c. 1031, s. 1; 1973, c. 476, s. 128; 1977, c. 163, s. 1; 1983, c. 891, s. 2.)

§ 130A-92. Duties of the State Registrar.

(a)   The State Registrar shall secure and maintain all vital records required under this Article and shall do all things necessary to carry out its provisions. The State Registrar shall:

(1)   Examine vital records received from local registrars to determine if these records are complete and satisfactory, and require the provision of information necessary to make the records complete and satisfactory;

(2)   Permanently preserve the information from the vital records in a systematic manner in adequate fireproof space which shall be provided in a State building by the Department of Administration, and maintain a comprehensive and continuous index of all vital records;

(3)   Prepare and supply or approve all forms used in carrying out the provisions of this Article;

(4)   Appoint local registrars as required by G.S. 130A-95 and exercise supervisory authority over local registrars, deputy local registrars and sub-registrars;

(5)   Enforce the provisions of this Article, investigate cases of irregularity or violations and report violations to law-enforcement officials for prosecution under G.S. 130A-26;

(6)   Conduct studies and research and recommend to the General Assembly any additional legislation necessary to carry out the purposes of this Article; and

(7)   Adopt rules necessary to carry out the provisions of this Article.

(b)   The State Registrar may retain payments made in excess of the fees established by this Article if the overpayment is in the amount of three dollars ($3.00) or less and the payor does not request a refund of the overpayment. The State Registrar is not required to notify the payor of any overpayment of three dollars ($3.00) or less. (1913, c. 109, s. 1; C.S., s. 7086; 1957, c. 1357, s. 1; 1969, c. 1031, s. 1; 1971, c. 444, s. 3; 1973, c. 476, s. 128; 1983, c. 891, s. 2; 1985, c. 366; 1993, c. 146, s. 2.)

§ 130A-93. Access to vital records; copies.

(a)   Only the State Registrar shall have access to original vital records and to indices to the original vital records. County offices authorized to issue certificates and the North Carolina State Archives also shall have access to indices to these original vital records, when specifically authorized by the State Registrar.

(b)   The following birth data, in any form and on any medium, in the possession of the Department, local health departments, or local register of deeds offices shall not be public records pursuant to Chapter 132 of the General Statutes: the names of children and parents, the addresses of parents (other than county of residence and postal code), and the social security numbers of parents. Access to copies and abstracts of these data shall be provided in accordance with G.S. 130A-99, Chapter 161 of the General Statutes, and this section. All other birth data shall be public records pursuant to Chapter 132 of the General Statutes. All birth records and data are State property and shall be managed only in accordance with official disposition instructions prepared by the Department of Cultural Resources. The application of this Chapter is subject to the provisions of Article 1 of Chapter 121 of the General Statutes, the North Carolina Archives and History Act. The State Registrar and other officials authorized to issue certified copies of vital records shall provide copies or abstracts of vital records, except those described in subsections (d), (e), (f) and (g) of this section, to any person upon request.

(c)   The State Registrar and other officials authorized to issue certified copies of vital records shall provide certified copies of vital records, except those described in subsections (d), (e), (f), and (g) of this section, only to the following:

(1)   A person requesting a copy of the person's own vital records or that of the person's spouse, sibling, direct ancestor or descendant, or stepparent or stepchild;

(2)   A person seeking information for a legal determination of personal or property rights; or

(3)   An authorized agent, attorney or legal representative of a person described above.

(c1)   A funeral director or funeral service licensee shall be entitled upon request to a certified copy of a death certificate.

(c2)   An agency acting as a confidential intermediary in accordance with G.S. 48-9-104 shall be entitled to a certified copy of a death certificate upon request.

(d)   Copies, certified copies or abstracts of birth certificates of adopted persons shall be provided in accordance with G.S. 48-9-107.

(e)   Copies or abstracts of the health and medical information contained on birth certificates shall be provided only to a person requesting a copy of the health and medical information contained on the person's own birth certificate, a person authorized by that person, or a person who will use the information for medical research purposes. Copies of or abstracts from any computer or microform database which contains individual-specific health or medical birth data, whether the database is maintained by the Department, a local health department, or any other public official, shall be provided only to an individual requesting his or her own data, a person authorized by that individual, or a person who will use the information for medical research purposes. The State Registrar shall adopt rules providing for the use of this information for medical research purposes. The rules shall, at a minimum, require a written description of the proposed use of the data, including protocols for protecting confidentiality of the data.

(f)   Copies, certified copies or abstracts of new birth certificates issued to persons in the federal witness protection program shall be provided only to a

188

person requesting a copy of the person's own birth certificate and that person's supervising federal marshall.

(g)   No copies, certified copies or abstracts of vital records shall be provided to a person purporting to request copies, certified copies or abstracts of that person's own vital records upon determination that the person whose vital records are being requested is deceased.

(h)   A certified copy issued under the provisions of this section shall have the same evidentiary value as the original and shall be prima facie evidence of the facts stated in the document. The State Registrar may appoint agents who shall have the authority to issue certified copies under a facsimile signature of the State Registrar. These copies shall have the same evidentiary value as those issued by the State Registrar.

(i)   Fees for issuing any copy of a vital record or for conducting a search of the files when no copy is made shall be as established in G.S. 130A-93.1 and G.S. 161-10.

(j)   No person shall prepare or issue any certificate which purports to be an official certified copy of a vital record except as authorized in this Article or the rules. (1983, c. 891, s. 2; 1985, c. 325, s. 1; 1991, c. 343, s. 1; 1993, c. 146, s. 3; 1995, c. 457, s. 7; 1997-242, s. 1; 2010-116, s. 4.)

§ 130A-93.1. Fees for vital records copies or search; automation fund.

(a)   The State Registrar shall collect, process, and utilize fees for services as follows:

(1)   A fee not to exceed twenty-four dollars ($24.00) shall be charged for issuing a first copy of a vital record or for conducting a routine search of the files for the record when no copy is made. A fee of fifteen dollars ($15.00) shall be charged for each additional certificate copy requested from the same search. When certificates are issued or searches conducted for statewide issuance by local agencies using databases maintained by the State Registrar, the local agency shall charge and forward to the State Registrar for the purposes established in subsection (b) of this section fourteen dollars ($14.00) and shall charge and retain ten dollars ($10.00) if a copy of the record is made. Provided,

however, that a local agency may waive the ten dollar ($10.00) charge for its retention when the copy is issued to a person over the age of 62 years.

(2)   A fee not to exceed fifteen dollars ($15.00) for in-State requests and not to exceed twenty dollars ($20.00) for out-of-state requests shall be charged in addition to the fee charged under subdivision (1) of this subsection and to all shipping and commercial charges when expedited service is specifically requested.

(2a)   The fee for a copy of a computer or microform database shall not exceed the cost to the agency of making and providing the copy.

(3)   Except as provided in subsection (b) of this section, fees collected under this subsection shall be used by the Department for public health purposes.

(b)   The Vital Records Automation Account is established as a nonreverting account within the Department. Five dollars ($5.00) of each fee collected pursuant to subdivision (a)(1) shall be credited to this Account. The Department shall use the revenue in the Account to fully automate and maintain the vital records system. When funds sufficient to fully automate and maintain the system have accumulated in the Account, fees shall no longer be credited to the Account but shall be used as specified in subdivision (a)(3) of this section.

(c)   Upon verification of voter registration, the State Registrar shall not charge any fee under subsection (a) of this section to a registered voter who signs a declaration stating the registered voter is registered to vote in this State and does not have a certified copy of that registered voter's birth certificate or marriage license necessary to obtain photo identification acceptable under G.S. 163-166.13. Any declaration shall prominently include the penalty under G.S. 163-275(13) for falsely or fraudulently making the declaration. (1991, c. 343, s. 2; 1991 (Reg. Sess., 1992), c. 1039, s. 5; 1997-242, s. 2; 2002-126, s. 29A.18(a); 2009-451, s. 10.22; 2012-18, s. 2.1; 2013-381, s. 3.2.)

§ 130A-94. Local registrar.

The local health director shall serve, ex officio, as the local registrar of each county within the jurisdiction of the local health department. (1983, c. 891, s. 2.)

§ 130A-95. Control of local registrar.

The State Registrar shall direct, control and supervise the activities of local registrars. (1913, c. 109, s. 4; 1915, c. 20; C.S., ss. 7089, 7090; 1955, c. 951, s. 6; 1957, c. 1357, s. 1; 1969, c. 1031, s. 1; 1983, c. 891, s. 2; 1985, c. 462, s. 14.)

§ 130A-96. Appointment of deputy and sub-registrars.

(a)   Each local registrar shall immediately upon appointment, appoint a deputy whose duty shall be to assist the local registrar and to act as local registrar in case of absence, illness, disability or removal of the local registrar. The deputy shall be designated in writing and be subject to all rules and statutes governing local registrars. The local registrar shall direct, control and supervise the activities of the deputy registrar and may remove a deputy registrar for cause.

(b)   The local registrar may, when necessary and with the approval of the State Registrar, appoint one or more persons to act as sub-registrars. Sub-registrars shall be authorized to receive certificates and issue burial-transit permits in and for designated portions of the county. Each sub-registrar shall enter the date the certificate was received and shall forward all certificates to the local registrar within three days.

(c)   The State Registrar shall direct, control and supervise sub-registrars and may remove a sub-registrar for cause. (1913, c. 109, s. 4; C.S., s. 7091; 1955, c. 951, s. 8; 1957, c. 1357, s. 1; 1969, c. 1031, s. 1; 1983, c. 891, s. 2.)

§ 130A-97. Duties of local registrars.

The local registrar shall:

(1)   Administer and enforce provisions of this Article and the rules, and immediately report any violation to the State Registrar;

(2)   Furnish certificate forms and instructions supplied by the State Registrar to persons who require them;

191

(3) Examine each certificate when submitted to determine if it has been completed in accordance with the provisions of this Article and the rules. If a certificate is incomplete or unsatisfactory, the responsible person shall be notified and required to furnish the necessary information. All birth and death certificates shall be typed or written legibly in permanent black, blue-black, or blue ink;

(4) Enter the date on which a certificate is received and sign as local registrar;

(5) Transmit to the register of deeds of the county a copy of each certificate registered within seven days of receipt of a birth or death certificate. The copy transmitted shall include the race of the father and mother if that information is contained on the State copy of the certificate of live birth. Copies transmitted may be on blanks furnished by the State Registrar or may be photocopies made in a manner approved by the register of deeds. The local registrar may also keep a copy of each certificate for no more than two years;

(6) On the fifth day of each month or more often, if requested, send to the State Registrar all original certificates registered during the preceding month; and

(7) Maintain records, make reports and perform other duties required by the State Registrar. (1913, c. 109, s. 18; 1915, c. 85, s. 2; c. 164, s. 2; C.S., s. 7109; Ex. Sess. 1920, c. 58, s. 1; 1931, c. 79; 1933, c. 9, s. 1; 1943, c. 673; 1949, c. 133; 1955, c. 951, ss. 20, 21; 1957, c. 1357, s. 1; 1963, c. 492, ss. 4, 8; 1969, c. 1031, s. 1; 1971, c. 444, s. 8; 1979, c. 95, s. 9; 1981, c. 554; 1983, c. 891, s. 2; 2003-60, s. 1.)

§ 130A-98. Pay of local registrars.

A local health department shall provide sufficient staff, funds and other resources necessary for the proper administration of the local vital records registration program. (1913, c. 109, s. 19; Ex. Sess. 1913, c. 15, s. 1; 1915, c. 85, s. 3; 1919, c. 210, s. 1; C.S., s 7110; Ex. Sess. 1920, c. 58, s. 2; 1949, c. 306; 1957, c. 1357, s. 1; 1969, c. 1031, s. 1; 1983, c. 891, s. 2.)

§ 130A-99. Register of deeds to preserve copies of birth and death records.

(a)   The register of deeds of each county shall file and preserve the copies of birth and death certificates furnished by the local registrar under the provisions of G.S. 130A-97, and shall make and keep a proper index of the certificates. These certificates shall be open to inspection and examination. Copies or abstracts of these certificates shall be provided to any person upon request. Certified copies of these certificates shall be provided only to those persons described in G.S. 130A-93(c).

(b)   The register of deeds may remove from the records and destroy copies of birth or death certificates for persons born or dying in counties other than the county in which the office of the register of deeds is located, only after confirming that copies of the birth or death certificates removed and destroyed are maintained by the State Registrar or North Carolina State Archives. (1957, c. 1357, s. 1; 1969, c. 80, s. 3; c. 1031, s. 1; 1983, c. 891, s. 2; 1997-309, s. 11.)

§ 130A-100. Register of deeds may perform notarial acts.

(a)   The register of deeds is authorized to take acknowledgments, administer oaths and affirmations and to perform all other notarial acts necessary for the registration or issuance of certificates relating to births, deaths or marriages. The register of deeds shall be entitled to a fee as prescribed in G.S. 161-10.

(b)   All acknowledgments taken, affirmations or oaths administered or other notarial acts performed by the register of deeds relating to the registration of certificates of births, deaths or marriages prior to June 16, 1959, are validated. (1945, c. 100; 1957, c. 1357, s. 1; 1959, c. 986; 1969, c. 80, s. 9; c. 1031, s. 1; 1983, c. 891, s. 2.)

§ 130A-101. Birth registration.

(a)   A certificate of birth for each live birth, regardless of the gestation period, which occurs in this State shall be filed with the local registrar of the county in which the birth occurs within 10 days after the birth and shall be

193

registered by the registrar if it has been completed and filed in accordance with this Article and the rules.

(b)   When a birth occurs in a hospital or other medical facility, the person in charge of the facility shall obtain the personal data, prepare the certificate, secure the signatures required by the certificate and file it with the local registrar within 10 days after the birth. The physician or other person in attendance shall provide the medical information required by the certificate.

(c)   When a birth occurs outside a hospital or other medical facility, the certificate shall be prepared and filed by one of the following in the indicated order of priority:

(1)   The physician in attendance at or immediately after the birth, or in the absence of such a person;

(2)   Any other person in attendance at or immediately after the birth, or in the absence of such a person;

(3)   The father, the mother or, in the absence or inability of the father and the mother, the person in charge of the premises where the birth occurred.

(d)   When a birth occurs on a moving conveyance and the child is first moved from the conveyance in this State, the birth shall be registered in the county where the child is first removed from the conveyance, and that place shall be considered the place of birth.

(e)   If the mother was married at the time of either conception or birth, or between conception and birth, the name of the husband shall be entered on the certificate as the father of the child, except as provided in this subsection. The surname of the child shall be the same as that of the husband, except that upon agreement of the husband and mother, or upon agreement of the mother and father if paternity has been otherwise determined, any surname may be chosen. The name of the putative father shall be entered on the certificate as the father of the child if one of the following conditions exists:

(1)   Paternity has been otherwise determined by a court of competent jurisdiction, in which case the name of the father as determined by the court shall be entered.

(2)   The child's mother, mother's husband, and putative father complete an affidavit acknowledging paternity that contains all of the following:

a.   A sworn statement by the mother consenting to the assertion of paternity by the putative father and declaring that the putative father is the child's natural father.

b.   A sworn statement by the putative father declaring that he believes he is the natural father of the child.

c.   A sworn statement by the mother's husband consenting to the assertion of paternity by the putative father.

d.   Information explaining in plain language the effect of signing the affidavit, including a statement of parental rights and responsibilities and an acknowledgment of the receipt of this information.

e.   The social security numbers of the putative father, mother, and mother's husband.

f.   The results of a DNA test that has confirmed the paternity of the putative father.

(f)   If the mother was unmarried at all times from date of conception through date of birth, the name of the father shall not be entered on the certificate unless the child's mother and father complete an affidavit acknowledging paternity which contains the following:

(1)   A sworn statement by the mother consenting to the assertion of paternity by the father and declaring that the father is the child's natural father and that the mother was unmarried at all times from the date of conception through the date of birth;

(2)   A sworn statement by the father declaring that he believes he is the natural father of the child;

(3)   Information explaining in plain language the effect of signing the affidavit, including a statement of parental rights and responsibilities and an acknowledgment of the receipt of this information; and

(4)   The social security numbers of both parents.

195

The State Registrar, in consultation with the Child Support Enforcement Section of the Division of Social Services, shall develop and disseminate a form affidavit for use in compliance with this section, together with an information sheet that contains all the information required to be disclosed by subdivision (3) of this subsection.

Upon the execution of the affidavit, the declaring father shall be listed as the father on the birth certificate, subject to the declaring father's right to rescind under G.S. 110-132. The executed affidavit shall be filed with the registrar along with the birth certificate. In the event paternity is properly placed at issue, a certified copy of the affidavit shall be admissible in any action to establish paternity. The surname of the child shall be determined by the mother, except if the father's name is entered on the certificate, the mother and father shall agree upon the child's surname. If there is no agreement, the child's surname shall be the same as that of the mother.

The execution and filing of this affidavit with the registrar does not affect rights of inheritance unless the affidavit is also filed with the clerk of court in accordance with G.S. 29-19(b)(2).

(g)   Each parent shall provide his or her social security number to the person responsible for preparing and filing the certificate of birth. (1913, c. 109, s. 13; 1915, c. 85, s. 1; C.S., s. 7010; 1957, c. 1357, s. 1; 1969, c. 1031, s. 1; 1979, c. 95, s. 4; c. 417; 1983, c. 891, s. 2; 1989, c. 199, ss. 1, 2; 1989 (Reg. Sess., 1990), c. 1004, s. 6; 1993, c. 333, s. 1; 1995, c. 428, s. 1; 1997-433, s. 4.12; 1998-17, s. 1; 2005-389, s. 4; 2009-285, s. 1; 2013-378, s. 8.)

§ 130A-102. Contents of birth certificate.

The certificate of birth shall contain those items recommended by the federal agency responsible for national vital statistics, except as amended or changed by the State Registrar. Medical information contained in a birth certificate shall not be public records open to inspection. (1913, c. 109, s. 14; C.S., s. 7102; 1949, c. 161, s. 2; 1955, c. 951, s. 15; 1957, c. 1357, s. 1; 1969, c. 1031, s. 1; 1979, c. 95, s. 7; 1983, c. 891, s. 2.)

§ 130A-103. Registration of birth certificates more than five days and less than one year after birth.

Any birth may be registered more than five days and less than one year after birth in the same manner as births are registered under this Article within five days of birth. The registration shall have the effect as if the registration had occurred within five days of birth. The registration however, shall not relieve any person of criminal liability for the failure to register the birth within five days of birth as required by G.S. 130A-101. (1941, c. 126; 1957, c. 1357, s. 1; 1969, c. 1031, s. 1; 1979, c. 95, s. 5; 1983, c. 891, s. 2.)

§ 130A-104. Registration of birth one year or more after birth.

(a)   When the birth of a person born in this State has not been registered within one year after birth, a delayed certificate may be filed with the register of deeds in the county in which the birth occurred. An applicant for a delayed certificate must submit the minimum documentation prescribed by the State Registrar.

(b)   A certificate of birth registered one year or more after the date of the birth shall be marked "delayed" and show the date of the delayed registration. A summary statement of evidence submitted in support of the delayed registration shall be endorsed on the certificate. The register of deeds shall forward the original and a duplicate to the State Registrar for final approval. If the certificate complies with the rules and has not been previously registered, the State Registrar shall file the original and return the duplicate to the register of deeds for recording.

(c)   When an applicant does not submit the minimum documentation required or when the State Registrar finds reason to question the validity or adequacy of the certificate or documentary evidence, the State Registrar shall not register the delayed certificate and shall advise the applicant of the reasons for this action. If the deficiencies are not corrected, the applicant shall be advised of the right to an administrative hearing and of the availability of a judicial determination under G.S. 130A-106.

(d)   Delayed certificates shall have the same evidentiary value as those registered within five days. (1941, c. 126; 1957, c. 1357, s. 1; 1969, c. 80, s. 8; c. 1031, s. 1; 1973, c. 476, s. 128; 1979, c. 95, s. 6; 1983, c. 891, s. 2.)

197

§ 130A-105. Validation of irregular registration of birth certificates.

The registration and filing with the State Registrar prior to April 1, 1941, of the birth certificate of a person whose birth was not registered within five days of birth is validated. All copies of birth certificates filed prior to April 9, 1941, properly certified by the State Registrar, shall have the same evidentiary value as those registered within five days. (1941, c. 126; 1957, c. 1357, s. 1; 1969, c. 1031, s. 1; 1973, c. 476, s. 128; 1983, c. 891, s. 2.)

§ 130A-106. Establishing fact of birth by persons without certificates.

(a)   A person born in this State not having a recorded certificate of birth, may file a verified petition with the clerk of the superior court in the county of the petitioner's legal residence or place of birth, setting forth the date, place of birth and parentage, and petitioning the clerk to hear evidence, and to find and adjudge the date, place and parentage of the birth of the petitioner. Upon the filing of a petition, the clerk shall set a hearing date, and shall conduct the proceeding in the same manner as other special proceedings. At the time set for the hearing, the petitioner shall present evidence to establish the facts of birth. If the evidence offered satisfies the court, the court shall enter judgment establishing the date, place of birth and parentage of the petitioner, and record it in the record of special proceedings. The clerk shall certify the judgment to the State Registrar who shall keep a record of the judgment. A copy shall be certified to the register of deeds of the county in which the petitioner was born.

(b)   Repealed by Session Laws 2007-323, s. 30.10(f), effective August 1, 2007, and applicable to all costs assessed or collected on or after that date.

(c)   The record of birth established under this section, when recorded, shall have the same evidentiary value as other records covered by this Article. (1941, c. 122; 1957, c. 1357, s. 1; 1969, c. 1031, s. 1; 1973, c. 476, s. 128; 1983, c. 891, s. 2; 2007-323, s. 30.10(f).)

§ 130A-107. Establishing facts relating to a birth of unknown parentage; certificate of identification.

(a)   A person of unknown parentage whose place and date of birth are unknown may file a verified petition with the clerk of the superior court in the county where the petitioner was abandoned. The petition shall set forth the facts concerning abandonment, the name, date and place of birth of petitioner and the names of any persons acting in loco parentis to the petitioner.

(b)   The clerk shall find facts and, if there is insufficient evidence to establish the place of birth, it shall be conclusively presumed that the person was born in the county of abandonment. The clerk shall enter and record judgment in the record of special proceedings. The clerk shall certify the judgment to the State Registrar who shall keep a record of the judgment. A copy shall be certified to the register of deeds of the county of abandonment.

(c)   A certificate of identification for a person of unknown parentage shall be filed by the clerk with the local registrar of vital statistics of the district in which the person was found.

(d)   Repealed by Session Laws 2007-323, s. 30.10(g), effective August 1, 2007, and applicable to all costs assessed or collected on or after that date. (1959, c. 492; 1969, c. 1031, s. 1; 1973, c. 476, s. 128; 1983, c. 891, s. 2; 2007-323, s. 30.10(g).)

§ 130A-108. Certificate of identification for individual of foreign birth.

(a)   In the case of an adopted individual born in a foreign country and residing in this State at the time of application, the State Registrar shall, upon the presentation of a certified copy of the original birth certificate from the country of birth and a certified copy of the final order of adoption signed by the clerk of court or other appropriate official, prepare a certificate of identification for the individual. The certificate shall contain the same information required by G.S. 48-9-107(a) for individuals adopted in this State, except that the country of birth shall be specified in lieu of the state of birth.

(b)   In the case of an adopted individual born in a foreign country and readopted in this State, the State Registrar shall, upon receipt of a report of that adoption from the Division of Social Services pursuant to G.S. 48-9-102(f), prepare a certificate of identification for that individual. The certificate shall contain the same information required by G.S. 48-9-107(a) for individuals adopted in this State, except the country of birth shall be specified in lieu of the state of birth. (1949, c. 160, s. 2; 1955, c. 951, s. 16; 1957, c. 1357, s. 1; 1969, c. 1031, s. 1; 1983, c. 891, s. 2; 1995, c. 457, s. 8; 1997-215, s. 13; 2001-208, s. 13; 2001-487, s. 101.)

§ 130A-109. Birth certificate as evidence.

Certified copies of birth certificates shall be accepted by public school authorities in this State as prima facie evidence of the age of children registering for school attendance, and no other proof shall be required. In addition, certified copies of birth certificates shall be required by all factory inspectors and employers of youthful labor, as prima facie proof of age, and no other proof shall be required. However, when it is not possible to secure a certified copy of a birth certificate, factory inspectors and employers may accept as secondary proof of age any competent evidence by which the age of persons is usually established. School authorities may accept only competent and verifiable evidence as secondary proof of age, specifically including but not limited to: (i) a certified copy of any medical record of the child's birth issued by the treating physician or the hospital in which the child was born, or (ii) a certified copy of a birth certificate issued by a church, mosque, temple, or other religious institution that maintains birth records of its members. (1913, c. 109, s. 17; C.S., s. 7107; 1957, c. 1357, s. 1; 1969, c. 1031, s. 1; 1983, c. 891, s. 2; 2011-388, s. 3.)

§ 130A-110. Registration of marriage certificates.

(a)   On or before the fifteenth day of the month, the register of deeds shall transmit to the State Registrar a record of each marriage ceremony performed during the preceding calendar month for which a license was issued by the register of deeds. The State Registrar shall prescribe a form containing the information required by G.S. 51-16 and additional information to conform with the requirements of the federal agency responsible for national vital statistics. The form shall be the official form of a marriage license, certificate of marriage and application for marriage license.

(b)   Each form signed and issued by the register of deeds, assistant register of deeds or deputy register of deeds shall constitute an original or a duplicate original. Upon request, the State Registrar shall furnish a true copy of the marriage registration. The copy shall have the same evidentiary value as the original.

(c)   The register of deeds shall provide copies or abstracts of marriage certificates to any person upon request. Certified copies of these certificates shall be provided only to those persons described in G.S. 130A-93(c).

(d)   Marriage certificates maintained by the local register of deeds shall be open to inspection and examination. (1961, c. 862; 1969, c. 1031, s. 1; 1973, c. 476, s. 128; 1977, c. 1110, s. 3; 1983, c. 891, s. 2; 1985, c. 325, s. 2; 2001-62, s. 15; 2001-487, s. 83.)

§ 130A-111. Registration of divorces and annulments.

For each divorce and annulment of marriage granted by a court of competent jurisdiction in this State, a report shall be prepared and filed by the clerk of court with the State Registrar. On or before the fifteenth day of each month, the clerk shall forward to the State Registrar the report of each divorce and annulment granted during the preceding calendar month. (1957, c. 983; 1969, c. 1031, s. 1; 1973, c. 476, s. 128; 1977, c. 1110, s. 2; 1983, c. 891, s. 2; 1985, c. 325, s. 3.)

§ 130A-112. Notification of death.

A funeral director or person acting as such who first assumes custody of a dead body or fetus of 20 completed weeks gestation or more shall submit a notification of death to the local registrar in the county where death occurred, within 24 hours of taking custody of the body or fetus. The notification of death shall identify the attending physician responsible for medical certification, except that for deaths under the jurisdiction of the medical examiner, the notification shall identify the medical examiner and certify that the medical examiner has released the body to a funeral director or person acting as such for final disposition. (1913, c. 109, s. 5; 1915, c. 164, s. 1; C.S., s. 7092; 1955, c. 951, s. 9; 1957, c. 1357, s. 1; 1969, c. 1031, s. 1; 1973, c. 873, s. 1; 1983, c. 891, s. 2.)

§ 130A-113. Permits for burial-transit, authorization for cremation and disinterment-reinterment.

(a)   The funeral director or person acting as such who first assumes custody of a dead body or fetus which is under the jurisdiction of the medical examiner shall obtain a burial-transit permit signed by the medical examiner prior to final disposition or removal from the State and within five days after death.

(b)   A dead body shall not be cremated or buried at sea unless the provisions of G.S. 130A-388 are met.

(c)   A permit for disinterment-reinterment shall be required prior to disinterment of a dead body or fetus except as otherwise authorized by law or rule. The permit shall be issued by the local registrar to a funeral director, embalmer or other person acting as such upon proper application.

(d)   No dead body or fetus shall be brought into this State unless accompanied by a burial-transit or disposal permit issued under the law of the state in which death or disinterment occurred. The permit shall be final authority for final disposition of the body or fetus in this State.

(e)   The local registrar shall issue a burial-transit permit for the removal of a dead body or fetus from this State if the requirements of G.S. 130A-112 are met and that the death is not under the jurisdiction of the medical examiner. (1973, c. 873, s. 2; 1977, c. 163, s. 2; 1983, c. 891, s. 2.)

§ 130A-114. Fetal death registration; certificate of birth resulting in stillbirth.

(a)   Each spontaneous fetal death occurring in the State of 20 completed weeks gestation or more, as calculated from the first day of the last normal menstrual period until the day of delivery, shall be reported within 10 days after delivery to the local registrar of the county in which the delivery occurred. The report shall be made on a form prescribed and furnished by the State Registrar.

(b)   When fetal death occurs in a hospital or other medical facility, the person in charge of the facility shall obtain the cause of fetal death and other required medical information over the signature of the attending physician, and shall prepare and file the report with the local registrar.

202

(c)   When a fetal death occurs outside of a hospital or other medical facility, the physician in attendance at or immediately after the delivery shall prepare and file the report. When a fetal death is attended by a person authorized to attend childbirth, the supervising physician shall prepare and file the report. Fetal deaths attended by lay midwives and all other persons shall be treated as deaths without medical attendance as provided for in G.S. 130A-115 and the medical examiner shall prepare and file the report.

(d)   For any spontaneous fetal death occurring in this State, either parent of the stillborn child may file an application with the State Registrar requesting a certificate of birth resulting in stillbirth. The certificate of birth resulting in stillbirth (i) shall be based upon the information available from the fetal death report filed pursuant to this section, (ii) shall not include any reference to the name of the stillborn child if the fetal death report does not include the name of the stillborn child and the parent filing the application does not elect to provide a name, and (iii) shall clearly indicate that it is not proof of a live birth. If the spontaneous fetal death occurred in this State prior to July 1, 2001, the State Registrar may not issue a certificate of birth resulting in stillbirth unless the application for the certificate is accompanied by a certified copy of the fetal death report. Issuance of a certificate of birth resulting in stillbirth does not replace the requirement to file a report of fetal death under this section. (1913, c. 109, s. 6; C.S., s. 7093; 1933, c. 9, s. 2; 1951, c. 1091, s. 1; 1955, c. 951, s. 10; 1957, c. 1357, s. 1; 1969, c. 1031, s. 1; 1973, c. 873, s. 3; 1979, c. 95, s. 1; 1983, c. 891, s. 2; 1989, c. 199, s. 3; 2011-357, s. 1.)

§ 130A-115. Death registration.

(a)   A death certificate for each death which occurs in this State shall be filed with the local registrar of the county in which the death occurred within five days after the death. If the place of death is unknown, a death certificate shall be filed within five days in the county where the dead body is found. If the death occurs in a moving conveyance, a death certificate shall be filed in the county in which the dead body was first removed from the conveyance.

(b)   The funeral director or person acting as such who first assumes custody of a dead body shall file the death certificate with the local registrar. The personal data shall be obtained from the next of kin or the best qualified person or source available. The funeral director or person acting as such is responsible for obtaining the medical certification of the cause of death, stating facts relative

203

to the date and place of burial, and filing the death certificate with the local registrar within five days of the death.

(c)   The medical certification shall be completed and signed by the physician in charge of the patient's care for the illness or condition which resulted in death, except when the death falls within the circumstances described in G.S. 130A-383. In the absence of the physician or with the physician's approval, the certificate may be completed and signed by an associate physician, a physician assistant in a manner consistent with G.S. 90-18.1(e1), a nurse practitioner in a manner consistent with G.S. 90-18.2(e1), the chief medical officer of the hospital or facility in which the death occurred or a physician who performed an autopsy upon the decedent under the following circumstances: the individual has access to the medical history of the deceased; the individual has viewed the deceased at or after death; and the death is due to natural causes. When specifically approved by the State Registrar, an electronic signature or facsimile signature of the physician, physician assistant, or nurse practitioner shall be acceptable. As used in this section, the term electronic signature has the same meaning as applies in G.S. 66-58.2. The physician, physician assistant, or nurse practitioner shall state the cause of death on the certificate in definite and precise terms. A certificate containing any indefinite terms or denoting only symptoms of disease or conditions resulting from disease as defined by the State Registrar, shall be returned to the person making the medical certification for correction and more definite statement.

(d)   The physician, physician assistant, nurse practitioner, or medical examiner making the medical certification as to the cause of death shall complete the medical certification no more than three days after death. The physician, physician assistant, nurse practitioner, or medical examiner may, in appropriate cases, designate the cause of death as unknown pending an autopsy or upon some other reasonable cause for delay, but shall send the supplementary information to the local registrar as soon as it is obtained.

(e)   In the case of death or fetal death without medical attendance, it shall be the duty of the funeral director or person acting as such and any other person having knowledge of the death to notify the local medical examiner of the death. The body shall not be disposed of or removed without the permission of the medical examiner. If there is no county medical examiner, the Chief Medical Examiner shall be notified. (1913, c. 109, ss. 7, 9; C.S., ss. 7094, 7096; 1949, c. 161, s. 1; 1955, c. 951, ss. 11, 12; 1957, c. 1357, s. 1; 1963, c. 492, ss. 1, 2, 4; 1969, c. 1031, s. 1; 1973, c. 476, s. 128; c. 873, s. 5; 1979, c. 95, ss. 2, 3; 1981, c. 187, s. 1; 1983, c. 891, s. 2; 1999-247, s. 1; 2011-197, s. 3.)

§ 130A-116. Contents of death certificate.

The certificate of death shall contain those items prescribed and specified on the standard certificate of death as prepared by the federal agency responsible for national vital statistics. The State Registrar may require additional information. (1913, c. 109, s. 7; C.S., s. 7094; 1949, c. 161, s. 1; 1955, c. 951, s. 11; 1957, c. 1357, s. 1; 1963, c. 492, ss. 1, 4; 1969, c. 1031, s. 1; 1983, c. 891, s. 2.)

§ 130A-117. Persons required to keep records and provide information.

(a)   All persons in charge of hospitals or other institutions, public or private, to which persons resort for confinement or treatment of diseases or to which persons are committed by process of law, shall make a record of personal data concerning each person admitted or confined to the institution. The record shall include information required for the certificates of birth and death and the reports of spontaneous fetal death required by this Article. The record shall be made at the time of admission from information provided by the person being admitted or confined. When this information cannot be obtained from this person, it shall be obtained from relatives or other knowledgeable persons.

(b)   When a dead body or dead fetus of 20 weeks gestation or more is released or disposed of by an institution, the person in charge of the institution shall keep a record showing the name of the decedent, date of death, name and address of the person to whom the body or fetus is released and the date of removal from the institution. If final disposition is made by the institution, the date, place, and manner of disposition shall also be recorded.

(c)   A funeral director, embalmer, or other person who removes from the place of death, transports or makes final disposition of a dead body or fetus, shall keep a record which shall identify the body, and information pertaining to the receipt, removal, delivery, burial, or cremation of the body, as may be required by the State Registrar. In addition, that person shall file a certificate or other report required by this Article or the rules of the Commission.

(d)   Records maintained under this section shall be retained for a period of not less than three years and shall be made available for inspection by the State Registrar upon request. (1913, c. 109, s. 16; C.S., s. 7104; 1957, c. 1357, s. 1; 1969, c. 1031, s. 1; 1979, c. 95, s. 8; 1983, c. 891, s. 2.)

205

§ 130A-118. Amendment of birth and death certificates.

(a)   After acceptance for registration by the State Registrar, no record made in accordance with this Article shall be altered or changed, except by a request for amendment. The State Registrar may adopt rules governing the form of these requests and the type and amount of proof required.

(b)   A new certificate of birth shall be made by the State Registrar when:

(1)   Proof is submitted to the State Registrar that the previously unwed parents of a person have intermarried subsequent to the birth of the person;

(2)   Notification is received by the State Registrar from the clerk of a court of competent jurisdiction of a judgment, order or decree disclosing different or additional information relating to the parentage of a person;

(3)   Satisfactory proof is submitted to the State Registrar that there has been entered in a court of competent jurisdiction a judgment, order or decree disclosing different or additional information relating to the parentage of a person; or

(4)   A written request from an individual is received by the State Registrar to change the sex on that individual's birth record because of sex reassignment surgery, if the request is accompanied by a notarized statement from the physician who performed the sex reassignment surgery or from a physician licensed to practice medicine who has examined the individual and can certify that the person has undergone sex reassignment surgery.

(c)   A new birth certificate issued under subsection (b) may reflect a change in surname when:

(1)   A child is legitimated by subsequent marriage and the parents agree and request that the child's surname be changed; or

(2)   A child is legitimated under G.S. 49-10 and the parents agree and request that the child's surname be changed, or the court orders a change in surname after determination that the change is in the best interests of the child.

(d)   For the amendment of a certificate of birth or death after its acceptance for filing, or for the making of a new certificate of birth under this Article, the

206

State Registrar shall be entitled to a fee not to exceed fifteen dollars ($15.00) to be paid by the applicant.

(e)   When a new certificate of birth is made, the State Registrar shall substitute the new certificate for the certificate of birth then on file, and shall forward a copy of the new certificate to the register of deeds of the county of birth. The copy of the certificate of birth on file with the register of deeds, if any, shall be forwarded to the State Registrar within five days. The State Registrar shall place under seal the original certificate of birth, the copy forwarded by the register of deeds and all papers relating to the original certificate of birth. The seal shall not be broken except by an order of a court of competent jurisdiction. Thereafter, when a certified copy of the certificate of birth of the person is issued, it shall be a copy of the new certificate of birth, except when an order of a court of competent jurisdiction shall require the issuance of a copy of the original certificate of birth. (1957, c. 1357, s. 1; 1969, c. 1031, s. 1; 1975, c. 556; 1977, c. 1110, s. 4; 1983, c. 891, s. 2; 2002-126, s. 29A.18(b).)

§ 130A-119. Clerk of Court to furnish State Registrar with facts as to paternity of children born out of wedlock when judicially determined.

Upon the entry of a judgment determining the paternity of a child born out of wedlock, the clerk of court of the county in which the judgment is entered shall notify the State Registrar in writing of the name of the person against whom the judgment has been entered, together with the other facts disclosed by the record as may assist in identifying the record of the birth of the child as it appears in the office of the State Registrar. If the judgment is modified or vacated, that fact shall be reported by the clerk to the State Registrar in the same manner. Upon receipt of the notification, the State Registrar shall record the information upon the birth certificate of the child. (1941, c. 297, s. 1; 1955, c. 951, s. 19; 1957, c. 1357, s. 1; 1969, c. 1031, s. 1; 1971, c. 444, s. 5; 1983, c. 891, s. 2; 2013-198, s. 26.)

§ 130A-120. Certification of birth dates furnished to veterans' organizations.

Upon application by any veterans' organization in this State in connection with junior or youth baseball, the State Registrar shall furnish certification of dates of birth without the payment of the fees prescribed in this Article. (1931, c. 318;

1939, c. 353; 1945, c. 996; 1955, c. 951, s. 24; 1957, c. 1357, s. 1; 1969, c. 1031, s. 1; 1973, c. 476, s. 128; 1983, c. 891, s. 2.)

§ 130A-121. List of deceased residents for county jury commission and Commissioner of Motor Vehicles.

(a)   Repealed by Session Laws 2012-180, s. 12, effective July 12, 2012.

(b)   The State Registrar shall provide to the Commissioner of Motor Vehicles an alphabetical list of all residents of the State who have died in the two years prior to July 1 of each odd-numbered year, unless an annual jury list is being prepared under G.S. 9-2(a), in which case the list shall be of all residents of the State who have died in the year prior to July 1 of each year. The list shall include the name and address of each deceased resident and may be in either printed or computerized form, as requested by the Commissioner of Motor Vehicles. (2007-512, s. 2; 2012-180, s. 12.)

§ 130A-122. Reserved for future codification purposes.

§ 130A-123. Reserved for future codification purposes.

Article 5.

Maternal and Child Health and Women's Health.

Part 1. In General.

§ 130A-124. Department to establish maternal and child health program.

(a)   The Department shall establish and administer a maternal and child health program for the delivery of preventive, diagnostic, therapeutic and habilitative health services to women of childbearing years, children and other persons who require these services. The program may include, but shall not be limited to, providing professional education and consultation, community coordination and direct care and counseling.

(b)   The Commission shall adopt rules necessary to implement the program.

208

(c)   Prior year refunds received by the Children's Special Health Services Program that are not encumbered or spent during a fiscal year shall not revert to the General Fund but shall remain in the Department for purchase of care and contracts in the Program. Funds appropriated for the purchase of care and contracts in the Program that are encumbered and not spent during a fiscal year shall not revert to the General Fund but shall remain in the Department for the purchase of care and contracts in the Program. (1983, c. 891, s. 2; 1993, c. 321, s. 275(a); 1997-172, s. 1; 1997-456, s. 54.)

§ 130A-125. Screening of newborns for metabolic and other hereditary and congenital disorders.

(a)   The Department shall establish and administer a Newborn Screening Program. The program shall include, but shall not be limited to:

(1)   Development and distribution of educational materials regarding the availability and benefits of newborn screening.

(2)   Provision of laboratory testing.

(3)   Development of follow-up protocols to assure early treatment for identified children, and the provision of genetic counseling and support services for the families of identified children.

(4)   Provision of necessary dietary treatment products or medications for identified children as medically indicated and when not otherwise available.

(5)   For each newborn, provision of physiological screening in each ear for the presence of permanent hearing loss.

(6)   For each newborn, provision of pulse oximetry screening to detect congenital heart defects.

(b)   The Commission shall adopt rules necessary to implement the Newborn Screening Program. The rules shall include, but shall not be limited to, the conditions for which screening shall be required, provided that screening shall not be required when the parents or the guardian of the infant object to such screening. If the parents or guardian object to the screening, the objection shall be presented in writing to the physician or other person responsible for administering the test, who shall place the written objection in the infant's medical record.

(b1)   The Commission shall adopt temporary and permanent rules to include newborn hearing screening and pulse oximetry screening in the Newborn Screening Program established under this section.

(b2)   The Commission's rules for pulse oximetry screening shall address at least all of the following:

(1)   Follow-up protocols to ensure early treatment for newborn infants diagnosed with a congenital heart defect, including by means of telemedicine. As used in this subsection, "telemedicine" is the use of audio and video between places of lesser and greater medical capability or expertise to provide and support health care when distance separates participants who are in different geographical locations.

(2)   A system for tracking both the process and outcomes of newborn screening utilizing pulse oximetry, with linkage to the Birth Defects Monitoring Program established pursuant to G.S. 130A-131.16.

(c)   A fee of nineteen dollars ($19.00) applies to a laboratory test performed by the State Laboratory of Public Health pursuant to this section. The fee for a laboratory test is a departmental receipt of the Department and shall be used to offset the cost of the Newborn Screening Program. (1991, c. 661, s. 1; 1991 (Reg. Sess., 1992), c. 1039, s. 6; 1998-131, s. 13; 2000-67, s. 11.31(a); 2005-276, s. 41.1(a); 2007-182, s. 2; 2008-107, s. 29.4(a); 2013-45, s. 1.)

§ 130A-126. Rule-making authority for birth - three-year-old early intervention program.

The rule-making authority for the birth - three-year-old early intervention program through Part C of the Individuals with Disabilities Act (IDEA) is transferred from the Commission for Mental Health, Developmental Disabilities, and Substance Abuse Services to the Commission for Public Health. (2005-276, s. 10.54A; 2007-182, s. 2.)

Part 2. Perinatal Health Care.

§ 130A-127. Department to establish program.

(a)   The Department shall establish and administer a perinatal health care program. The program may include, but shall not be limited to:

(1)   Prenatal health care services including health education and identification of high-risk pregnancies;

(2)   Prenatal, delivery and newborn health care services provided at hospitals participating at graduated levels of complexity; and

(3)   Regionalized perinatal health care services including a plan for effective communication, consultation, referral and transportation links among hospitals, health departments, physicians, schools and other relevant community resources for mothers and infants at high risk for mortality and morbidity.

(b)   The Commission shall adopt rules necessary to implement the program. (1973, c. 1240, s. 1; 1983, c. 891, s. 2.)

§ 130A-128: Repealed by Session Laws 1991, c. 518, s. 1.

§ 130A-128A: Recodified as G. S. 130A-128.1 by Session Laws 2009-570, s. 43.1, effective August 28, 2009.

§ 130A-128.1. Department to provide free educational information about umbilical cord stem cells and umbilical cord blood banking.

(a)   As used in this section:

(1)   Health care professional. - A person who is licensed pursuant to Chapter 90 of the General Statutes to practice as a physician, physician assistant, or registered nurse or who is approved pursuant to Chapter 90 of the General Statutes to practice midwifery.

211

(2)   Umbilical cord blood. - The blood that remains in the umbilical cord and placenta after the birth of a newborn child.

(b)   Effective January 1, 2010, the Department of Health and Human Services shall make available free of charge to the general public on its Internet Web site printable publications, in a format that can be downloaded, containing medically accurate information regarding umbilical cord stem cells and umbilical cord blood banking that is sufficient to allow a pregnant woman to make an informed decision about whether to participate in a public or private umbilical cord blood banking program. The publications shall include at least all of the following information:

(1)   An explanation of the medical processes involved in the collection of umbilical cord blood.

(2)   An explanation of any risks associated with umbilical cord blood collection to the mother and the newborn child.

(3)   The options available to a mother regarding stem cells contained in the umbilical cord blood after delivery of the mother's newborn child, including:

a.   Having the stem cells discarded.

b.   Donating the stem cells to a public umbilical cord blood bank.

c.   Storing the stem cells in a private umbilical cord blood bank for use by immediate and extended family members.

d.   Storing the stem cells for use by the family through a family or sibling donor banking program that provides free collection, processing, and storage of the stem cells where there is a medical need.

(4)   The current and potential future medical uses, risks, and benefits of umbilical cord blood collection to (i) the mother, newborn child, and biological family and (ii) individuals who are not biologically related to the mother or newborn child.

(5)   An explanation of the differences between public and private umbilical cord blood banking.

212

(6)   Options for ownership and future use of the donated umbilical cord blood.

(c)   The Department may satisfy the requirements of subsection (b) of this section by including on its Internet Web site a link to a federally sponsored Internet Web site that North Carolina citizens may access so long as the federally sponsored Internet Web site contains all of the information specified in subdivisions (1) through (6) of subsection (b) of this section.

(d)   The Department shall encourage health care professionals who provide health care services that are directly related to a woman's pregnancy to provide each woman with the publications described in subsection (b) of this section prior to the woman's third trimester of pregnancy.

(e)   A health care professional or health care institution shall not be liable for damages in a civil action, subject to prosecution in a criminal proceeding, or subject to disciplinary action by the North Carolina Medical Board or the North Carolina Board of Nursing for acting in good faith with respect to informing a pregnant woman prior to her third trimester of pregnancy about the publications described in subsection (b) of this section. (2009-67, s. 1; 2009-570, s. 43.1.)

Part 3. Sickle Cell.

§ 130A-129. Department to establish program.

The Department shall establish and administer a Sickle Cell Program. The Commission shall, after consultation with the Council on Sickle Cell Syndrome, adopt rules for the program that shall include, but not be limited to, programs for education, voluntary testing, counseling, and medical reimbursement services for sickle cell syndrome. "Sickle cell syndrome" includes sickle cell disease, sickle cell trait, sickle cell thalassemia and variants. (1987, c. 822, s. 2.)

§ 130A-130. Duties of local health departments.

Local health departments shall provide sickle cell syndrome testing and counseling at no cost to persons requesting these services. If an individual is found to have any aspect of sickle cell syndrome, the local health department

213

shall inform the individual to that effect. The State Laboratory of Public Health shall, upon request, provide a person's sickle cell screening test results to any local health department or Sickle Cell Program contracting agency which has been requested to provide sickle cell services to that person. (1987, c. 822, s. 2.)

Part 3A. Council on Sickle Cell Syndrome.

§ 130A-131. Council on Sickle Cell Syndrome; appointment; expenses; terms.

A Council on Sickle Cell Syndrome is created. The Council shall consist of a chairperson and 14 other members appointed by the Governor. Members shall serve without compensation except for reimbursement for travel and expenses in pursuit of Council business. Except as provided in this subsection, Council members shall serve a term of three years. To achieve a staggered term structure, five members shall be appointed for a term of one year, five members for a term of two years, and five members for a term of three years. (1973, c. 570, s. 1; 1987, c. 822, s. 3; 1989, c. 727, s. 179.)

§ 130A-131.1. Council membership.

In making appointments, consideration shall be given to persons representing the following areas:

(1)   Members of community agencies interested in sickle cell syndrome;

(2)   State and local officials concerned with public health, social services and rehabilitation;

(3)   Teachers and members of State and local school boards;

(4)   Physicians in medical centers and physicians in community practice who are interested in sickle cell syndrome;

(5)   Persons or relatives of persons with sickle cell disease. (1973, c. 570, s. 2; 1987, c. 822, s. 3; 1989, c. 727, s. 179.)

214

§ 130A-131.2. Council role.

The Council shall advise the Department and the Commission for Public Health on the needs of persons with sickle cell syndrome, and shall make recommendations to meet these needs. Such recommendations shall include but not be limited to recommendations for legislative action and for rules regarding the services of the Sickle Cell Program. The Council shall develop procedures to facilitate its operation. All clerical and other services required by the Council shall be furnished by the Department without budget limitations. (1973, c. 570, s. 3; 1987, c. 822, s. 3; 1989, c. 727, ss. 179, 180; 1997-443, s. 11A.76; 2007-182, s. 2.)

§ 130A-131.3. Reserved for future codification purposes.

§ 130A-131.4. Reserved for future codification purposes.

Part 4. Lead Poisoning in Children.

§ 130A-131.5. Commission to adopt rules.

(a)   For the protection of the public health, the Commission shall adopt rules for the prevention and control of lead poisoning in children in accordance with this Part.

(b)   Repealed by Session Laws 1998-209, s. 1. (1989, c. 333; c. 751, s. 15; 1991, c. 300, s. 1; 1997-506, s. 45; 1998-209, s. 1.)

§ 130A-131.6. Reserved for future codification purposes.

§ 130A-131.7. Definitions.

The following definitions apply in this Part:

(1)   "Abatement" means undertaking any of the following measures to eliminate a lead-based paint hazard:

a.   Removing lead-based paint from a surface and repainting the surface.

b.   Removing a component, such as a windowsill, painted with lead-based paint and replacing the component.

c.   Enclosing a surface painted with lead-based paint with paneling, vinyl siding, or another approved material.

d.   Encapsulating a surface painted with lead-based paint with a sealant.

e.   Any other measure approved by the Commission.

(2)   "Child-occupied facility" means a building, or portion of a building, constructed before 1978, regularly visited by a child who is less than six years of age. Child-occupied facilities may include, but are not limited to, child care facilities, preschools, nurseries, kindergarten classrooms, schools, clinics, or treatment centers including the common areas, the grounds, any outbuildings, or other structures appurtenant to the facility.

(3)   "Confirmed lead poisoning" means a blood lead concentration of 20 micrograms per deciliter or greater determined by the lower of two consecutive blood tests within a six-month period.

(4)   "Department" means the Department of Environment and Natural Resources or its authorized agent.

(5)   "Elevated blood lead level" means a blood lead concentration of 10 micrograms per deciliter or greater determined by the lower of two consecutive blood tests within a six-month period.

(6)   "Lead-based paint hazard" means a condition that is likely to result in exposure to lead-based paint or to soil or dust that contains lead at a concentration that constitutes a lead poisoning hazard.

(7)   "Lead poisoning hazard" means any of the following:

a.   Any lead-based paint or other substance that contains lead in an amount equal to or greater than 1.0 milligrams lead per square centimeter as determined by X-ray fluorescence or five-tenths of a percent (0.5%) lead by weight as determined by chemical analysis: (i) on any readily accessible substance or chewable surface on which there is evidence of teeth marks or

216

mouthing; or (ii) on any other deteriorated or otherwise damaged interior or exterior surface.

b.   Any substance that contains lead intended for use by children less than six years of age in an amount equal to or greater than 0.06 percent (0.06%) lead by weight as determined by chemical analysis.

c.   Any concentration of lead dust that is equal to or greater than 40 micrograms per square foot on floors or 250 micrograms per square foot on interior windowsills, vinyl miniblinds, bathtubs, kitchen sinks, or lavatories.

d.   Any lead-based paint or other substance that contains lead on a friction or impact surface that is subject to abrasion, rubbing, binding, or damage by repeated contact and where the lead dust concentrations on the nearest horizontal surface underneath the friction or impact surface are equal to or greater than 40 micrograms per square foot on floors or 250 micrograms per square foot on interior windowsills.

e.   Any concentration of lead in bare soil in play areas, gardens, pet sleeping areas, and areas within three feet of a residential housing unit or child-occupied facility equal to or greater than 400 parts per million. Any concentration of lead in bare soil in other locations of the yard equal to or greater than 1,200 parts per million.

f.   Any ceramic ware generating equal to or greater than three micrograms of lead per milliliter of leaching solution for flatware or 0.5 micrograms of lead per milliliter for cups, mugs, and pitchers as determined by Method 973.32 of the Association of Official Analytical Chemists.

g.   Any concentration of lead in drinking water equal to or greater than 15 parts per billion.

(8)   "Lead-safe housing" is housing that was built since 1978 or has been tested by a person that has been certified to perform risk assessments and found to have no lead-based paint hazard within the meaning of the Residential Lead-Based Paint Reduction Act of 1992, 42 U.S.C. § 4851b(15).

(9)   "Maintenance standard" means the following:

a.   Using safe work practices, repairing and repainting areas of deteriorated paint inside a residential housing unit and for single-family and duplex

217

residential dwelling built before 1950, repairing and repainting areas of deteriorated paint on interior and exterior surfaces;

b.   Cleaning the interior of the unit to remove dust that constitutes a lead poisoning hazard;

c.   Adjusting doors and windows to minimize friction or impact on surfaces;

d.   Subject to the occupant's approval, appropriately cleaning any carpets;

e.   Taking such steps as are necessary to ensure that all interior surfaces on which dust might collect are readily cleanable; and

f.   Providing the occupant or occupants all information required to be provided under the Residential Lead-Based Paint Hazard Reduction Act of 1992, and amendments thereto.

(10)   "Managing agent" means any person who has charge, care, or control of a building or part thereof in which dwelling units or rooming units are leased.

(11), (12)   Repealed by Session Laws 2003-150, s. 1, effective July 1, 2003.

(13)   "Readily accessible substance" means any substance that can be ingested or inhaled by a child less than six years of age. Readily accessible substances include deteriorated paint that is peeling, chipping, cracking, flaking, or blistering to the extent that the paint has separated from the substrate. Readily accessible substances also include soil, water, toys, vinyl miniblinds, bathtubs, lavatories, doors, door jambs, stairs, stair rails, windows, interior windowsills, baseboards, and paint that is chalking.

(14)   "Regularly visits" means the presence at a residential housing unit or child-occupied facility on at least two different days within any week, provided that each day's visit lasts at least three hours and the combined weekly visits last at least six hours, and the combined annual visits last at least 60 hours.

(15)   "Remediation" means the elimination or control of lead poisoning hazards by methods approved by the Department.

(16)   "Residential housing unit" means a dwelling, dwelling unit, or other structure, all or part of which is designed or used for human habitation, including

218

the common areas, the grounds, any outbuildings, or other structures appurtenant to the residential housing unit.

(17)   "Supplemental address" means a residential housing unit or child-occupied facility where a child with confirmed lead poisoning regularly visits or attends. Supplemental address also means a residential housing unit or child-occupied facility where a child resided, regularly visited, or attended within the six months immediately preceding the determination of confirmed lead poisoning. (1997-443, ss. 11A.123, 15.30(b); 1998-209, s. 2; 2003-150, s. 1.)

§ 130A-131.8. Laboratory reports.

(a)   All laboratories doing business in this State shall report to the Department all environmental lead test results and blood lead test results for children less than six years of age and for individuals whose ages are unknown at the time of testing. Reports shall be made by electronic submission within five working days after test completion.

(b)   Reports of blood lead test results shall contain all of the following:

(1)   The child's full name, date of birth, sex, race, ethnicity, address, and Medicaid number, if any.

(2)   The name, address, and telephone number of the requesting health care provider.

(3)   The name, address, and telephone number of the testing laboratory.

(4)   The laboratory results, whether the specimen type is venous or capillary; the laboratory sample number, and the dates the sample was collected and analyzed.

(c)   Reports of environmental lead test results shall contain all of the following:

(1)   The address where the samples were collected.

(2)   Sample type, such as dust, paint, soil, or water.

219

(3)   Surface type, such as floor, window sill, or window trough.

(4)   Collection location.

(5)   The name, address, and telephone number of the testing laboratory.

(6)   The laboratory results, unit of measurement, the laboratory sample number, and the dates the sample was collected and analyzed. (1997-443, s. 15.30(b); 2003-150, s. 2; 2009-484, s. 1.)

§ 130A-131.9. Examination and testing.

When the Department has a reasonable suspicion that a child less than six years of age has an elevated blood lead level or a confirmed lead poisoning, the Department may require that child to be examined and tested within 30 days. The Department shall require from the owner, managing agent, or tenant of the residential housing unit or child-occupied facility information on each child who resides in, regularly visits, or attends, or, who has within the past six months, resided in, regularly visited, or attended the unit or facility. The information required shall include each child's name and date of birth, the names and addresses of each child's parents, legal guardian, or full-time custodian. The owner, managing agent, or tenant shall submit the required information within 10 days of receipt of the request from the Department. (1997-443, s. 15.30(b); 2003-150, s. 3.)

§ 130A-131.9A. Investigation to identify lead poisoning hazards.

(a)   When the Department learns of confirmed lead poisoning, the Department shall conduct an investigation to identify the lead poisoning hazards to children. The Department shall investigate the residential housing unit where the child with confirmed lead poisoning resides. The Department shall also investigate the supplemental addresses of the child who has confirmed lead poisoning.

(a1)   When the Department learns of an elevated blood lead level, the Department shall, upon informed consent, investigate the residential housing unit where the child with the elevated blood level resides. When consent to

220

investigate is denied, the child with the elevated blood lead level cannot be located, or the child's parent or guardian fails to respond, the Department shall document the denial of consent, inability to locate, or failure to respond.

(b)   The Department shall also conduct an investigation when it reasonably suspects that a lead poisoning hazard to children exists in a residential housing unit or child-occupied facility occupied, regularly visited, or attended by a child less than six years of age.

(c)   In conducting an investigation, the Department may take samples of surface materials, or other materials suspected of containing lead, for analysis and testing. If samples are taken, chemical determination of the lead content of the samples shall be by atomic absorption spectroscopy or equivalent methods approved by the Department. (1997-443, s. 15.30(b); 2003-150, s. 4.)

§ 130A-131.9B. Notification.

Upon determination that a lead poisoning hazard exists, the Department shall give written notice of the lead poisoning hazard to the owner or managing agent of the residential housing unit or child-occupied facility and to all persons residing in, attending, or regularly visiting the unit or facility. The written notice to the owner or managing agent shall include a list of possible methods of remediation. (1997-443, s. 15.30(b); 2003-150, s. 5.)

§ 130A-131.9C. Abatement and Remediation.

(a)   Upon determination that a child less than six years of age has a confirmed lead poisoning of 20 micrograms per deciliter or greater and that child resides in a residential housing unit containing lead poisoning hazards, the Department shall require remediation of the lead poisoning hazards. The Department shall also require remediation of the lead poisoning hazards identified at the supplemental addresses of a child less than six years of age with a confirmed lead poisoning of 20 micrograms per deciliter or greater.

(b)   When remediation of lead poisoning hazards is required under subsection (a) of this section, the owner or managing agent shall submit a written remediation plan to the Department within 14 days of receipt of the lead

221

poisoning hazard notification and shall obtain written approval of the plan before initiating remediation activities. The remediation plan shall comply with subsections (g), (h), and (i) of this section.

(c)   If the remediation plan submitted fails to meet the requirements of this section, the Department shall issue an order requiring submission of a modified plan. The order shall indicate the modifications that shall be made to the remediation plan and the date that the plan as modified shall be submitted to the Department.

(d)   If the owner or managing agent does not submit a remediation plan within 14 days, the Department shall issue an order requiring submission of a remediation plan within five days of receipt of the order.

(e)   The owner or managing agent shall notify the Department and the occupants of the dates of remediation activities at least three days before commencement of the activities.

(f)   Remediation of the lead poisoning hazards shall be completed within 60 days of the Department's approval of the remediation plan. If the remediation activities are not completed within 60 days, the Department shall issue an order requiring completion of the activities. An owner or managing agent may apply to the Department for an extension of the deadline. The Department may issue an order extending the deadline for 30 days upon proper written application by the owner or managing agent.

(g)   All of the following methods of remediation of lead-based paint hazards are prohibited:

(1)   Stripping paint on-site with methylene chloride-based solutions.

(2)   Torch or flame burning.

(3)   Heating paint with a heat gun above 1,100 degrees Fahrenheit.

(4)   Covering with new paint or wallpaper unless all readily accessible lead-based paint has been removed.

(5)   Uncontrolled abrasive blasting, machine sanding, or grinding, except when used with High Efficiency Particulate Air (HEPA) exhaust control that

removes particles of 0.3 microns or larger from the air at ninety-nine and seven-tenths percent (99.7%) or greater efficiency.

(6)   Uncontrolled waterblasting.

(7)   Dry scraping, unless used in conjunction with heat guns, or around electrical outlets, or when treating no more than two square feet on interior surfaces, or no more than 20 square feet on exterior surfaces.

(h)   All lead-containing waste and residue shall be removed and disposed of in accordance with applicable federal, State, and local laws and rules. Other substances containing lead that are intended for use by children less than six years of age and vinyl miniblinds that constitute a lead poisoning hazard shall be removed and disposed of in accordance with applicable federal, State, and local laws and rules.

(i)   All remediation plans shall require that the lead poisoning hazards be reduced to the following levels:

(1)   Fewer than 40 micrograms per square foot for lead dust on floors.

(2)   Fewer than 250 micrograms per square foot for lead dust on interior windowsills, bathtubs, kitchen sinks, and lavatories.

(3)   Fewer than 400 micrograms per square foot for lead dust on window troughs.

(4)   Fewer than 400 parts per million for lead in bare soil in play areas, gardens, pet sleeping areas, and areas within three feet of the residential housing unit or child-occupied facility. Lead in bare soil in other locations of the yard shall be reduced to less than 1,200 parts per million.

(5)   Fewer than 15 parts per billion for lead in drinking water.

(j)   The Department shall verify by visual inspection that the approved remediation plan has been completed. The Department may also verify plan completion by residual lead dust monitoring and soil or drinking water lead level measurement.

(j1)   Compliance with the maintenance standard satisfies the remediation requirements for confirmed lead poisoning cases identified on or after 1 October

223

1990 as long as all lead poisoning hazards identified on interior and exterior surfaces are addressed by remediation. Except for owner-occupied residential housing units, continued compliance shall be verified by means of an annual monitoring inspection conducted by the Department. For owner-occupied residential housing units, continued compliance shall be verified (i) by means of an annual monitoring inspection, (ii) by documentation that no child less than six years of age has resided in or regularly visited the residential housing unit within the past year, or (iii) by documentation that no child less than six years of age residing in or regularly visiting the unit has an elevated blood lead level.

(k)   Removal of children from the residential housing unit or child-occupied facility shall not constitute remediation if the property continues to be used for a residential housing unit or child-occupied facility. The remediation requirements imposed in subsection (a) of this section apply so long as the property continues to be used as a residential housing unit or child-occupied facility. (1997-443, s. 15.30(b); 1998-209, s. 3; 2003-150, s. 6.)

§ 130A-131.9D. Effect of compliance with maintenance standard.

Any owner of a residential housing unit constructed prior to 1978 who is sued by a current or former occupant seeking damages for injuries allegedly arising from exposure to lead-based paint or lead-contaminated dust, shall not be deemed liable (i) for any injuries sustained by that occupant after the owner first complied with the maintenance standard defined under G.S. 130A-131.7 provided the owner has repeated the steps provided for in the maintenance standard annually for units in which children of less than six years of age have resided or regularly visited within the past year and obtained a certificate of compliance under G.S. 130A-131.9E annually during such occupancy; or (ii) if the owner is able to show by other documentation that compliance with the maintenance standard has been maintained during the period when the injuries were sustained; or (iii) if the owner is able to show that the unit was lead-safe housing containing no lead-based paint hazards during the period when the injuries were sustained. (1997-443, s. 15.30(b); 1998-209, s. 4.)

§ 130A-131.9E. Certificate of evidence of compliance.

An owner of a unit who has complied with the maintenance standard may apply annually to the Department for a certificate of compliance. Upon presentation of acceptable proof of compliance, the Department shall provide to the owner a certificate evidencing compliance. The Department may issue a certificate based solely on information provided by the owner and may revoke the certificate upon showing that any of the information is erroneous or inadequate, or upon finding that the unit is no longer in compliance with the maintenance standard. (1997-443, s. 15.30(b).)

§ 130A-131.9F. Discrimination in financing.

(a)   No bank or financial institution in the business of lending money for the purchase, sale, construction, rehabilitation, improvement, or refinancing of real property of the lending of money secured by an interest in real property may refuse to make such loans merely because of the presence of lead-based paint on the residential real property or in the residential housing unit provided that the owner is in compliance with the maintenance standard and has obtained a certificate of compliance under G.S. 130A-131.9E annually.

(b)   Nothing in this section shall (i) require a financial institution to extend a loan or otherwise provide financial assistance if it is clearly evident that health-related issues, other than those related to lead-based paint, made occupancy of the housing accommodation an imminent threat to the health or safety of the occupant, or (ii) be construed to preclude a financial institution from considering the fair market value of the property which will secure the proposed loan.

(c)   Failure to meet the maintenance standard shall not be deemed a default under existing mortgages. (1997-443, s. 15.30(b).)

§ 130A-131.9G. Resident responsibilities.

In any residential housing unit occupied by a child less than six years of age who has an elevated blood lead level of 10 micrograms per deciliter or greater, the Department shall advise, in writing, the owner or managing agent and the child's parents or legal guardian of the importance of carrying out routine cleaning activities in the units they occupy, own, or manage. The cleaning activities shall include all of the following:

(1)   Wiping clean all windowsills with a damp cloth or sponge at least weekly.

(2)   Regularly washing all surfaces accessible to children.

(3)   In the case of a leased residential housing unit, identifying any deteriorated paint in the unit and notifying the owner or managing agent of the conditions within 72 hours of discovery.

(4)   Identifying and understanding potential lead poisoning hazards in the environment of each child less than six years of age in the unit (including toys, vinyl miniblinds, playground equipment, drinking water, soil, and painted surfaces), and taking steps to prevent children from ingesting lead such as encouraging children to wash their faces and hands frequently and especially after playing outdoors. (1997-443, s. 15.30(b); 2003-150, s. 7.)

§ 130A-131.9H. Application fees for certificates of compliance.

The Department shall collect an application fee of ten dollars ($10.00) for each certificate of compliance. Fee receipts shall be used to support the program that is developed to implement this Part. Fee receipts also may be used to provide for relocation and medical expenses incurred by children with confirmed lead poisoning. (1998-209, s. 5.)

Part 5. Disposition of Remains of Terminated Pregnancies.

§ 130A-131.10. Manner of disposition of remains of pregnancies.

(a)   The Commission for Public Health shall adopt rules to ensure that all facilities authorized to terminate pregnancies, and all medical or research laboratories or facilities to which the remains of terminated pregnancies are sent by facilities authorized to terminate pregnancies, shall dispose of the remains in a manner limited to burial, cremation, or, except as prohibited by subsection (b) of this section, approved hospital type of incineration.

226

(b)   A hospital or other medical facility or a medical or research laboratory or facility shall dispose of the remains of a recognizable fetus only by burial or cremation. The Commission shall adopt rules to implement this subsection.

(c)   A hospital or other medical facility is relieved from the obligation to dispose of the remains in accordance with subsections (a) and (b) of this section if it sends the remains to a medical or research laboratory or facility.

(d)   This section does not impose liability on a permitted medical waste treatment facility for a hospital's or other medical facility's violation of this section nor does it impose any additional duty on the treatment facility to inspect waste received from the hospital or medical facility to determine compliance with this section. (1989, c. 85; 1997-517, s. 4; 2007-182, s. 2.)

§§ 130A-131.11 through 130A-131.14. Reserved for future codification purposes.

Part 6. Teen Pregnancy Prevention.

§ 130A-131.15: Repealed by Session Laws 2001-424, s. 21.89(b), effective July 1, 2001.

§ 130A-131.15A. Department to establish program.

(a)   The Department shall establish and administer Teen Pregnancy Prevention Initiatives. The Department shall establish initiatives for primary prevention, secondary prevention, and special projects.

(b)   The Commission shall adopt rules necessary to implement this section. The rules shall include a maximum annual funding level for initiatives and a requirement for local match.

(c)   Initiatives shall be funded in accordance with selection criteria established by the Commission. In funding initiatives, the Department shall target counties with the highest teen pregnancy rates, increasingly higher rates, high rates within demographic subgroups, or greatest need for parenting programs. Grants shall be awarded on an annual basis.

227

(d)   Initiatives shall be funded on a four-year funding cycle. The Department may end funding prior to the end of the four-year period if programmatic requirements and performance standards are not met. At the end of four years of funding, a local initiative shall be eligible to reapply for funding.

(e)   Administrative costs in implementing this section shall not exceed ten percent (10%) of the total funds administered pursuant to this section.

(f)   Programs are not required to provide a cash match for these funds; however, the Department may require an in-kind match.

(g)   The Department shall periodically evaluate the effectiveness of teen pregnancy prevention programs. (2001-424, s. 21.89(c).)

Part 7. Birth Defects.

§ 130A-131.16. Birth defects monitoring program established; definitions.

(a)   The Birth Defects Monitoring Program is established within the State Center for Health and Environmental Statistics. The Birth Defects Monitoring Program shall compile, tabulate, and publish information related to the incidence and prevention of birth defects.

(b)   As used in this Part, unless the context clearly requires otherwise, the term:

(1)   "Birth defect" means any physical, functional, or chemical abnormality present at birth that is of possible genetic or prenatal origin.

(2)   "Program" means the Birth Defects Monitoring Program established under this Part.

(c)   Physicians and persons in charge of licensed medical facilities shall, upon request, permit staff of the Program to examine, review, and obtain a copy of any medical record in their possession or under their control that pertains to a diagnosed or suspected birth defect, including the records of the mother.

(d)   A physician or person in charge of a licensed medical facility who permits examination, review, or copying of medical records pursuant to this section shall

228

be immune from civil or criminal liability that might otherwise be incurred or imposed for providing access to these medical records based upon invasion of privacy or breach of physician-patient confidentiality. (1995, c. 268, s. 1.)

§ 130A-131.17. Confidentiality of information; research.

(a)   All information collected and analyzed by the Program pursuant to this Part shall be confidential insofar as the identity of the individual patient is concerned. This information shall not be considered public record open to inspection. Access to the information shall be limited to Program staff authorized by the Director of the State Center for Health and Environmental Statistics. The Director of the State Center for Health and Environmental Statistics may also authorize access to this information to persons engaged in demographic, epidemiological, or other similar scientific studies related to health. The Commission shall adopt rules that establish strict criteria for the use of monitoring Program information for scientific research. All persons given authorized access to Program information shall agree, in writing, to maintain confidentiality.

(b)   All scientific research proposed to be conducted by persons other than authorized Program staff using the information from the Program, shall first be reviewed and approved by the Director of the State Center for Health and Environmental Statistics and an appropriate committee for the protection of human subjects which is approved by the United States Department of Health and Human Services pursuant to Part 46 of Title 45 of the Code of Federal Regulations. Satisfaction of the terms of the Commission's rules for data access shall entitle the researcher to obtain information from the Program and, if part of the research protocol, to contact case subjects.

(c)   Whenever authorized Program staff propose a research protocol that includes contacting case subjects, the Director of the State Center for Health and Environmental Statistics shall submit a protocol describing the research to the State Health Director and to an appropriate committee for the protection of human subjects which is approved by the United States Department of Health and Human Services pursuant to Part 46 of Title 45 of the Code of Federal Regulations. If and when the protocol is approved by the committee and by the State Health Director pursuant to the rules of the Commission, then Program staff shall be entitled to complete the approved project and to contact case subjects.

(d)   The Program shall maintain a record of all persons who are given access to the information in the system. The record shall include the following:

(1)   The name of the person authorizing access;

(2)   The name, title, and organizational affiliation of persons given access;

(3)   The dates of access; and

(4)   The specific purposes for which information is to be used.

The record required under this subsection shall be open to public inspection during normal operating hours.

(e)   Nothing in this section prohibits the Program from publishing statistical compilations relating to birth defects that do not in any way identify individual patients. (1995, c. 268, s. 1.)

§§ 130A-131.18 through 130A-131.24. Reserved for future codification purposes.

Part 8. Office of Women's Health.

§ 130A-131.25. Office of Women's Health established.

(a)   There is established in the Department the Office of Women's Health. The purpose of the office is to expand the State's public health concerns and focus to include a comprehensive outlook on the overall health status of women. The primary goals of the Office shall be the prevention of disease and improvement in the quality of life for women over their entire lifespan. The Department shall develop strategies for achieving these goals, which shall include but not be limited to:

(1)   Developing a strategic plan to improve public services and programs targeting women;

(2)   Conducting policy analyses on specific issues related to women's health;

(3)   Facilitating communication among the Department's programs and between the Department and external women's health groups and community-based organizations;

(4)   Building public health awareness and capacity regarding women's health issues by providing a series of services including evaluation, recommendation, technical assistance, and training; and

(5)   Developing initiatives for modification or expansion of women-oriented services with the intent of establishing meaningful public/private partnerships in the future.

(b)   The Office shall study the feasibility of establishing initiatives for:

(1)   Early intervention services for women infected with HIV; and

(2)   Outreach, treatment, and follow-up services to women at high risk for contracting sexually transmitted diseases.

In conducting the study the Department shall take into consideration related services already in place in the Department and at the local level. (1997-172, s. 2.)

§ 130A-131.32. Reserved for future codification purposes.

Article 6.

Communicable Diseases.

Part 1. In General.

§ 130A-133: Repealed by Session Laws 2002-179, s. 3, effective October 1, 2002.

§ 130A-134. Reportable diseases and conditions.

The Commission shall establish by rule a list of communicable diseases and communicable conditions to be reported. (1983, c. 891, s. 2; 1987, c. 782, s. 4.)

§ 130A-135. Physicians to report.

A physician licensed to practice medicine who has reason to suspect that a person about whom the physician has been consulted professionally has a communicable disease or communicable condition declared by the Commission to be reported, shall report information required by the Commission to the local health director of the county or district in which the physician is consulted. The Commission shall declare confirmed HIV infection to be a reportable communicable condition. (1893, c. 214, s. 11; Rev., s. 3448; 1917, c. 263, s. 7; C.S., s. 7151; 1921, c. 223, s. 1; 1957, c. 1357, s. 1; 1973, c. 476, s. 128; 1983, c. 891, s. 2; 1987, c. 782, s. 5; 1989, c. 698, s. 3.)

§ 130A-136. School principals and child care operators to report.

A principal of a school and an operator of a child care facility, as defined in G.S. 110-86(3), who has reason to suspect that a person within the school or child care facility has a communicable disease or communicable condition declared by the Commission to be reported, shall report information required by the Commission to the local health director of the county or district in which the school or facility is located. (1979, c. 192, s. 2; 1983, c. 891, s. 2; 1987, c. 782, s. 6; 1997-506, s. 46.)

§ 130A-137. Medical facilities may report.

A medical facility, in which there is a patient reasonably suspected of having a communicable disease or condition declared by the Commission to be reported, may report information specified by the Commission to the local health director of the county or district in which the facility is located. (1983, c. 891, s. 2; 1987, c. 782, s. 7.)

§ 130A-138. Operators of restaurants and other food or drink establishments to report.

An operator of a restaurant or other establishment where food or drink is prepared or served for pay, as defined in G.S. 130A-247(4) and (5), shall report information required by the Commission to the local health director of the county or district in which the restaurant or food establishment is located when the operator has reason to suspect an outbreak of food-borne illness in its customers or employees or when it has reason to suspect that a food handler at the establishment has a food-borne disease or food-borne condition required by the Commission to be reported. (1917, c. 263, s. 9; C.S., s. 7153; 1921, c. 223, s. 3; 1957, c. 1357, s. 1; 1973, c. 476, s. 128; 1979, c. 192, s. 3; 1983, c. 891, s. 2; 1987, c. 782, s. 8.)

§ 130A-139. Persons in charge of laboratories to report.

A person in charge of a laboratory providing diagnostic service in this State shall report information required by the Commission to a public health agency specified by the Commission when the laboratory makes any of the following findings:

(1)   Sputa, gastric contents, or other specimens which are smear positive for acid fast bacilli or culture positive for Mycobacterium tuberculosis;

(2)   Urethral smears positive for Gram-negative intracellular diplococci or any culture positive for Neisseria gonorrhoeae;

(3)   Positive serological tests for syphilis or positive darkfield examination;

(4)   Any other positive test indicative of a communicable disease or communicable condition for which laboratory reporting is required by the Commission. (1981, c. 81, s. 1; 1983, c. 891, s. 2; 1987, c. 782, s. 9; 2001-28, s. 1.)

§ 130A-140. Local health directors to report.

A local health director shall report to the Department all cases of diseases or conditions or laboratory findings of residents of the jurisdiction of the local health department which are reported to the local health director pursuant to this Article. A local health director shall report all other cases and laboratory findings reported pursuant to this Article to the local health director of the county, district, or authority where the person with the reportable disease or condition or laboratory finding resides. (1919, c. 206, s. 2; C.S., s. 7192; 1957, c. 1357, s. 1; 1961, c. 753; 1973, c. 476, s. 128; 1983, c. 891, s. 2; 1987, c. 782, s. 10; 1997-502, s. 10.)

§ 130A-141. Form, content and timing of reports.

The Commission shall adopt rules which establish the specific information to be submitted when making a report required by this Article, time limits for reporting, the form of the reports and to whom reports of laboratory findings are to be made. (1983, c. 891, s. 2; 1987, c. 782, s. 11.)

§ 130A-141.1. Temporary order to report.

(a)   The State Health Director may issue a temporary order requiring health care providers to report symptoms, diseases, conditions, trends in use of health care services, or other health-related information when necessary to conduct a public health investigation or surveillance of an illness, condition, or symptoms that may indicate the existence of a communicable disease or condition that presents a danger to the public health. The order shall specify which health care providers must report, what information is to be reported, and the period of time for which reporting is required. The period of time for which reporting is required pursuant to a temporary order shall not exceed 90 days. The Commission may adopt rules to continue the reporting requirement when necessary to protect the public health.

(b)   For the purposes of this section, the term "health care provider" has the same meaning as that term is defined in G.S. 130A-476(g). (2004-80, s. 5.)

§ 130A-142. Immunity of persons who report.

234

A person who makes a report pursuant to the provisions of this Article shall be immune from any civil or criminal liability that might otherwise be incurred or imposed as a result of making that report. (1983, c. 891, s. 2; 1987, c. 782, s. 12.)

§ 130A-143. Confidentiality of records.

All information and records, whether publicly or privately maintained, that identify a person who has AIDS virus infection or who has or may have a disease or condition required to be reported pursuant to the provisions of this Article shall be strictly confidential. This information shall not be released or made public except under the following circumstances:

(1)   Release is made of specific medical or epidemiological information for statistical purposes in a way that no person can be identified;

(2)   Release is made of all or part of the medical record with the written consent of the person or persons identified or their guardian;

(3)   Release is made for purposes of treatment, payment, research, or health care operations to the extent that disclosure is permitted under 45 Code of Federal Regulations §§ 164.506 and 164.512(i). For purposes of this section, the terms "treatment," "payment," "research," and "health care operations" have the meaning given those terms in 45 Code of Federal Regulations § 164.501;

(4)   Release is necessary to protect the public health and is made as provided by the Commission in its rules regarding control measures for communicable diseases and conditions;

(5)   Release is made pursuant to other provisions of this Article;

(6)   Release is made pursuant to subpoena or court order. Upon request of the person identified in the record, the record shall be reviewed in camera. In the trial, the trial judge may, during the taking of testimony concerning such information, exclude from the courtroom all persons except the officers of the court, the parties and those engaged in the trial of the case;

(7)   Release is made by the Department or a local health department to a court or a law enforcement official for the purpose of enforcing this Article or

Article 22 of this Chapter, or investigating a terrorist incident using nuclear, biological, or chemical agents. A law enforcement official who receives the information shall not disclose it further, except (i) when necessary to enforce this Article or Article 22 of this Chapter, or when necessary to conduct an investigation of a terrorist incident using nuclear, biological, or chemical agents, or (ii) when the Department or a local health department seeks the assistance of the law enforcement official in preventing or controlling the spread of the disease or condition and expressly authorizes the disclosure as necessary for that purpose;

(8)   Release is made by the Department or a local health department to another federal, state or local public health agency for the purpose of preventing or controlling the spread of a communicable disease or communicable condition;

(9)   Release is made by the Department for bona fide research purposes. The Commission shall adopt rules providing for the use of the information for research purposes;

(10)   Release is made pursuant to G.S. 130A-144(b); or

(11)   Release is made pursuant to any other provisions of law that specifically authorize or require the release of information or records related to AIDS. (1983, c. 891, s. 2; 1987, c. 782, s. 13; 2002-179, s. 7; 2011-314, s. 4.)

§ 130A-144. Investigation and control measures.

(a)   The local health director shall investigate, as required by the Commission, cases of communicable diseases and communicable conditions reported to the local health director pursuant to this Article.

(b)   Physicians, persons in charge of medical facilities or laboratories, and other persons shall, upon request and proper identification, permit a local health director or the State Health Director to examine, review, and obtain a copy of medical or other records in their possession or under their control which the State Health Director or a local health director determines pertain to the (i) diagnosis, treatment, or prevention of a communicable disease or communicable condition for a person infected, exposed, or reasonably suspected of being infected or exposed to such a disease or condition, or (ii) the

236

investigation of a known or reasonably suspected outbreak of a communicable disease or communicable condition.

(c)   A physician or a person in charge of a medical facility or laboratory who permits examination, review or copying of medical records pursuant to subsection (b) shall be immune from any civil or criminal liability that otherwise might be incurred or imposed as a result of complying with a request made pursuant to subsection (b).

(d)   The attending physician shall give control measures prescribed by the Commission to a patient with a communicable disease or communicable condition and to patients reasonably suspected of being infected or exposed to such a disease or condition. The physician shall also give control measures to other individuals as required by rules adopted by the Commission.

(e)   The local health director shall ensure that control measures prescribed by the Commission have been given to prevent the spread of all reportable communicable diseases or communicable conditions and any other communicable disease or communicable condition that represents a significant threat to the public health. The local health department shall provide, at no cost to the patient, the examination and treatment for tuberculosis disease and infection and for sexually transmitted diseases designated by the Commission.

(f)   All persons shall comply with control measures, including submission to examinations and tests, prescribed by the Commission subject to the limitations of G.S. 130A-148.

(g)   The Commission shall adopt rules that prescribe control measures for communicable diseases and conditions subject to the limitations of G.S. 130A-148. Temporary rules prescribing control measures for communicable diseases and conditions shall be adopted pursuant to G.S. 150B-13.

(h)   Anyone who assists in an inquiry or investigation conducted by the State Health Director for the purpose of evaluating the risk of transmission of HIV or Hepatitis B from an infected health care worker to patients, or who serves on an expert panel established by the State Health Director for that purpose, shall be immune from civil liability that otherwise might be incurred or imposed for any acts or omissions which result from such assistance or service, provided that the person acts in good faith and the acts or omissions do not amount to gross negligence, willful or wanton misconduct, or intentional wrongdoing. This qualified immunity does not apply to acts or omissions which occur with respect

237

to the operation of a motor vehicle. Nothing in this subsection provides immunity from liability for a violation of G.S. 130A-143. (1893, c. 214, s. 16; Rev., s. 4459; 1909, c. 793, s. 8; C.S., s. 7158; 1957, c. 1357, s. 1; 1973, c. 476, s. 128; 1983, c. 891, s. 2; 1987, c. 782, s. 14; 1991, c. 225, s. 1; 1995, c. 228, s. 1; 2001-28, s. 2; 2004-80, s. 6; 2009-501, s. 2.)

§ 130A-145. Quarantine and isolation authority.

(a)   The State Health Director and a local health director are empowered to exercise quarantine and isolation authority. Quarantine and isolation authority shall be exercised only when and so long as the public health is endangered, all other reasonable means for correcting the problem have been exhausted, and no less restrictive alternative exists.

(b)   No person other than a person authorized by the State Health Director or local health director shall enter quarantine or isolation premises. Nothing in this subsection shall be construed to restrict the access of authorized health care, law enforcement, or emergency medical services personnel to quarantine or isolation premises as necessary in conducting their duties.

(c)   Before applying quarantine or isolation authority to livestock or poultry for the purpose of preventing the direct or indirect conveyance of an infectious agent to persons, the State Health Director or a local health director shall consult with the State Veterinarian in the Department of Agriculture and Consumer Services.

(d)   When quarantine or isolation limits the freedom of movement of a person or animal or of access to a person or animal whose freedom of movement is limited, the period of limited freedom of movement or access shall not exceed 30 calendar days. Any person substantially affected by that limitation may institute in superior court in Wake County or in the county in which the limitation is imposed an action to review that limitation. The official who exercises the quarantine or isolation authority shall give the persons known by the official to be substantially affected by the limitation reasonable notice under the circumstances of the right to institute an action to review the limitation. If a person or a person's representative requests a hearing, the hearing shall be held within 72 hours of the filing of that request, excluding Saturdays and Sundays. The person substantially affected by that limitation is entitled to be represented by counsel of the person's own choice or if the person is indigent, the person shall be represented by counsel appointed in accordance with Article 36 of Chapter 7A of the General Statutes and the rules adopted by the Office of

238

Indigent Defense Services. The court shall reduce or terminate the limitation unless it determines, by the preponderance of the evidence, that the limitation is reasonably necessary to prevent or limit the conveyance of a communicable disease or condition to others.

If the State Health Director or the local health director determines that a 30-calendar-day limitation on freedom of movement or access is not adequate to protect the public health, the State Health Director or local health director must institute in superior court in the county in which the limitation is imposed an action to obtain an order extending the period of limitation of freedom of movement or access. If the person substantially affected by the limitation has already instituted an action in superior court in Wake County, the State Health Director must institute the action in superior court in Wake County or as a counterclaim in the pending case. Except as provided below for persons with tuberculosis, the court shall continue the limitation for a period not to exceed 30 days if it determines, by the preponderance of the evidence, that the limitation is reasonably necessary to prevent or limit the conveyance of a communicable disease or condition to others. The court order shall specify the period of time the limitation is to be continued and shall provide for automatic termination of the order upon written determination by the State Health Director or local health director that the quarantine or isolation is no longer necessary to protect the public health. In addition, where the petitioner can prove by a preponderance of the evidence that quarantine or isolation was not or is no longer needed for protection of the public health, the person quarantined or isolated may move the trial court to reconsider its order extending quarantine or isolation before the time for the order otherwise expires and may seek immediate or expedited termination of the order. Before the expiration of an order issued under this section, the State Health Director or local health director may move to continue the order for additional periods not to exceed 30 days each. If the person whose freedom of movement has been limited has tuberculosis, the court shall continue the limitation for a period not to exceed one calendar year if it determines, by a preponderance of the evidence, that the limitation is reasonably necessary to prevent or limit the conveyance of tuberculosis to others. The court order shall specify the period of time the limitation is to be continued and shall provide for automatic termination of the order upon written determination by the State Health Director or local health director that the quarantine or isolation is no longer necessary to protect the public health. In addition, where the petitioner can prove by a preponderance of the evidence that quarantine or isolation was not or is no longer needed for protection of the public health, the person quarantined or isolated may move the trial court to reconsider its order extending quarantine or isolation before the time for the

239

order otherwise expires and may seek immediate or expedited termination of the order. Before the expiration of an order limiting the freedom of movement of a person with tuberculosis, the State Health Director or local health director may move to continue the order for additional periods not to exceed one calendar year each. (1957, c. 1357, s. 1; 1983, c. 891, s. 2; 1987, c. 782, s. 15; 2002-179, s. 5; 2004-80, s. 2.)

§ 130A-146. Transportation of bodies of persons who have died of reportable diseases.

No person shall transport in this State the remains of any person who has died of a disease declared by the Commission to be reported until the body has been encased in a manner as prescribed by rule by the Commission. Only persons who have complied with the rules of the Commission concerning the removal of dead bodies shall be issued a burial-transit permit. (1893, c. 214, s. 16; Rev., s. 4459; C.S., s. 7161; 1953, c. 675, s. 16; 1957, c. 1357, s. 1; 1973, c. 476, s. 128; 1983, c. 891, s. 2.)

§ 130A-147. Rules of the Commission.

For the protection of the public health, the Commission is authorized to adopt rules for the detection, control and prevention of communicable diseases. (1983, c. 891, s. 2.)

§ 130A-148. Laboratory tests for AIDS virus infection.

(a)   For the protection of the public health, the Commission shall adopt rules establishing standards for the certification of laboratories to perform tests for Acquired Immune Deficiency Syndrome (AIDS) virus infection. The rules shall address, but not be limited to, proficiency testing, record maintenance, adequate staffing and confirmatory testing. Tests for AIDS virus infection shall be performed only by laboratories certified pursuant to this subsection and only on specimens submitted by a physician licensed to practice medicine. This subsection shall not apply to testing performed solely for research purposes under the approval of an institutional review board.

240

(b)   Prior to obtaining consent for donation of blood, semen, tissue or organs, a facility or institution seeking to obtain blood, tissue, semen or organs for transfusion, implantation, transplantation or administration shall provide the potential donor with information about AIDS virus transmission, and information about who should not donate.

(c)   No blood or semen may be transfused or administered when blood from the donor has not been tested or has tested positive for AIDS virus infection by a standard laboratory test.

(d)   No tissue or organs may be transplanted or implanted when blood from the donor has not been tested or has tested positive for AIDS virus infection by a standard laboratory test unless consent is obtained from the recipient, or from the recipient's guardian or a responsible adult relative of the recipient if the recipient is not competent to give such consent.

(e)   Any facility or institution that obtains or transfuses, implants, transplants, or administers blood, tissue, semen, or organs shall be immune from civil or criminal liability that otherwise might be incurred or imposed for transmission of AIDS virus infection if the provisions specified in subsections (b), (c), and (d) of this section have been complied with.

(f)   Specimens may be tested for AIDS virus infection for research or epidemiologic purposes without consent of the person from whom the specimen is obtained if all personal identifying information is removed from the specimen prior to testing.

(g)   Persons tested for AIDS virus infection shall be notified of test results and counseled appropriately. This subsection shall not apply to tests performed by or for entities governed by Article 39 of Chapter 58 of the General Statutes, the Insurance Information and Privacy Protection Act, provided that said entities comply with the notice requirements thereof.

(h)   The Commission may authorize or require laboratory tests for AIDS virus infection when necessary to protect the public health.

A test for AIDS virus infection may also be performed upon any person solely by order of a physician licensed to practice medicine in North Carolina who is rendering medical services to that person when, in the reasonable medical judgment of the physician, the test is necessary for the appropriate treatment of the person; however, the person shall be informed that a test for AIDS virus

241

infection is to be conducted, and shall be given clear opportunity to refuse to submit to the test prior to it being conducted, and further if informed consent is not obtained, the test may not be performed. A physician may order a test for AIDS virus infection without the informed consent of the person tested if the person is incapable of providing or incompetent to provide such consent, others authorized to give consent for the person are not available, and testing is necessary for appropriate diagnosis or care of the person.

An unemancipated minor may be tested for AIDS virus infection without the consent of the parent or legal guardian of the minor when the parent or guardian has refused to consent to such testing and there is reasonable suspicion that the minor has AIDS virus or HIV infection or that the child has been sexually abused.

(i)   Except as provided in this section, no test for AIDS virus infection shall be required, performed or used to determine suitability for continued employment, housing or public services, or for the use of places of public accommodation as defined in G.S. 168A-3(8), or public transportation.

Further it shall be unlawful to discriminate against any person having AIDS virus or HIV infection on account of that infection in determining suitability for continued employment, housing, or public services, or for the use of places of public accommodation, as defined in G.S. 168A-3(8), or public transportation.

Any person aggrieved by an act or discriminatory practice prohibited by this subsection relating to housing shall be entitled to institute a civil action pursuant to G.S. 41A-7 of the State Fair Housing Act. Any person aggrieved by an act or discriminatory practice prohibited by this subsection other than one relating to housing may bring a civil action to enforce rights granted or protected by this subsection.

The action shall be commenced in superior court in the county where the alleged discriminatory practice or prohibited conduct occurred or where the plaintiff or defendant resides. Such action shall be tried to the court without a jury. Any relief granted by the court shall be limited to declaratory and injunctive relief, including orders to hire or reinstate an aggrieved person or admit such person to a labor organization.

In a civil action brought to enforce provisions of this subsection relating to employment, the court may award back pay. Any such back pay liability shall not accrue from a date more than two years prior to the filing of an action under this subsection. Interim earnings or amounts earnable with reasonable diligence by the aggrieved person shall operate to reduce the back pay otherwise allowable. In any civil action brought under this subsection, the court, in its discretion, may award reasonable attorney's fees to the substantially prevailing party as a part of costs.

A civil action brought pursuant to this subsection shall be commenced within 180 days after the date on which the aggrieved person became aware or, with reasonable diligence, should have become aware of the alleged discriminatory practice or prohibited conduct.

Nothing in this section shall be construed so as to prohibit an employer from:

(1)   Requiring a test for AIDS virus infection for job applicants in preemployment medical examinations required by the employer;

(2)   Denying employment to a job applicant based solely on a confirmed positive test for AIDS virus infection;

(3)   Including a test for AIDS virus infection performed in the course of an annual medical examination routinely required of all employees by the employer; or

(4)   Taking the appropriate employment action, including reassignment or termination of employment, if the continuation by the employee who has AIDS virus or HIV infection of his work tasks would pose a significant risk to the health of the employee, coworkers, or the public, or if the employee is unable to perform the normally assigned duties of the job.

(j)   It shall not be unlawful for a licensed health care provider or facility to:

(1)   Treat a person who has AIDS virus or HIV infection differently from persons who do not have that infection when such treatment is appropriate to protect the health care provider or employees of the provider or employees of the facility while providing appropriate care for the person who has the AIDS virus or HIV infection; or

(2)   Refer a person who has AIDS virus or HIV infection to another licensed health care provider or facility when such referral is for the purpose of providing more appropriate treatment for the person with AIDS virus or HIV infection. (1987, c. 782, s. 16; 1989, c. 698, s. 1; 1991, c. 720, s. 78.)

243

§ 130A-149: Recodified as G.S. 130A-479 by Session Laws 2002-179, s. 2, effective October 1, 2002.

Part 1A. Health Care-Associated Infections.

§ 130A-150. Statewide surveillance and reporting system.

(a)   By December 31, 2011, the Department, in consultation with the State HAI Advisory Group and in accordance with rules adopted by the Commission pursuant to subsection (b) of this section, shall establish a statewide surveillance and reporting system for specified health care-associated infections.

(b)   The Commission shall adopt rules necessary to implement the statewide surveillance and reporting system established pursuant to subsection (a) of this section. The rules shall specify uniform standards for surveillance and reporting of specified health care-associated infections under the statewide surveillance and reporting system. The uniform standards shall include at least all of the following:

(1)   A preference for electronic surveillance of specified health care-associated infections to the greatest extent practicable.

(2)   A requirement for electronic reporting of specified health care-associated infections.

(c)   Each hospital, as defined in G.S. 131E-76(3), is subject to the statewide surveillance and reporting system established in accordance with subsection (a) of this section and shall be responsible for health care-associated infections surveillance and reporting of specified health care-associated infections data to the Department through the Centers for Disease Control and Prevention National Health Care Safety Network.

(d)   The Department shall release to the public aggregated and provider-specific data on health care-associated infections that does not contain social security numbers or other personal identifying information only if it deems the release of this data to be reliable and necessary to protect the public's health.

(e)   Repealed by Session Laws 2013-360, s. 12A.8(d), effective July 1, 2013. (2011-386, ss. 1, 2; 2013-360, s. 12A.8(d).)

§ 130A-151. Reserved for future codification purposes.

Part 2. Immunization.

§ 130A-152. Immunization required.

(a)   Every child present in this State shall be immunized against diphtheria, tetanus, whooping cough, poliomyelitis, red measles (rubeola) and rubella. In addition, every child present in this State shall be immunized against any other disease upon a determination by the Commission that the immunization is in the interest of the public health. Every parent, guardian, person in loco parentis and person or agency, whether governmental or private, with legal custody of a child shall have the responsibility to ensure that the child has received the required immunization at the age required by the Commission. If a child has not received the required immunizations by the specified age, the responsible person shall obtain the required immunization for the child as soon as possible after the lack of the required immunization is determined.

(b)   Repealed by Session Laws 2002-179, s. 10, effective October 1, 2002.

(c)   The Commission shall adopt and the Department shall enforce rules concerning the implementation of the immunization program. The rules shall provide for:

(1)   The child's age at administration of each vaccine;

(2)   The number of doses of each vaccine;

(3)   Exemptions from the immunization requirements where medical practice suggests that immunization would not be in the best health interests of a specific category of children;

(4)   The procedures and practices for administering the vaccine; and

(5)   Redistribution of vaccines provided to local health departments.

(c1)   The Commission for Public Health shall, pursuant to G.S. 130A-152 and G.S. 130A-433, adopt rules establishing reasonable fees for the administration of vaccines and rules limiting the requirements that can be placed on children, their parents, guardians, or custodians as a condition for receiving vaccines provided by the State. These rules shall become effective January 1, 1994.

(d)   Only vaccine preparations which meet the standards of the United States Food and Drug Administration or its successor in licensing vaccines and are approved for use by the Commission may be used.

(e)   When the Commission requires immunization against a disease not listed in paragraph (a) of this section, or requires an additional dose of a vaccine, the Commission is authorized to exempt from the new requirement children who are or who have been enrolled in school (K-12) on or before the effective date of the new requirement. (1957, c. 1357, s. 1; 1971, c. 191; 1973, c. 476, s. 128; c. 632, s. 1; 1975, c. 84; 1977, c. 160; 1979, c. 56, s. 1; 1983, c. 891, s. 2; 1985, c. 158; 1993, c. 321, s. 281(a); 2002-179, s. 10; 2007-182, s. 2.)

§ 130A-153. Obtaining immunization; reporting by local health departments; access to immunization information in patient records; immunization of minors.

(a)   The required immunization may be obtained from a physician licensed to practice medicine, from a local health department, or in the case of a person at least 18 years of age, from an immunizing pharmacist. Local health departments shall administer required and State-supplied immunizations at no cost to uninsured or underinsured patients with family incomes below two hundred percent (200%) of the federal poverty level. A local health department may redistribute these vaccines only in accordance with the rules of the Commission.

(b)   Local health departments shall file monthly immunization reports with the Department. The report shall be filed on forms prepared by the Department and shall state, at a minimum, each patient's age and the number of doses of each type of vaccine administered.

(c)   Immunization certificates and information concerning immunizations contained in medical or other records shall, upon request, be shared with the Department, local health departments, an immunizing pharmacist, and the patient's attending physician. In addition, an insurance institution, agent, or insurance support organization, as those terms are defined in G.S. 58-39-15, may share immunization information with the Department. The Commission may, for the purpose of assisting the Department in enforcing this Part, provide by rule that other persons may have access to immunization information, in whole or in part.

(d)   A physician or local health department may immunize a minor with the consent of a parent, guardian, or person standing in loco parentis to the minor. A physician or local health department may also immunize a minor who is presented for immunization by an adult who signs a statement that he or she is authorized by a parent, guardian, or person standing in loco parentis to the minor to obtain the immunization for the minor. (1957, c. 1357, s. 1; 1959, c. 177; 1965, c. 652; 1971, c. 191; 1973, c. 476, s. 128; 1979, c. 56, s. 1; 1983, c. 891, s. 2; 1985, c. 743, ss. 1, 2; 1993, c. 134, s. 1; 1999-110, s. 2; 2009-451, s. 10.29A(a); 2010-31, s. 10.13(b); 2013-246, s. 5.)

§ 130A-154. Certificate of immunization.

(a)   A physician or local health department administering a required vaccine shall give a certificate of immunization to the person who presented the child for immunization. The certificate shall state the name of the child, the name of the child's parent, guardian, or person responsible for the child obtaining the required immunization, the address of the child and the parent, guardian or responsible person, the date of birth of the child, the sex of the child, the number of doses of the vaccine given, the date the doses were given, the name and address of the physician or local health department administering the required immunization and other relevant information required by the Commission.

(b)   Except as otherwise provided in this subsection, a person who received immunizations in a state other than North Carolina shall present an official certificate or record of immunization to the child care facility, school (K-12), or college or university. This certificate or record shall state the person's name, address, date of birth, and sex; the type and number of doses of administered vaccine; the dates of the first MMR and the last DTP and polio; the name and address of the physician or local health department administering the required immunization; and other relevant information required by the Commission. (1957, c. 1357, s. 1; 1959, c. 177; 1965, c. 652; 1971, c. 191; 1979, c. 56, s. 1; 1983, c. 891, s. 2; 1999-110, s. 3.)

§ 130A-155. Submission of certificate to child care facility, preschool and school authorities; record maintenance; reporting.

(a)   No child shall attend a school (pre K-12), whether public, private or religious, a child care facility as defined in G.S. 110-86(3), unless a certificate of immunization indicating that the child has received the immunizations required by G.S. 130A-152 is presented to the school or facility. The parent, guardian, or responsible person must present a certificate of immunization on the child's first day of attendance to the principal of the school or operator of the facility, as defined in G.S. 110-86(7). If a certificate of immunization is not presented on the first day, the principal or operator shall present a notice of deficiency to the parent, guardian or responsible person. The parent, guardian or responsible person shall have 30 calendar days from the first day of attendance to obtain the required immunization for the child. If the administration of vaccine in a series of doses given at medically approved intervals requires a period in excess of 30 calendar days, additional days upon certification by a physician may be allowed to obtain the required immunization. Upon termination of 30 calendar days or the extended period, the principal or operator shall not permit the child to attend the school or facility unless the required immunization has been obtained.

(b)   The school or child care facility shall maintain on file immunization records for all children attending the school or facility which contain the information required for a certificate of immunization as specified in G.S. 130A-154. These certificates shall be open to inspection by the Department and the local health department during normal business hours. When a child transfers to another school or facility, the school or facility which the child previously attended shall, upon request, send a copy of the child's immunization record at no charge to the school or facility to which the child has transferred.

(c)   The school shall file an annual immunization report with the Department by November 1. The child care facility shall file an immunization report annually with the Department. The report shall be filed on forms prepared by the Department and shall state the number of children attending the school or facility, the number of children who had not obtained the required immunization within 30 days of their first attendance, the number of children who received a medical exemption and the number of children who received a religious exemption.

(d)   Any adult who attends school (pre K-12), whether public, private or religious, shall obtain the immunizations required in G.S. 130A-152 and shall

248

present to the school a certificate in accordance with this section. The physician or local health department administering a required vaccine to the adult shall give a certificate of immunization to the person. The certificate shall state the person's name, address, date of birth and sex; the number of doses of the vaccine given; the date the doses were given; the name and addresses of the physician or local health department administering the required immunization; and other relevant information required by the Commission. (1957, c. 1357, s. 1; 1959, c. 177; 1965, c. 652; 1971, c. 191; 1973, c. 632, s. 2; 1979, c. 56, s. 1; 1981, c. 44; 1983, c. 891, s. 2; 1997-506, s. 47; 1999-110, s. 4; 2007-187, s. 2.)

§ 130A-155.1. Submission of certificate to college or universities.

(a)   Except as otherwise provided in this section, no person shall attend a college or university, whether public, private, or religious, unless a certificate of immunization or a record of immunization from a high school located in North Carolina indicating that the person has received immunizations required by G.S. 130A-152 is presented to the college or university. The person shall present a certificate or record of immunization on or before the date the person first registers for a quarter or semester during which the student will reside on the campus or first registers for more than four traditional day credit hours to the registrar of the college or university. If a certificate or record of immunization is not in the possession of the college or university on the date of first registration, the college or university shall present a notice of deficiency to the student. The student shall have 30 calendar days from the date of the student's first registration to obtain the required immunization. If immunization requires a series of doses and the period necessary to give the vaccine at standard intervals extends beyond the date of the first registration, the student shall be allowed to attend the college or university upon written certification by a physician that the standard series is in progress. The physician shall state the time period needed to complete the series. Upon termination of this time period, the college or university shall not permit the student to continue in attendance unless the required immunization has been obtained.

(b)   The college or university shall maintain on file immunization records for all students attending the school which contain the information required for a certificate of immunization as specified in G.S. 130A-154. These certificates shall be open to inspection by the Department and the local health department during normal business hours. When a student transfers to another college or university, the college or university which the student previously attended shall,

249

upon request, send a copy of the student's immunization record at no charge to the college or university to which the student has transferred.

(c)   Within 60 calendar days after the commencement of a new school year, the college or university shall file an immunization report with the Department. The report shall be filed on forms prepared by the Department and shall state the number of students attending the school or facility, the number of students who had not obtained the required immunization within 30 days of their first attendance, the number of students who received a medical exemption and the number of students who received a religious exemption.

(d)   Repealed by Session Laws 1999-110, s. 5.

(e)   The provisions of this section shall not apply to:

(1)   Educational institutions established under Chapter 115D of the General Statutes.

(2)   Students residing off-campus and registering for any combination of:

a.   Off-campus courses.

b.   Evening courses.

c.   Weekend courses.

d.   No more than four traditional day credit hours in on-campus courses. (1985, c. 692, s. 1; 1987, c. 782, s. 17; 1991, c. 381, s. 1; 1999-110, s. 5; 2007-99, s. 1.)

§ 130A-156. Medical exemption.

The Commission for Public Health shall adopt by rule medical contraindications to immunizations required by G.S. 130A-152. If a physician licensed to practice medicine in this State certifies that a required immunization is or may be detrimental to a person's health due to the presence of one of the contraindications adopted by the Commission, the person is not required to receive the specified immunization as long as the contraindication persists. The State Health Director may, upon request by a physician licensed to practice

250

medicine in this State, grant a medical exemption to a required immunization for a contraindication not on the list adopted by the Commission. (1957, c. 1357, s. 1; 1959, c. 177; 1965, c. 652; 1971, c. 191; 1979, c. 56, s. 1; 1983, c. 891, s. 2; 1987, c. 782, s. 18; 1989, c. 122; 1999-110, s. 6; 2007-182, s. 2.)

§ 130A-157. Religious exemption.

If the bona fide religious beliefs of an adult or the parent, guardian or person in loco parentis of a child are contrary to the immunization requirements contained in this Chapter, the adult or the child shall be exempt from the requirements. Upon submission of a written statement of the bona fide religious beliefs and opposition to the immunization requirements, the person may attend the college, university, school or facility without presenting a certificate of immunization. (1957, c. 1357, s. 1; 1959, c. 177; 1965, c. 652; 1971, c. 191; 1979, c. 56, s. 1; 1983, c. 891, s. 2; 1985, c. 692, s. 2; 2002-179, s. 17.)

§ 130A-158. Restitution required when vaccine spoiled due to provider negligence.

Immunization program providers shall be liable for restitution to the State for the cost of replacement vaccine when vaccine in the provider's inventory has become spoiled or unstable due to the provider's negligence and unreasonable failure to properly handle or store the vaccine. (2001-424, s. 21.86(a).)

§ 130A-159. Reserved for future codification purposes.

Part 3. Venereal Disease.

§§ 130A-160 through 130A-166: Repealed by Session Laws 1991, c. 225, s. 2.

§ 130A-171: Repealed.

§ 130A-172: Repealed.

§ 130A-173: Repealed.

§ 130A-174: Repealed.

§ 130A-175. Reserved for future codification purposes.

§ 130A-176. Reserved for future codification purposes.

§ 130A-177: Repealed.

§ 130A-178: Repealed.

§ 130A-179. Repealed by Session Laws 1987, c. 782, s. 20.

§§ 130A-180 through 130A-183. Reserved for future codification purposes.

Part 6. Rabies.

§ 130A-184. Definitions.

The following definitions apply in this Part:

(1)   Animal Control Officer. - A city or county employee whose responsibility includes animal control. The term "Animal Control Officer" also includes agents of a private organization that is operating an animal shelter under contract with a city or county whenever those agents are performing animal control functions at the shelter.

(2)   Cat. - A domestic feline of the genus and species Felis catus.

(3)   Certified rabies vaccinator. - A person appointed and certified to administer rabies vaccine to animals in accordance with this Part.

(4)   Dog. - A domestic canine of the genus, species, and subspecies Canis lupus familiaris.

(4a)   Feral. - An animal that is not socialized.

252

(4b)   Ferret. - A domestic mammal of the genus, species, and subspecies Mustela putorius furo.

(5)   Rabies vaccine. - An animal rabies vaccine licensed by the United States Department of Agriculture and approved for use in this State by the Commission.

(6)   State Public Heath Veterinarian. - A person appointed by the Secretary to direct the State public health veterinary program.

(6a)   Stray. - An animal that meets both of the following conditions:

a.   Is beyond the limits of confinement or lost.

b.   Is not wearing any tags, microchips, tattoos, or other methods of identification.

(7)   Vaccination. - The administration of rabies vaccine by a person authorized to administer it under G.S. 130A-185. (1935, c. 122, s. 1; 1949, c. 645, s. 1; 1953, c. 876, s. 1; 1957, c. 1357, s. 3; 1973, c. 476, s. 128; 1983, c. 891, s. 2; 2009-304, s. 2; 2009-327, s. 1.)

§ 130A-185. Vaccination required.

(a)   Vaccination required. - The owner of an animal listed in this subsection over four months of age shall have the animal vaccinated against rabies:

(1)   Cat.

(2)   Dog.

(3)   Ferret.

(b)   Vaccination. - Only animal rabies vaccine licensed by the United States Department of Agriculture and approved by the Commission shall be used on animals in this State. A rabies vaccine may only be administered by one or more of the following:

(1)   A licensed veterinarian.

(2)   A registered veterinary technician under the direct supervision of a licensed veterinarian.

(3)   A certified rabies vaccinator. (1935, c. 122, s. 1; 1941, c. 259, s. 2; 1953, c. 876, s. 2; 1973, c. 476, s. 128; 1983, c. 891, s. 2; 2009-327, s. 2.)

§ 130A-186. Appointment and certification of certified rabies vaccinator.

In those counties where licensed veterinarians are not available to participate in all scheduled county rabies control clinics, the local health director shall appoint one or more persons for the purpose of administering rabies vaccine to animals in that county. Whether or not licensed veterinarians are available, the local health director may appoint one or more persons for the purpose of administering rabies vaccine to animals in their county and these persons will make themselves available to participate in the county rabies control program. The State Public Health Veterinarian shall provide at least four hours of training to those persons appointed by the local health director to administer rabies vaccine. Upon satisfactory completion of the training, the State Public Health Veterinarian shall certify in writing that the appointee has demonstrated a knowledge and procedure acceptable for the administration of rabies vaccine to animals. A certified rabies vaccinator shall be authorized to administer rabies vaccine to animals in the county until the appointment by the local health director has been terminated. (1935, c. 122, s. 3; 1941, c. 259, s. 3; 1953, c. 876, s. 3; 1957, c. 1357, s. 4; 1983, c. 891, s. 2.)

§ 130A-187. County rabies vaccination clinics.

(a)   Local Clinics. - The local health director shall organize or assist other county departments to organize at least one countywide rabies vaccination clinic per year for the purpose of vaccinating animals required to be vaccinated under this Part. Public notice of the time and place of rabies vaccination clinics shall be published in a newspaper having general circulation within the area.

(b)   Fee. - The county board of commissioners may establish a fee to be charged for a rabies vaccination given at a county rabies vaccination clinic. The fee amount may consist of the following:

(1)   A charge for administering and storing the vaccine, not to exceed ten dollars ($10.00).

(2)   The actual cost of the rabies vaccine, the vaccination certificate, and the rabies vaccination tag. (1983, c. 891, s. 2; 1987, c. 219; 2009-327, s. 3.)

§ 130A-188: Repealed by Session Laws 2009-327, s. 4, effective October 1, 2009.

§ 130A-189. Rabies vaccination certificates.

A person who administers a rabies vaccine shall complete a rabies vaccination certificate. The Commission shall adopt rules specifying the information that must be included on the certificate. An original rabies vaccination certificate shall be given to the owner of the animal that receives the rabies vaccine. A copy of the rabies vaccination certificate shall be retained by the licensed veterinarian or the certified rabies vaccinator. A copy shall also be given to the county agency responsible for animal control, provided the information given to the county agency shall not be used for commercial purposes. (1935, c. 122, s. 6; 1941, c. 259, s. 5; 1959, c. 352; 1983, c. 891, s. 2; 1993, c. 245, s. 1; 2009-327, s. 5.)

§ 130A-190. Rabies vaccination tags.

(a)   Issuance. - A person who administers a rabies vaccine shall issue a rabies vaccination tag to the owner of the animal. The rabies vaccination tag shall show the year issued, a vaccination number, the words "North Carolina" or the initials "N.C." and the words "rabies vaccine." Dogs shall wear rabies vaccination tags at all times. Cats and ferrets must wear rabies vaccination tags unless they are exempt from wearing the tags by local ordinance.

(b)   Fee. - Rabies vaccination tags, links, and rivets may be obtained from the Department of Health and Human Services. The Secretary is authorized to collect a fee for the rabies tags, links, and rivets in accordance with this subsection. The fee for each tag is the sum of the following:

(1)   The actual cost of the rabies tag, links, and rivets.

255

(2)   Transportation costs.

(3)   Fifteen cents (15¢). This portion of the fee shall be used to fund rabies education and prevention programs.

(4)   Repealed by Session Laws 2010-31, s. 11.4(h), effective October 1, 2010.

(c)   Repealed by Session Laws 2007-487, s. 1, effective January 1, 2008. (1935, c. 122, s. 6; 1941, c. 259, s. 5; 1959, c. 352; 1983, c. 891, s. 2; 1997-69, s. 1; 2000-163, s. 2; 2007-487, s. 1; 2009-327, s. 6; 2010-31, s. 11.4(h).)

§ 130A-191. Possession and distribution of rabies vaccine.

It shall be unlawful for persons other than licensed veterinarians, certified rabies vaccinators and persons engaged in the distribution of rabies vaccine to possess rabies vaccine. Persons engaged in the distribution of vaccines may distribute, sell and offer to sell rabies vaccine only to licensed veterinarians and certified rabies vaccinators. (1987, c. 218.)

§ 130A-192. Animals not wearing required rabies vaccination tags.

(a)   The Animal Control Officer shall canvass the county to determine if there are any animals not wearing the required rabies vaccination tag. If an animal required to wear a tag is found not wearing one, the Animal Control Officer shall check to see if the owner's identification can be found on the animal. If the animal is wearing an owner identification tag with information enabling the owner of the animal to be contacted, or if the Animal Control Officer otherwise knows who the owner is, the Animal Control Officer shall notify the owner in writing to have the animal vaccinated against rabies and to produce the required rabies vaccination certificate to the Animal Control Officer within three days of the notification. If the animal is not wearing an owner identification tag and the Animal Control Officer does not otherwise know who the owner is, the Animal Control Officer may impound the animal. The duration of the impoundment of these animals shall be established by the county board of commissioners, but the duration shall not be less than 72 hours. During the impoundment period, the Animal Control Officer shall make a reasonable effort

256

to locate the owner of the animal. If the Animal Control Officer has access at no cost or at a reasonable cost to a microchip scanning device, the Animal Control Officer shall scan the animal and utilize any information that may be available through a microchip to locate the owner of the animal, if possible. If the animal is not reclaimed by its owner during the impoundment period, the animal shall be disposed of in one of the following manners: returned to the owner; adopted as a pet by a new owner; or put to death by a procedure approved by rules adopted by the Department of Agriculture and Consumer Services or, in the absence of such rules, by a procedure approved by the American Veterinary Medical Association, the Humane Society of the United States or of the American Humane Association.

(a1)   Before an animal may be put to death, it shall be made available for adoption as provided in G.S. 19A-32.1.

(a2)   Repealed by Session Laws 2013-377, s. 3, effective July 29, 2013.

(a3)   The Animal Control Officer shall maintain a record of all animals impounded under this section which shall include the date of impoundment, the length of impoundment, the method of disposal of the animal and the name of the person or institution to whom any animal has been released.

(b)   through (e) Repealed by Session Laws 2013-377, s. 3, effective July 29, 2013. (1935, c. 122, s. 8; 1983, c. 891, s. 2; 2009-304, s. 1; 2009-327, s. 7; 2013-377, s. 3.)

§ 130A-193. Vaccination and confinement of animals brought into this State.

(a)   Vaccination Required. - An animal brought into this State that is required to be vaccinated under this Part shall immediately be securely confined and shall be vaccinated against rabies within one week after entry. The animal shall remain confined for two weeks after vaccination.

(b)   Exceptions. - The provisions of subsection (a) shall not apply to:

(1)   An animal brought into this State for exhibition purposes if the animal is confined and not permitted to run at large.

(2)   An animal brought into this State accompanied by a certificate issued by a licensed veterinarian showing that the animal is apparently free from and has not been exposed to rabies and that the animal is currently vaccinated against rabies. (1935, c. 122, s. 11; 1983, c. 891, s. 2; 2009-327, s. 8.)

§ 130A-194. Quarantine of districts infected with rabies.

An area may be declared under quarantine against rabies by the local health director when the disease exists to the extent that the lives of persons are endangered. When quarantine is declared, each animal in the area that is required to be vaccinated under this Part shall be confined on the premises of the owner or in a veterinary hospital unless the animal is on a leash or under the control and in the sight of a responsible adult. (1935, c. 122, s. 12; 1941, c. 259, s. 9; 1949, c. 645, s. 3; 1953, c. 876, s. 8; 1957, c. 1357, s. 8; 1983, c. 891, s. 2; 2009-327, s. 9.)

§ 130A-195. Destroying stray or feral animals in quarantine districts.

When quarantine has been declared and stray or feral animals continue to run uncontrolled in the area, any peace officer or Animal Control Officer shall have the right, after reasonable effort has been made to apprehend the animals, to destroy the stray or feral animals and properly dispose of their bodies. (1935, c. 122, s. 13; 1953, c. 876, s. 9; 1983, c. 891, s. 2; 2009-327, s. 10.)

§ 130A-196. Notice and confinement of biting animals.

(a)   Notice. - When a person has been bitten by an animal required to be vaccinated under this Part, the person or parent, guardian or person standing in loco parentis of the person, and the person owning the animal or in control or possession of the animal shall notify the local health director immediately and give the name and address of the person bitten and the owner of the animal. If the animal that bites a person is a stray or feral animal, the local agency responsible for animal control shall make a reasonable attempt to locate the owner of the animal. If the owner cannot be identified within 72 hours of the event, the local health director may authorize the animal be euthanized, and the

258

head of the animal shall be immediately sent to the State Laboratory of Public Health for rabies diagnosis. If the event occurs on a weekend or State holiday the time period for owner identification shall be extended 24 hours.

A physician who attends a person bitten by an animal known to be a potential carrier of rabies shall report the incident within 24 hours to the local health director. The report must include the name, age, and sex of the person.

(b) Confinement. - When an animal required to be vaccinated under this Part bites a person, the animal shall be immediately confined for 10 days in a place designated by the local health director. The local health director may authorize a dog trained and used by a law enforcement agency to be released from confinement to perform official duties upon submission of proof that the dog has been vaccinated for rabies in compliance with this Part. After reviewing the circumstances of the particular case, the local health director may allow the owner to confine the animal on the owner's property. An owner who fails to confine an animal in accordance with the instructions of the local health director shall be guilty of a Class 2 misdemeanor. If the owner or the person who controls or possesses the animal that has bitten a person refuses to confine the animal as required by this subsection, the local health director may order seizure of the animal and its confinement for 10 days at the expense of the owner. (1935, c. 122, s. 17; 1941, c. 259, s. 11; 1953, c. 876, s. 13; 1957, c. 1357, s. 9; 1977, c. 628; 1983, c. 891, s. 2; 1985, c. 674; 1989, c. 298; 1993, c. 539, s. 950; 1994, Ex. Sess., c. 24, s. 14(c); 2009-327, s. 11.)

§ 130A-197. Infected animals to be destroyed; protection of vaccinated animals.

When the local health director reasonably suspects that an animal required to be vaccinated under this Part has been exposed to the saliva or nervous tissue of a proven rabid animal or animal reasonably suspected of having rabies that is not available for laboratory diagnosis, the animal shall be considered to have been exposed to rabies. An animal exposed to rabies shall be destroyed immediately by its owner, the county Animal Control Officer or a peace officer unless the animal has been vaccinated against rabies in accordance with this Part and the rules of the Commission more than 28 days prior to being exposed, and is given a booster dose of rabies vaccine within five days of the exposure. As an alternative to destruction, the animal may be quarantined at a facility approved by the local health director for a period up to six months, and under reasonable conditions imposed by the local health director. (1935, c. 122, s. 14; 1953, c. 876, s. 10; 1983, c. 891, s. 2; 2000-163, s. 4; 2009-327, s. 12.)

§ 130A-198. Confinement.

A person who owns or has possession of an animal which is suspected of having rabies shall immediately notify the local health director or county Animal Control Officer and shall securely confine the animal in a place designated by the local health director. The animal shall be confined for a period of 10 days. Other animals may be destroyed at the discretion of the State Public Health Veterinarian. (1935, c. 122, s. 15; c. 344; 1941, c. 259, s. 10; 1953, c. 876, s. 11; 1983, c. 891, s. 2; 2009-327, s. 13.)

§ 130A-199. Rabid animals to be destroyed; heads to be sent to State Laboratory of Public Health.

An animal diagnosed as having rabies by a licensed veterinarian shall be destroyed and its head sent to the State Laboratory of Public Health. The heads of all animals that die during a confinement period required by this Part shall be immediately sent to the State Laboratory of Public Health for rabies diagnosis. (1935, c. 122, s. 16; 1953, c. 876, s. 12; 1973, c. 476, s. 128; 1983, c. 891, s. 2; 2009-327, s. 14.)

§ 130A-200. Confinement or leashing of vicious animals.

A local health director may declare an animal to be vicious and a menace to the public health when the animal has attacked a person causing bodily harm without being teased, molested, provoked, beaten, tortured or otherwise harmed. When an animal has been declared to be vicious and a menace to the public health, the local health director shall order the animal to be confined to its owner's property. However, the animal may be permitted to leave its owner's property when accompanied by a responsible adult and restrained on a leash. (1935, c. 122, s. 18; 1953, c. 876, s. 14; 1983, c. 891, s. 2.)

§ 130A-201. Rabies emergency.

A local health director in whose county or district rabies is found in the wild animal population as evidenced by a positive diagnosis of rabies in the past year in any wild animal, except a bat, may petition the State Health Director to declare a rabies emergency in the county or district. In determining whether a rabies emergency exists, the State Health Director shall consult with the Public Health Veterinarian and the State Agriculture Veterinarian and may consult with any other source of veterinary expertise the State Health Director deems advisable. Upon finding that a rabies emergency exists in a county or district, the State Health Director shall petition the Executive Director of the Wildlife Resources Commission to develop a plan pursuant to G.S. 113-291.2(a1) to reduce the threat of rabies exposure to humans and domestic animals by foxes, raccoons, skunks, or bobcats in the county or district. Upon determination by the State Health Director that the rabies emergency no longer exists for a county or district, the State Health Director shall immediately notify the Executive Director of the Wildlife Resources Commission. (1997-402, s. 1.)

§ 130A-202. Reserved for future codification purposes.

§ 130A-203. Reserved for future codification purposes.

§ 130A-204. Reserved for future codification purposes.

Article 7.

Chronic Disease.

Part 1. Cancer.

§ 130A-205. Administration of program; rules.

(a)   The Department shall establish and administer a program for the prevention and detection of cancer and the care and treatment of persons with cancer.

(b)   The Commission shall adopt rules necessary to implement the program. (1945, c. 1050, s. 1; 1957, c. 1357, s. 1; 1973, c. 476, s. 128; 1981, c. 345, s. 2; 1983, c. 891, s. 2.)

§ 130A-206. Financial aid for diagnosis and treatment.

The Department shall provide financial aid for diagnosis and treatment of cancer to indigent citizens of this State having or suspected of having cancer. The Department may make facilities for diagnosis and treatment of cancer available to all citizens. Reimbursement shall only be provided for diagnosis and treatment performed in a medical facility which meets the minimum requirements for cancer control established by the Commission. The Commission shall adopt rules specifying the terms and conditions by which the patients may receive financial aid. (1945, c. 1050, s. 2; 1957, c. 1357, s. 1; 1973, c. 476, s. 128; 1981, c. 345, s. 2; 1983, c. 891, s. 2.)

§ 130A-207. Cancer clinics.

The Department is authorized to provide financial aid to sponsored cancer clinics in medical facilities and local health departments. The Commission shall adopt rules to establish minimum standards for the staffing, equipment and operation of the clinics sponsored by the Department. (1945, c. 1050, s. 3; 1949, c. 1071; 1957, c. 1357, s. 1; 1973, c. 476, s. 128; 1981, c. 345, s. 2; 1983, c. 891, s. 2.)

§ 130A-208. Central cancer registry.

A central cancer registry is established within the Department. The central cancer registry shall compile, tabulate and preserve statistical, clinical and other reports and records relating to the incidence, treatment and cure of cancer received pursuant to this Part. The central cancer registry shall provide assistance and consultation for public health work. (1945, c. 1050, s. 7; 1957, c. 1357, s. 1; 1973, c. 476, s. 128; 1981, c. 345, s. 2; 1983, c. 891, s. 2.)

§ 130A-209. Incidence reporting of cancer; charge for collection if failure to report.

(a)   By no later than October 1, 2014, all health care facilities and health care providers that detect, diagnose, or treat cancer or benign brain or central nervous system tumors shall submit by electronic transmission a report to the central cancer registry each diagnosis of cancer or benign brain or central nervous system tumors in any person who is screened, diagnosed, or treated by the facility or provider. The electronic transmission of these reports shall be in a format prescribed by the United States Department of Health and Human Services, Centers for Disease Control and Prevention, National Program of Cancer Registries. The reports shall be made within six months after diagnosis. Diagnostic, demographic and other information as prescribed by the rules of the Commission shall be included in the report.

(b)   If a health care facility or health care provider fails to report as required under this section, then the central cancer registry may conduct a site visit to the facility or provider or be provided access to the information from the facility or provider and report it in the appropriate format. The Commission may adopt rules requiring that the facility or provider reimburse the registry for its cost to access and report the information in an amount not to exceed one hundred dollars ($100.00) per case. Thirty days after the expiration of the six-month period for reporting under subsection (a) of this section, the registry shall send notice to each facility and provider that has not submitted a report as of that date that failure to file a report within 30 days shall result in collection of the data by the registry and liability for reimbursement imposed under this section. Failure to receive or send the notice required under this section shall not be construed as a waiver of the reporting requirement. For good cause, the central cancer registry may grant an additional 30 days for reporting.

(c)   As used in this section, the term:

(1)   "Health care facility" or "facility" means any hospital, clinic, or other facility that is licensed to administer medical treatment or the primary function of which is to provide medical treatment in this State. The term includes health care facility laboratories and independent pathology laboratories;

(2)   "Health care provider" or "provider" means any person who is licensed or certified to practice a health profession or occupation under Chapter 90 of the General Statutes and who diagnoses or treats cancer or benign brain or central nervous system tumors. (1949, c. 499; 1957, c. 1357, s. 1; 1973, c. 476, s. 128; 1981, c. 345, s. 2; 1983, c. 891, s. 2; 1999-33, s. 1; 2005-373, s. 1; 2013-378, s. 9.)

§ 130A-210. Repealed by Session Laws 1999-33, s. 2.

§ 130A-211. Immunity of persons who report cancer.

A person who makes a report pursuant to G.S. 130A-209 to the central cancer registry shall be immune from any civil or criminal liability that might otherwise be incurred or imposed. (1967, c. 859; 1969, c. 5; 1973, c. 476, s. 128; 1981, c. 345, s. 2; 1983, c. 891, s. 2; 2013-321, s. 2.)

§ 130A-212. Confidentiality of records.

The clinical records or reports of individual patients shall be confidential and shall not be public records open to inspection. The Commission shall provide by rule for the use of the records and reports for medical research. (1981, c. 345, s. 2; 1983, c. 891, s. 2.)

§ 130A-213. Cancer Committee of the North Carolina Medical Society.

In implementing this Part, the Department shall consult with the Cancer Committee of the North Carolina Medical Society. The Committee shall consist of at least one physician from each congressional district. Any proposed rules or reports affecting the operation of the cancer control program shall be reviewed by the Committee for comment prior to adoption. (1945, c. 1050, s. 9; 1957, c. 1357, s. 1; 1973, c. 476, s. 128; 1981, c. 345, s. 2; 1983, c. 891, s. 2.)

§ 130A-214. Duties of Department.

The Department shall study the entire problem of cancer including its causes, including environmental factors; prevention; detection; diagnosis and treatment. The Department shall provide or assure the availability of cancer educational resources to health professionals, interested private or public organizations and the public. (1967, c. 186, s. 2; 1973, c. 476, s. 128; 1981, c. 345, s. 2; 1983, c. 891, s. 2.)

§ 130A-215. Reports.

The Secretary shall make a report to the Governor and the General Assembly specifying the activities of the cancer control program and its budget. The report shall be made to the Governor annually and to the General Assembly biennially. (1981, c. 345, s. 2; 1983, c. 891, s. 2.)

§ 130A-215.1: Reserved for future codification purposes.

§ 130A-215.2: Reserved for future codification purposes.

§ 130A-215.3: Reserved for future codification purposes.

§ 130A-215.4: Reserved for future codification purposes.

§ 130A-215.5. Communication of mammographic breast density information to patients.

(a)   All health care facilities that perform mammography examinations shall include in the summary of the mammography report, required by federal law to be provided to a patient, information that identifies the patient's individual breast density classification based on the Breast Imaging Reporting and Data System established by the American College of Radiology. If the facility determines that a patient has heterogeneously or extremely dense breasts, the summary of the mammography report shall include the following notice:

"Your mammogram indicates that you may have dense breast tissue. Dense breast tissue is relatively common and is found in more than forty percent (40%) of women. The presence of dense tissue may make it more difficult to detect abnormalities in the breast and may be associated with an increased risk of breast cancer. We are providing this information to raise your awareness of this important factor and to encourage you to talk with your physician about this and other breast cancer risk factors. Together, you can decide which screening options are right for you. A report of your results was sent to your physician."

(b)   Patients who receive diagnostic or screening mammograms may be directed to informative material about breast density. This informative material may include the American College of Radiology's most current brochure on the subject of breast density. (2013-321, s. 1.)

265

§ 130A-216. Cancer patient navigation program.

The Department shall establish a cancer patient navigation program under the Breast and Cervical Cancer Control Program. The purpose of the program shall be to provide education about and assistance with the management of cancer. At a minimum, the program shall do the following:

(1)   Initially serve breast and cervical cancer patients statewide with the intent of future expansion to all other cancer types.

(2)   Employ a multidisciplinary team approach to assist cancer patients in identifying and gaining access to available health care, financial and legal assistance, transportation, psychological support, and other related issues.

(3)   Work with an existing cancer service agency that is not affiliated with a particular health care institution so that program clients may have access to any cancer health care facility in the State. (2009-502, s. 1.)

§ 130A-217. Reserved for future codification purposes.

§ 130A-218. Reserved for future codification purposes.

§ 130A-219. Reserved for future codification purposes.

Part 2. Chronic Renal Disease.

§ 130A-220. Department to establish program.

(a)   The Department shall establish and administer a program for the detection and prevention of chronic renal disease and the care and treatment of persons with chronic renal disease. The program may include:

(1)   Development of services for the prevention of chronic renal disease;

(2)   Development and expansion of services for the care and treatment of persons with chronic renal disease, including techniques which will have a lifesaving effect in the care and treatment of those persons;

(3)   Provision of financial assistance on the basis of need for diagnosis and treatment of persons with chronic renal disease;

(4)   Equipping dialysis and transplantation centers; and

(5)   Development of an education program for physicians, hospitals, local health departments and the public concerning chronic renal disease.

(b)   The Commission is authorized to adopt rules necessary to implement the program. (1971, c. 1027, s. 1; 1973, c. 476, s. 128; 1983, c. 891, s. 2.)

Part 3. Glaucoma and Diabetes.

§ 130A-221. Department authorized to establish program.

(a)   The Department may establish and administer a program for the detection and prevention of glaucoma and diabetes and the care and treatment of persons with glaucoma and diabetes. The program may include:

(1)   Education of patients, health care personnel and the public;

(2)   Development and expansion of services to persons with glaucoma and diabetes; and

(3)   Provision of supplies, equipment and medication for detection and control of glaucoma and diabetes.

(b)   The Commission is authorized to adopt rules necessary to implement the program. (1977, 2nd Sess., c. 1257, s. 1; 1983, c. 891, s. 2; 1997-137, s. 2.)

§ 130A-221.1. Coordination of diabetes programs.

(a)   The Division of Medical Assistance and the Diabetes Prevention and Control Branch of the Division of Public Health, within the Department of Health and Human Services; in addition to the State Health Plan Division within the Department of State Treasurer; shall work collaboratively to each develop plans to reduce the incidence of diabetes, to improve diabetes care, and to control the complications associated with diabetes. Each entity's plans shall be tailored to the population the entity serves and must establish measurable goals and objectives.

(b)   On or before December 1 of each even-numbered year, the entities referenced in subsection (a) of this section shall collectively submit a report to the Joint Legislative Oversight Committee on Health and Human Services and the Fiscal Research Division. The report shall provide the following:

(1)   An assessment of the financial impact that each type of diabetes has on each entity and collectively on the State. This assessment shall include: the number of individuals with diabetes served by the entity, the cost of diabetes prevention and control programs implemented by the entity, the financial toll or impact diabetes and related complications places on the program, and the financial toll or impact diabetes and related complications places on each program in comparison to other chronic diseases and conditions.

(2)   A description and an assessment of the effectiveness of each entity's programs and activities implemented to prevent and control diabetes. For each program and activity, the assessment shall document the source and amount of funding provided to the entity, including funding provided by the State.

(3)   A description of the level of coordination that exists among the entities referenced in subsection (a) of this section, as it relates to activities, programs, and messaging to manage, treat, and prevent all types of diabetes and the complications from diabetes.

(4)   The development of and revisions to detailed action plans for preventing and controlling diabetes and related complications. The plans shall identify proposed action steps to reduce the impact of diabetes, pre-diabetes, and related diabetic complications; identify expected outcomes for each action step; and establish benchmarks for preventing and controlling diabetes.

(5)   A detailed budget identifying needs, costs, and resources required to implement the plans identified in subdivision (4) of this subsection, including a list of actionable items for consideration by the Committee. (2013-192, s. 1.)

Part 4. Arthritis.

§ 130A-222. Department to establish program.

(a)   The Department shall establish and administer a program for the detection and prevention of arthritis and the care and treatment of persons with arthritis. The purpose of the program shall be:

(1)   To improve professional education for physicians and allied health professionals including nurses, physical and occupational therapists and social workers;

(2)   To conduct programs of public education and information;

(3)   To provide detection and treatment programs and services for the at-risk population of this State;

(4)   To utilize the services available at the State medical schools, existing arthritis rehabilitation centers and existing local arthritis clinics and agencies;

(5)   To develop an arthritis outreach clinical system;

(6)   To develop and train personnel at clinical facilities for diagnostic work-up, laboratory analysis and consultations with primary physicians regarding patient management; and

(7)   To develop the epidemiologic studies to determine frequency and distribution of the disease.

(b)   The Commission is authorized to adopt rules necessary to implement the program. (1979, c. 996, s. 2; 1983, c. 891, s. 2.)

§ 130A-222.1: Reserved for future codification purposes.

§ 130A-222.2: Reserved for future codification purposes.

§ 130A-222.3: Reserved for future codification purposes.

§ 130A-222.4: Reserved for future codification purposes.

Part 4A. Chronic Care Coordination.

§ 130A-222.5. Department to coordinate chronic care initiatives.

The Department's Divisions of Public Health and Medical Assistance and the Division in the Department of State Treasurer responsible for the State Health Plan for Teachers and State Employees shall collaborate to reduce the incidence of chronic disease and improve chronic care coordination within the State by doing all of the following:

(1)   Identifying goals and benchmarks for the reduction of chronic disease.

(2)   Developing wellness and prevention plans specifically tailored to each of the Divisions.

(3)   Submitting an annual report on or before January 1 of each odd-numbered year to the Senate Appropriations Committee on Health and Human Services, the House Appropriations Subcommittee on Health and Human Services, the Joint Legislative Oversight Committee on Health and Human Services, and the Fiscal Research Division that includes at least all of the following:

a.   The financial impact and magnitude of the chronic health conditions in this State that are most likely to cause death and disability, including, but not limited to, chronic cardiovascular disease, oncology, stroke, chronic lung disease, and chronic metabolic disease. As used in this subdivision, the term "chronic cardiovascular disease" includes heart disease and hypertension; the term "chronic metabolic disease" includes diabetes and obesity; and the term "chronic lung disease" means asthma and chronic obstructive pulmonary disease.

b.   An assessment of the benefits derived from wellness and prevention programs and activities implemented within the State with the goal of coordinating chronic care. This assessment shall include a breakdown of the amount of all State, federal, and other funds appropriated to the Department for wellness and prevention programs and activities for the detection, prevention, and treatment of persons with multiple chronic health conditions, at least one of which is a condition identified in sub-subdivision a. of this subdivision.

270

c.   A description of the level of coordination among the Divisions of Public Health and Medical Assistance and the Division in the Department of State Treasurer responsible for the State Health Plan for Teachers and State Employees with respect to activities, programs, and public education on the prevention, treatment, and management of the chronic health conditions identified in sub-subdivision a. of this subdivision.

d.   Detailed action plans for care coordination of multiple chronic health conditions in the same patient, including a range of recommended legislative actions. The action plans shall identify proposed action steps to reduce the financial impact of the chronic health conditions identified in sub-subdivision a. of this subdivision, including (i) adjustment of hospital readmission rates, (ii) development of transitional care plans, (iii) implementation of comprehensive medication management, as described by the Patient-Centered Primary Care Collaborative, to help patients achieve improved clinical and therapeutic outcomes, and (iv) adoption of standards related to quality that are publicly reported evidence-based measures endorsed through a multistakeholder process such as the National Quality Forum. The action plans shall also identify expected outcomes of these proposed action steps during the succeeding fiscal biennium and establish benchmarks for coordinating care and reducing the incidence of multiple chronic health conditions.

e.   A detailed budget identifying all costs associated with implementing the action plans identified in sub-subdivision d. of this subdivision. (2013-207, s. 2.)

Part 5. Adult Health.

§ 130A-223. Department to establish program.

(a)   The Department shall establish and administer a program for the prevention of diseases, disabilities and accidents that contribute significantly to mortality and morbidity among adults. The program may also provide for the care and treatment of persons with these diseases or disabilities.

(b)   The Commission is authorized to adopt rules necessary to implement the program. (1983, c. 891, s. 2.)

Part 5A. Men's Health.

271

§ 130A-223.1. Department to establish strategies for improving men's health.

The Department of Health and Human Services, Division of Public Health, Chronic Disease and Injury Prevention Section, shall work to expand the State's attention and focus on the prevention of disease and improvement in the quality of life for men over their entire lifespan. The Department shall develop strategies for achieving these goals, which shall include, but not be limited to, all of the following:

(1)   Developing a strategic plan to improve health care services.

(2)   Building public health awareness.

(3)   Developing initiatives within existing programs.

(4)   Pursuing federal and State funding for the screening, early detection, and treatment of prostate cancer and other diseases affecting men's health. (2013-360, s. 12E.7.)

Part 6. Injury Prevention.

§ 130A-224. Department to establish program.

To protect and enhance the public health, welfare, and safety, the Department shall establish and administer a comprehensive statewide injury prevention program. The Department shall designate the Division of Public Health as the lead agency for injury prevention activities. The Division of Public Health shall:

(1)   Develop a comprehensive State plan for injury prevention;

(2)   Maintain an injury prevention program that includes data collection, surveillance, and education and promotes injury control activities; and

(3)   Develop collaborative relationships with other State agencies and private and community organizations to establish programs promoting injury prevention. (2007-187, s. 3.)

§ 130A-225. Reserved for future codification purposes.

§ 130A-226. Reserved for future codification purposes.

Article 8.

Sanitation.

Part 1. General.

§ 130A-227. Department to establish program; definitions.

(a)   For the purpose of promoting a safe and healthful environment and developing corrective measures required to minimize environmental health hazards, the Department shall establish a sanitation program. The Department shall employ environmental engineers, sanitarians, soil scientists and other scientific personnel necessary to carry out the sanitation provisions of this Chapter and the rules of the Commission.

(b)   The following definitions shall apply throughout this Article:

(1)   "Department" means the Department of Health and Human Services.

(2)   "Secretary" means the Secretary of Health and Human Services. (1983, c. 891, s. 2; 1997-443, s. 11A.77A; 2011-145, s. 13.3(aaa).)

§ 130A-228: Repealed.

§ 130A-229: Repealed.

Part 3. Sanitation of Scallops, Shellfish and Crustacea.

§§ 130A-230, 130A-231: Repealed by Session Laws 2011-145, s. 13.3(ppp), effective July 1, 2011. See note for recodification of former G.S. 130A-230.

§ 130A-232: Reserved for future codification purposes.

Part 3A. Monitor Water Quality of Coastal Fishing and Recreation Waters.

§ 130A-233: Repealed by Session Laws 2011-145, s. 13.3(rrr), effective July 1, 2011. See note for recodification of former G.S. 130A-233.1.

§ 130A-233.1: Repealed by Session Laws 2011-145, s. 13.3(rrr), effective July 1, 2011. See note for recodification of former G.S. 130A-233.1.

§ 130A-233.2: Repealed by Session Laws 2011-145, s. 13.3(rrr), effective July 1, 2011. See note for recodification of former G.S. 130A-233.1.

§ 130A-234. Reserved for future codification purposes.

Part 4. Institutions and Schools.

§ 130A-235. Regulation of sanitation in institutions; setback requirements applicable to certain water supply wells.

(a)   For protection of the public health, the Commission shall adopt rules to establish sanitation requirements for all institutions and facilities at which individuals are provided room or board and for which a license to operate is required to be obtained or a certificate for payment is obtained from the Department. The rules shall also apply to facilities that provide room and board to individuals but are exempt from licensure under G.S. 131D-10.4(1). No other State agency may adopt rules to establish sanitation requirements for these institutions and facilities. The Department shall issue a license to operate or a certificate for payment to such an institution or facility only upon compliance with all applicable sanitation rules of the Commission, and the Department may suspend or revoke a license or a certificate for payment for violation of these rules. In adopting rules pursuant to this section, the Commission shall define categories of standards to which such institutions and facilities shall be subject and shall establish criteria for the placement of any such institution or facility into one of the categories. This section shall not apply to State institutions and facilities subject to inspection under G.S. 130A-5(10). This section shall not apply to a single-family dwelling that is used for a family foster home or a therapeutic foster home, as those terms are defined in G.S. 131D-10.2.

(a1)   Notwithstanding any law, rule, or policy to the contrary, the frequency of food service inspections in nursing homes or nursing home beds licensed under Part 1 of Article 5 of Chapter 131E of the General Statutes or Part 1 of Article 6

274

of Chapter 131E of the General Statutes that are also certified by the Centers for Medicare and Medicaid Services shall be reduced to a minimum of two inspections per year until October 1, 2012, and thereafter reduced to a minimum of one inspection per year, if the facility achieves a grade "A" sanitation score. If the facility receives a grade "B" or lower on its annual food service inspection, the county may conduct inspections until the food service operation achieves a grade "A" sanitation score. Nothing in this section prohibits the county from conducting an evaluation or inspection in response to a complaint or in the interest of public safety.

(b)   Rules that establish a minimum distance from a building foundation for a water supply well shall provide that an institution or facility located in a single-family dwelling served by a water supply well that is located closer to a building foundation than the minimum distance specified in the rules may be licensed or approved if the results of water testing meet or exceed standards established by the Commission and there are no other potential health hazards associated with the well. At the time of application for licensure or approval, water shall be sampled and tested for pesticides, nitrates, and bacteria. Thereafter, water shall be sampled and tested at intervals determined by the Commission but not less than annually. A registered sanitarian or other health official who is qualified by training and experience shall collect the water samples as required by this subsection and may examine the well location to determine if there are other potential health hazards associated with the well. A well shall comply with all other applicable sanitation requirements established by the Commission.

(c)   The Department may suspend or revoke a license or approval for a violation of this section or rules adopted by the Commission. (1945, c. 829, s. 1; 1957, c. 1357, s. 1; 1973, c. 476, s. 128; 1983, c. 891, s. 2; 1987, c. 543, s. 1; 1989, c. 727, s. 143; 1997-443, s. 11A.79; 1998-136, s. 1; 2001-109, s. 1; 2001-487, s. 84(a); 2011-226, s. 1.)

§ 130A-236. Regulation of sanitation in schools.

For the protection of the public health, the Commission shall adopt rules to establish sanitation requirements for public, private and religious schools. The rules shall address, but not be limited to, the cleanliness of floors, walls, ceilings, storage spaces and other areas; adequacy of lighting, ventilation, water supply, toilet and lavatory facilities; sewage collection, treatment and disposal facilities; and solid waste disposal. The Department shall inspect schools at least annually. The Department shall submit written inspection reports of public schools to the State Board of Education and written inspection reports of private and religious schools to the Department of Administration. (1973, c. 1239, s. 1; 1983, c. 891, s. 2; 1993, c. 522, s. 11.)

§ 130A-237. Corrective action.

A principal or administrative head of a public, private, or religious school shall immediately take action to correct conditions that do not satisfy the sanitation rules. (1973, c. 1239, s. 2; 1983, c. 891, s. 2; 1993, c. 262, s. 6.)

§ 130A-238: Repealed.

§ 130A-239: Repealed.

§ 130A-240: Repealed.

§ 130A-241: Repealed.

§ 130A-242: Repealed.

§ 130A-243: Repealed.

§ 130A-244: Repealed.

§ 130A-245: Repealed.

§ 130A-246: Repealed.

Part 6. Regulation of Food and Lodging Facilities.

§ 130A-247. Definitions.

The following definitions shall apply throughout this Part:

(1)   "Establishment" means (i) an establishment that prepares or serves drink, (ii) an establishment that prepares or serves food, (iii) an establishment

276

that provides lodging, (iv) a bed and breakfast inn, or (v) an establishment that prepares and sells meat food products as defined in G.S. 106-549.15(14) or poultry products as defined in G.S. 106-549.51(26).

(1a)   "Permanent house guest" means a person who receives room or board for periods of a week or longer. The term includes visitors of the permanent house guest.

(2)   "Private club" means an organization that (i) maintains selective members, is operated by the membership, does not provide food or lodging for pay to anyone who is not a member or a member's guest, and is either incorporated as a nonprofit corporation in accordance with Chapter 55A of the General Statutes or is exempt from federal income tax under the Internal Revenue Code as defined in G.S. 105-130.2(1) or (ii) meets the definition of a private club set forth in G.S. 18B-1000(5).

(3)   "Regular boarder" means a person who receives food for periods of a week or longer.

(4)   "Establishment that prepares or serves drink" means a business or other entity that prepares or serves beverages made from raw apples or potentially hazardous beverages made from other raw fruits or vegetables or that otherwise puts together, portions, sets out, or hands out drinks for human consumption.

(5)   "Establishment that prepares or serves food" means a business or other entity that cooks, puts together, portions, sets out, or hands out food for human consumption.

(5a)   "Bed and breakfast home" means a business in a private home of not more than eight guest rooms that offers bed and breakfast accommodations for a period of less than one week and that meets all of the following criteria:

a.   Does not serve food or drink to the general public for pay.

b.   Serves the breakfast meal, the lunch meal, the dinner meal, or a combination of all or some of these three meals, only to overnight guests of the home.

c.   Includes the price of any meals served in the room rate.

277

d.   Is the permanent residence of the owner or the manager of the business.

(6)   "Bed and breakfast inn" means a business of not more than 12 guest rooms that offers bed and breakfast accommodations to at least nine but not more than 23 persons per night for a period of less than one week, and that:

a.   Does not serve food or drink to the general public for pay;

b.   Serves only the breakfast meal, and that meal is served only to overnight guests of the business;

c.   Includes the price of breakfast in the room rate; and

d.   Is the permanent residence of the owner or the manager of the business.

(7)   "Limited food services establishment" means an establishment as described in G.S. 130A-248(a4), with food handling operations that are restricted by rules adopted by the Commission pursuant to G.S. 130A-248(a4) and that prepares or serves food only in conjunction with amateur athletic events.

(8)   "Temporary food establishment" means an establishment not otherwise exempted from this part pursuant to G.S. 130A-250 that (i) prepares or serves food, (ii) operates for a period of time not to exceed 21 days in one location, and (iii) is affiliated with and endorsed by a transitory fair, carnival, circus, festival, or public exhibition. (1983, c. 891, s. 2; 1987, c. 367; 1991, c. 733, s. 1; 1993, c. 262, s. 1; c. 513, s. 12; 1995, c. 123, s. 12; c. 507, s. 26.8(f); 1999-247, ss. 3, 4; 2013-360, s. 12E.1(a); 2013-413, ss. 7, 11(a).)

§ 130A-248. Regulation of food and lodging establishments.

(a)   For the protection of the public health, the Commission shall adopt rules governing the sanitation of establishments that prepare or serve drink or food for pay and establishments that prepare and sell meat food products or poultry products. However, any establishment that prepares or serves food or drink to the public, regardless of pay, shall be subject to the provisions of this Article if the establishment that prepares or serves food or drink holds an ABC permit, as defined in G.S. 18B-101, meets any of the definitions in G.S. 18B-1000, and does not meet the definition of a private club as provided in G.S. 130A-247(2).

278

(a1)   For the protection of the public health, the Commission shall adopt rules governing the sanitation of hotels, motels, tourist homes, and other establishments that provide lodging for pay.

(a2)   For the protection of the public health, the Commission shall adopt rules governing the sanitation of bed and breakfast homes, as defined in G.S. 130A-247, and rules governing the sanitation of bed and breakfast inns, as defined in G.S. 130A-247. In carrying out this function, the Commission shall adopt requirements that are the least restrictive so as to protect the public health and not unreasonably interfere with the operation of bed and breakfast homes and bed and breakfast inns.

(a3)   The rules adopted by the Commission pursuant to subsections (a), (a1), and (a2) of this section shall address, but not be limited to, the following:

(1)   Sanitation requirements for cleanliness of floors, walls, ceilings, storage spaces, utensils, ventilation equipment, and other areas and items;

(2)   Requirements for:

a.   Lighting and water supply;

b.   Wastewater collection, treatment, and disposal facilities; and

c.   Lavatory and toilet facilities, food protection, and waste disposal;

(3)   The cleaning and bactericidal treatment of eating and drinking utensils and other food-contact surfaces. A requirement imposed under this subdivision to sanitize multiuse eating and drinking utensils and other food-contact surfaces does not apply to utensils and surfaces provided in the guest room of the lodging unit for guests to prepare food while staying in the guest room.

(3a)   The appropriate and reasonable use of gloves or utensils by employees who handle unwrapped food;

(4)   The methods of food preparation, transportation, catering, storage, and serving;

(5)   The health of employees;

(6)   Animal and vermin control; and

279

(7)   The prohibition against the offering of unwrapped food samples to the general public unless the offering and acceptance of the samples are continuously supervised by an agent of the entity preparing or offering the samples or by an agent of the entity on whose premises the samples are made available. As used in this subdivision, "food samples" means unwrapped food prepared and made available for sampling by and without charge to the general public for the purpose of promoting the food made available for sampling. This subdivision does not apply to unwrapped food prepared and offered in buffet, cafeteria, or other style in exchange for payment by the general public or by the person or entity arranging for the preparation and offering of such unwrapped food. This subdivision shall not apply to open air produce markets nor to farmer market facilities operated on land owned or leased by the State of North Carolina or any local government.

The rules shall contain a system for grading establishments, such as Grade A, Grade B, and Grade C. The rules shall be written in a manner that promotes consistency in both the interpretation and application of the grading system.

(a4)   For the protection of the public health, the Commission shall adopt rules governing the sanitation of limited food service establishments. In adopting the rules, the Commission shall not limit the number of days that limited food service establishments may operate. Limited food service establishment permits shall be issued only to political subdivisions of the State, establishments operated by volunteers that prepare or serve food in conjunction with amateur athletic events, or for establishments operated by organizations that are exempt from federal income tax under section 501(c)(3) or section 501(c)(4) of the Internal Revenue Code.

(a5)   The Department of Health and Human Services may grant a variance from rules adopted pursuant to this section in accordance with the United States Food and Drug Administration Food Code 2009 if the Department determines that the issuance of the variance will not result in a health hazard or nuisance condition.

(b)   No establishment shall commence or continue operation without a permit or transitional permit issued by the Department. The permit or transitional permit shall be issued to the owner or operator of the establishment and shall not be transferable. If the establishment is leased, the permit or transitional permit shall be issued to the lessee and shall not be transferable. If the location of an establishment changes, a new permit shall be obtained for the establishment. A permit shall be issued only when the establishment satisfies all of the requirements of the rules and the requirements of subsection (g) of this section. The Commission shall adopt rules establishing the requirements that must be met before a transitional permit may be issued, and the period for which a transitional permit may be issued. The Department may also impose conditions on the issuance of a permit or transitional permit in accordance with rules adopted by the Commission. A permit or transitional permit shall be immediately revoked in accordance with G.S. 130A-23(d) for failure of the establishment to maintain a minimum grade of C. A permit or transitional permit may otherwise be suspended or revoked in accordance with G.S. 130A-23.

(b1)   A permit shall expire one year after an establishment closes unless the permit is the subject of a contested case pursuant to Article 3 of Chapter 150B of the General Statutes.

(c)   If ownership of an establishment is transferred or the establishment is leased, the new owner or lessee shall apply for a new permit. The new owner or lessee may also apply for a transitional permit. A transitional permit may be issued upon the transfer of ownership or lease of an establishment to allow the correction of construction and equipment problems that do not represent an immediate threat to the public health. Upon issuance of a new permit or a transitional permit for an establishment, any previously issued permit for an establishment in that location becomes void.

(c1)   The Commission shall adopt rules governing the sanitation of pushcarts and mobile food units. A permitted restaurant or commissary shall serve as a base of operations for a pushcart. A mobile food unit shall meet all of the sanitation requirements of a permitted commissary or shall have a permitted restaurant or commissary that serves as its base of operation.

(d)   The Department shall charge each establishment subject to this section, except nutrition programs for the elderly administered by the Division of Aging and Adult Services of the Department of Health and Human Services, establishments that prepare and sell meat food products or poultry products, temporary food establishments, limited food services establishments, and public school cafeterias, a fee of one hundred twenty dollars ($120.00) for each permit issued. This fee shall be reassessed annually for permits that do not expire. The Commission shall adopt rules to implement this subsection. Fees collected under this subsection shall be used for State and local food, lodging, and institution sanitation programs and activities. No more than fifty dollars ($50.00) of each fee collected under this subsection may be used to support State health programs and activities.

281

(d1)   The Department shall charge a twenty-five dollar ($25.00) late payment fee to any establishment subject to this section, except nutrition programs for the elderly administered by the Division of Aging of the Department of Health and Human Services, establishments that prepare and sell meat food products or poultry products, temporary food establishments, limited food services establishments, and public school cafeterias, that fails to pay the fee required by subsection (d) of this section within 45 days after billing by the Department. The Department may, in accordance with G.S. 130A-23, suspend the permit of an establishment that fails to pay the required fee within 60 days after billing by the Department. The Department shall charge a reinstatement fee of one hundred fifty dollars ($150.00) to any establishment that requests reinstatement of its permit after the permit has been suspended. The Commission shall adopt rules to implement this subsection.

The clear proceeds of civil penalties collected pursuant to this subsection shall be remitted to the Civil Penalty and Forfeiture Fund in accordance with G.S. 115C-457.2.

(d2)   A local health department shall charge each temporary food establishment and each limited food services establishment a fee of seventy-five dollars ($75.00) for each permit issued. A local health department shall use all fees collected under this subsection for local food, lodging, and institution sanitation programs and activities.

(e)   In addition to the fees under subsection (d) of this section, the Department may charge a fee of two hundred fifty dollars ($250.00) for plan review of plans for prototype franchised or chain facilities for food establishments subject to this section. All of the fees collected under this subsection may be used to support the State food, lodging, and institution sanitation programs and activities under this Part.

(f)   Any local health department may charge a fee not to exceed two hundred fifty dollars ($250.00) for plan review by that local health department of plans for food establishments subject to this section that are not subject to subsection (e) of this section. All of the fees collected under this subsection may be used for local food, lodging, and institution sanitation programs and activities. No food establishment that pays a fee under subsection (e) of this section is liable for a fee under this subsection.

(g)   (Effective until October 1, 2014) All hotels, motels, tourist homes, and other establishments that provide lodging for pay shall install either a battery-

282

operated or electrical carbon monoxide detector in every enclosed space having a fossil fuel burning heater, appliance, or fireplace and in any enclosed space, including a sleeping room, that shares a common wall, floor, or ceiling with an enclosed space having a fossil fuel burning heater, appliance, or fireplace. Carbon monoxide detectors shall be listed by a nationally recognized testing laboratory that is OSHA-approved to test and certify to American National Standards Institute/Underwriters Laboratories Standards ANSI/UL2034 or ANSI/UL2075, and installed in accordance with either the standard of the National Fire Protection Association or the minimum protection designated in the manufacturer's instructions, which the establishment shall retain or provide as proof of compliance. A carbon monoxide detector may be combined with smoke detectors if the combined detector complies with the requirements of this subdivision for carbon monoxide alarms and ANSI/UL217 for smoke detectors.

(g)   (Effective October 1, 2014) All hotels, motels, tourist homes, and other establishments that provide lodging for pay shall have carbon monoxide detectors installed in every enclosed space having a fossil fuel burning heater, appliance, or fireplace and in any enclosed space, including a sleeping room, that shares a common wall, floor, or ceiling with an enclosed space having a fossil fuel burning heater, appliance, or fireplace. Carbon monoxide detectors shall be (i) listed by a nationally recognized testing laboratory that is OSHA-approved to test and certify to American National Standards Institute/Underwriters Laboratories Standards ANSI/UL2034 or ANSI/UL2075, (ii) installed in accordance with either the standard of the National Fire Protection Association or the minimum protection designated in the manufacturer's instructions, which the establishment shall retain or provide as proof of compliance, (iii) receive primary power from the building's wiring, where such wiring is served from a commercial source, and (iv) receive power from a battery when primary power is interrupted. A carbon monoxide detector may be combined with smoke detectors if the combined detector complies with the requirements of this subdivision for carbon monoxide alarms and ANSI/UL217 for smoke detectors. (1941, c. 309, s. 1; 1955, c. 1030, s. 1; 1957, c. 1214, s. 1; 1973, c. 476, s. 128; 1983, c. 891, s. 2; 1987, c. 438, s. 2; 1989, c. 551, ss. 1, 4; 1989 (Reg. Sess., 1990), c. 1064, s. 1; 1991, c. 226, s. 1; c. 656, ss. 1, 2; c. 733, s. 2; 1991 (Reg. Sess., 1992), c. 1039, s. 7; 1993, c. 262, s. 2; c. 346, s. 1; c. 513, s. 13; 1995, c. 123, s. 13(a)-(d); c. 507, s. 26.8(b), (g); 1997-367, s. 1; 1997-443, s. 11A.118(a); 1997-479, s. 1; 2002-126, ss. 29A.15(a), 29A.16; 2003-340, ss. 1.5, 3; 2005-276, s. 6.37(s); 2009-451, s. 13.2(a)-(c); 2009-484, s. 2(b); 2011-145, s. 31.11A(a); 2011-391, s. 61A; 2011-394, s. 15(b); 2012-142, s. 10.15; 2012-187, s. 16.2; 2013-360, s. 12E.1(b)-(d), (f); 2013-413, ss. 11(b), 19(b), (c).)

§ 130A-249. Inspections; report and grade card.

The Secretary may enter any establishment that is subject to the provisions of G.S. 130A-248 for the purpose of making inspections. The Secretary shall inspect each food service establishment at a frequency established by the Commission. In establishing a schedule for inspections, the Commission shall consider the risks to the population served by the establishment and the type of food or drink served by the establishment. The person responsible for the management or control of an establishment shall permit the Secretary to inspect every part of the establishment and shall render all aid and assistance necessary for the inspection. The Secretary shall leave a copy of the inspection form and a card or cards showing the grade of the establishment with the responsible person. The Secretary shall post the grade card in a conspicuous place as determined by the Secretary where it may be readily observed by the public upon entering the establishment or upon picking up food prepared inside but received and paid for outside the establishment through delivery windows or other delivery devices. If a single establishment has one or more outside delivery service stations and an internal delivery system, that establishment shall have a grade card posted where it may be readily visible upon entering the establishment and one posted where it may be readily visible in each delivery window or delivery device upon picking up the food outside the establishment. The grade card or cards shall not be removed by anyone, except by or upon the instruction of the Secretary. (1941, c. 309, s. 2; 1955, c. 1030, s. 2; 1973, c. 476, s. 128; 1983, c. 891, s. 2; 1987, c. 145; c. 189; 1989, c. 551, s. 2; 1993, c. 262, s. 3; 2005-386, s. 4.1.)

§ 130A-250. Exemptions.

The following shall be exempt from this Part:

(1)   Establishments that provide lodging described in G.S. 130A-248(a1) with four or fewer lodging units.

(2)   Condominiums.

(3)   Establishments that prepare or serve food or provide lodging to regular boarders or permanent houseguests only. However, the rules governing food sanitation adopted under G.S. 130A-248 apply to establishments that are not regulated under G.S. 130A-235 and that prepare or serve food for pay to 13 or more regular boarders or permanent houseguests who are disabled or who are 55 years of age or older. Establishments to which the rules governing food

284

sanitation are made applicable by this subdivision that are in operation as of 1 July 2000 may continue to use equipment and construction in use on that date if no imminent hazard exists. Replacement equipment for these establishments shall comply with the rules governing food sanitation adopted under G.S. 130A-248.

(4)   Private homes that occasionally offer lodging accommodations, which may include the providing of food, for two weeks or less to persons attending special events, provided these homes are not bed and breakfast homes or bed and breakfast inns.

(5)   Private clubs.

(6)   Curb markets operated by the State Agricultural Extension Service.

(7)   Establishments (i) that are incorporated as nonprofit corporations in accordance with Chapter 55A of the General Statutes or (ii) that are exempt from federal income tax under the Internal Revenue Code, as defined in G.S. 105-228.90, or (iii) that are political committees as defined in G.S. 163-278.6(14) and that prepare or serve food or drink for pay no more frequently than once a month for a period not to exceed two consecutive days, including establishments permitted pursuant to this Part when preparing or serving food or drink at a location other than the permitted locations. A nutrition program for the elderly that is administered by the Division of Aging of the Department of Health and Human Services and that prepares and serves food or drink on the premises where the program is located in connection with a fundraising event is exempt from this Part if food and drink are prepared and served no more frequently than one day each month.

(8)   Establishments that put together, portion, set out, or hand out only beverages that do not include those made from raw apples or potentially hazardous beverages made from raw fruits or vegetables, using single service containers that are not reused on the premises.

(9)   Establishments where meat food products or poultry products are prepared and sold and which are under inspection by the North Carolina Department of Agriculture and Consumer Services or the United States Department of Agriculture.

(10)   Markets that sell uncooked cured country ham or uncooked cured salted pork and that engage in minimal preparation such as slicing, weighing, or

285

wrapping the ham or pork, when this minimal preparation is the only activity that would otherwise subject these markets to regulation under this Part.

(11) Establishments that only set out or hand out beverages that are regulated by the North Carolina Department of Agriculture and Consumer Services in accordance with Article 12 of Chapter 106 of the General Statutes.

(12) Establishments that only set out or hand out food that is regulated by the North Carolina Department of Agriculture and Consumer Services in accordance with Article 12 of Chapter 106 of the General Statutes.

(13) Traditional country stores that sell uncooked sandwiches or similar food items and that engage in minimal preparation such as slicing bananas, spreading peanut butter, mixing and spreading pimiento cheese, and assembling these items into sandwiches, when this minimal preparation is the only activity that would otherwise subject these establishments to regulation under this Part. For the purposes of this subsection, traditional country stores means for-profit establishments that sell an assortment of goods, including prepackaged foods and beverages, and have been in continuous operation for at least 75 years.

(14) Bona fide cooking schools, defined for the purpose of this subdivision as cooking schools that (i) primarily provide courses or instruction on food preparation techniques that participants can replicate in their homes, (ii) prepare or serve food for cooking school participants during instructional time only, and (iii) do not otherwise prepare or serve food to the public. (1955, c. 1030, s. 4; 1957, c. 1214, s. 3; 1983, c. 884, ss. 1, 2; c. 891, s. 2; 1985 (Reg. Sess., 1986), c. 926; 1989, c. 551, s. 3; 1991, c. 733, s. 3; 1993, c. 262, s. 4; c. 513, s. 14; 1995, c. 123, s. 14; 1997-261, s. 86; 1999-13, s. 1; 1999-247, s. 5; 2000-82, s. 1; 2001-440, s. 4; 2010-180, s. 18; 2011-335, s. 1.)

Part 7. Mass Gatherings.

§ 130A-251. Legislative intent and purpose.

The intent and purpose of this Part is to provide for the protection of the public health, safety and welfare of those persons in attendance at mass gatherings and of those persons who reside near or are located in proximity to the sites of mass gatherings or are directly affected by them. (1971, c. 712, s. 1; 1983, c. 891, s. 2.)

§ 130A-252. Definition of mass gathering; applicability of Part.

(a)   For the purposes of this Part, "mass gathering" means a congregation or assembly of more than 5,000 people in an open space or open air for a period of more than 24 hours. A mass gathering shall include all congregations and assemblies organized or held for any purpose, but shall not include assemblies in permanent buildings or permanent structures designed or intended for use by a large number of people. To determine whether a congregation or assembly extends for more than 24 hours, the period shall begin when the people expected to attend are first permitted on the land where the congregation or assembly will be held and shall end when the people in attendance are expected to depart. To determine whether a congregation or assembly shall consist of more than 5,000 people, the number reasonably expected to attend, as determined from the promotion, advertisement and preparation for the congregation or assembly and from the attendance at prior congregations or assemblies of the same type, shall be considered.

(b)   The provisions of this Part do not apply to a permanent stadium with an adjacent campground that hosts an annual event that has, within the previous five years, attracted crowds in excess of 70,000 people. The term "stadium" includes speedways and dragways. (1971, c. 712, s. 1; 1973, c. 476, s. 128; 1983, c. 891, s. 2; 1999-3, s. 1; 1999-171, s. 1.)

§ 130A-253. Permit required; information report; revocation of permit.

(a)   No person shall organize, sponsor or hold any mass gathering unless a permit has been issued to the person by the Secretary under the provisions of this Part. A permit shall be required for each mass gathering and is not transferable.

(b)   A permit may be revoked by the Secretary at any time if the Secretary finds that the mass gathering is being or has been maintained or operated in violation of this Part. A permit may be revoked upon the request of the permittee or upon abandonment of the operation. A permit will otherwise expire upon satisfactory completion of the post-gathering cleanup following the close of the mass gathering.

(c)   The Secretary, upon information that a congregation or assembly of people which may constitute a mass gathering is being organized or promoted, may direct the organizer or promoter to submit within five calendar days an information report to the Department. The report shall contain the information required for an application for permit under G.S. 130A-254(b) and other information concerning the promotion, advertisement and preparation for the congregation or assembly and prior congregations or assemblies, as the Secretary deems necessary. The Secretary shall consider all available information including any report received and shall determine if the proposed congregation or assembly is a mass gathering. If the Secretary determines that a proposed congregation or assembly is a mass gathering, the Secretary shall notify the organizer or promoter to submit an application for permit at least 30 days prior to the commencement of the mass gathering. (1971, c. 712, s. 1; 1973, c. 476, s. 128; 1983, c. 891, s. 2.)

§ 130A-254. Application for permit.

(a)   Application for a permit for a mass gathering shall be made to the Secretary on a form and in a manner prescribed by the Secretary. The application shall be filed with the Secretary at least 30 days prior to the commencement of the mass gathering. A fee as prescribed by the Secretary, not to exceed one hundred dollars ($100.00), shall accompany the application.

(b)   The application shall contain the following information: identification of the applicant; identification of any other person or persons responsible for organizing, sponsoring or holding the mass gathering; the location of the proposed mass gathering; the estimated maximum number of persons reasonably expected to be in attendance at any time; the date or dates and the hours during which the mass gathering is to be conducted; and a statement as to the total time period involved.

(c)   The application shall be accompanied by an outline map of the area to be used, to approximate scale, showing the location of all proposed and existing privies or toilets; lavatory and bathing facilities; all water supply sources including lakes, ponds, streams, wells and storage tanks; all areas of assemblage; all camping areas; all food service areas; all garbage and refuse storage and disposal areas; all entrances and exits to public highways; and emergency ingress and egress roads.

(d)   The application shall be accompanied by additional plans, reports and information required by the Secretary as necessary to carry out the provisions of this Part.

(e)   A charge shall be levied by the Secretary to cover the cost of additional services, including police, fire and medical services, provided by the State or units of local government on account of the mass gathering. The Secretary shall reimburse the State or the units of local government for the additional services upon receipt of payment. (1971, c. 712, s. 1; 1973, c. 476, s. 128; 1983, c. 891, s. 2.)

§ 130A-255. Provisional permit; performance bond; liability insurance.

(a)   Within 15 days after the receipt of the application, the Secretary shall review the application and inspect the proposed site for the mass gathering. If it is likely that the requirements of this Part and the rules of the Commission can be met by the applicant, a provisional permit shall be issued.

(b)   The Secretary shall require the permittee within five days after issuance of the provisional permit to file with the Secretary a performance bond or other surety to be executed to the State in the amount of five thousand dollars ($5,000) for up to 10,000 persons and an additional one thousand dollars ($1,000) for each additional 5,000 persons or fraction reasonably estimated to attend the mass gathering. The bond shall be conditioned on full compliance with this Part and the rules of the Commission and shall be forfeitable upon noncompliance and a showing by the Secretary of injury, damage or other loss to the State or local governmental agencies caused by the noncompliance.

(c)   The permittee shall in addition file satisfactory evidence of public liability and property damage insurance in an amount determined by the Secretary to be reasonable, not to exceed one million dollars ($1,000,000) in amount, in relation to the risks and hazards involved in the proposed mass gathering. (1971, c. 712, s. 1; 1973, c. 476, s. 128; 1983, c. 891, s. 2.)

289

§ 130A-256. Issuance of permit; revocation; forfeiture of bond; cancellation.

(a)   If, upon inspection by the Secretary five days prior to the starting date of the mass gathering, or earlier upon request of the permittee, the required facilities are found to be in place, satisfactory arrangements are found to have been made for required services, the charge for additional services levied in accordance with G.S. 130A-254(e) has been paid and other applicable provisions of this Part and the rules of the Commission are found to have been met, the Secretary shall issue a permit for the mass gathering. If, upon inspection, the facilities, arrangements or other provisions are not satisfactory, the provisional permit shall be revoked and no permit shall be issued.

(b)   Upon revocation of either the provisional permit or the permit, the permittee shall immediately announce cancellation of the mass gathering in as effective a manner as is reasonably possible including, but not limited to, the use or whatever methods were used for advertising or promoting the mass gathering.

(c)   If the provisional permit or the permit is revoked prior to or during the mass gathering, the Secretary may order the permittee to install facilities and make arrangements necessary to accommodate persons who may nevertheless attend or be present at the mass gathering despite its cancellation and to restore the site to a safe and sanitary condition. In the event the permittee fails to comply with the order of the Secretary, the Secretary may immediately proceed to install facilities and make other arrangements and provisions for cleanup as may be minimally required in the interest of public health and safety, utilizing any State and local funds and resources as may be available.

(d)   If the Secretary installs facilities or makes arrangements or provisions for cleanup pursuant to subsection (c), the Secretary may apply to a court of competent jurisdiction prior to or within 60 days after the action to order forfeiture of the permittee's performance bond or surety for violation of this Part or the rules of the Commission. The court may order that the proceeds shall be applied to the extent necessary to reimburse State and local governmental agencies for expenditures made pursuant to the action taken by the Secretary upon the permittee's failure to comply with the order. Any excess proceeds shall be returned to the insurer of the bond or to the surety after deducting court costs. (1971, c. 712, s. 1; 1973, c. 476, s. 128; 1983, c. 891, s. 2.)

§ 130A-257. Rules of the Commission.

For the protection of the public health, safety and welfare of those attending mass gatherings and of other persons who may be affected by mass gatherings, the Commission shall adopt rules to carry out the provisions of this Part and to establish requirements for the provision of facilities and services at mass gatherings. The rules shall include, but not be limited to, the establishment of requirements as follows:

(1)   General requirements relating to minimum size of activity area including camping and parking space, distance of activity area from dwellings, distance from public water supplies and watersheds and an adequate command post for use by personnel of health, law-enforcement and other governmental agencies;

(2)   Adequate ingress and egress roads, parking facilities and entrances and exits to public highways;

(3)   Plans for limiting attendance and crowd control, dust control and rapid emergency evacuation;

(4)   Medical care, including facilities, services and personnel;

(5)   Sanitary water supply, source and distribution; toilet facilities; sewage disposal; solid waste collection and disposal; food dispensing; insect and rodent control; and post-gathering cleanup; and

(6)   Noise level at perimeter; lighting and signs. (1971, c. 712, s. 1; 1973, c. 476, s. 128; 1983, c. 891, s. 2.)

§ 130A-258. Local ordinances not abrogated.

Nothing in this Part shall be construed to limit the authority of units of local government to adopt ordinances regulating, but not prohibiting, congregations and assemblies not covered by this Part. (1971, c. 712, s. 1; 1983, c. 891, s. 2.)

§§ 130A-259 through 130A-260. Reserved for future codification purposes.

291

Part 8. Bedding.

§§ 130A-261 through 130A-273: Recodified as Article 4H of Chapter 106, G.S. 106-65.95 through 106-65.107, by Session Laws 2011-145, s. 13.3(v), effective July 1, 2011.

Part 9. Milk Sanitation.

§§ 130A-274 through 130A-279: Recodified as Article 28C of Chapter 106, G.S. 106-266.30 through 106-266.35, by Session Laws 2011-145, s. 13.3(l), effective July 1, 2011.

§§ 130A-261 through 130A-273: Recodified as Article 4H of Chapter 106, G.S. 106-65.95 through 106-65.107, by Session Laws 2011-145, s. 13.3(v), effective July 1, 2011.

§§ 130A-274 through 130A-279: Recodified as Article 28C of Chapter 106, G.S. 106-266.30 through 106-266.35, by Session Laws 2011-145, s. 13.3(l), effective July 1, 2011.

Part 10. Public Swimming Pools.

§ 130A-280. Scope.

This Article provides for the regulation of public swimming pools in the State as they may affect the public health and safety. As used in this Article, the term "public swimming pool" means any structure, chamber, or tank containing an artificial body of water used by the public for swimming, diving, wading, recreation, or therapy, together with buildings, appurtenances, and equipment used in connection with the body of water, regardless of whether a fee is charged for its use. The term includes municipal, school, hotel, motel, apartment, boarding house, athletic club, or other membership facility pools and spas. This Article does not apply to a private pool serving a single family dwelling and used only by the residents of the dwelling and their guests. This Article also does not apply to therapeutic pools used in physical therapy programs operated by medical facilities licensed by the Department or operated by a licensed physical therapist, nor to therapeutic chambers drained, cleaned, and refilled after each individual use. (1989, c. 577, s. 1; 1997-443, s. 11A.80.)

§ 130A-281. Operation permit required.

No public swimming pool may be opened for use unless the owner or operator has obtained an operation permit issued by the Department pursuant to rules adopted under G.S. 130A-282. (1989, c. 577, s. 1.)

§ 130A-282. Commission to adopt rules; exception.

(a)   Rules Required. For protection of the public health and safety, the Commission shall adopt and the Department shall enforce rules concerning the construction and operation of public swimming pools. The Commission shall classify public swimming pools on the basis of size, usage, type, or any other appropriate factor and shall adopt requirements for each classification. The rules shall include requirements for:

(1)   Submission and review of plans prior to construction.

(2)   Application, review, expiration, renewal, and revocation or suspension of an operating permit.

(3)   Inspection.

(4)   Design and construction including materials, depth and other dimensions, and standards for the abatement of suction hazards.

(5)   Operation and safety including water source, water quality and testing, fencing, water treatment, chemical storage, toilet and bath facilities, measures to ensure the personal cleanliness of bathers, safety equipment and other safety measures, and sewage and other wastewater disposal.

(b)   Exception. Public swimming pools constructed or remodeled prior to May 1, 1993, that do not meet specific design and construction requirements of the rules for public swimming pools adopted by the Commission shall not be required to comply with design and construction requirements other than requirements related to the abatement of suction hazards. Public swimming pools constructed or remodeled prior to May 1, 1993, shall comply with all other rules for public swimming pools adopted by the Commission.

(c)   No single drain, single suction outlet public swimming pools less than 18 inches deep shall be allowed to operate. (1989, c. 577, s. 1; 1993, c. 215, s. 1; 1993 (Reg. Sess., 1994), c. 732, s. 1.)

Part 11. Tattooing.

§ 130A-283. Tattooing regulated.

(a)   Definition. - As used in this Part, the term "tattooing" means the inserting of permanent markings or coloration, or the producing of scars, upon or under human skin through puncturing by use of a needle or any other method.

(b)   Prohibited Practice. - No person shall engage in tattooing without first obtaining a tattooing permit from the Department. Licensed physicians, as well as physician assistants and nurse practitioners working under the supervision of a licensed physician, who perform tattooing within the normal course of their professional practice are exempt from the requirements of this Part.

(c)   Application. - To obtain a tattooing permit, a person must apply to the Department. Upon receipt of the application, the Department, acting through the local health department, shall inspect the premises, instruments, utensils, equipment, and procedures of the applicant to determine whether the applicant meets the requirements for a tattooing permit set by the Commission. If the applicant meets these requirements, the Department shall issue a permit to the applicant. A permit is valid for one year and must be renewed annually by applying to the Department for a permit renewal.

(d)   Violations. - The Department may deny an application for a tattooing permit if an applicant does not meet the requirements set by the Commission for the permit. The Department may suspend, revoke, or refuse to renew a permit if it finds that tattooing is being performed in violation of this Part. In accordance with G.S. 130A-24(a), Chapter 150B of the General Statutes, the Administrative Procedure Act, governs appeals concerning the enforcement of this Part.

(e)   Limitation. - A permit issued pursuant to this Part does not authorize a person to remove a tattoo from the body of a human being. Compliance with this Part is not a bar to prosecution for a violation of G.S. 14-400. (1993 (Reg. Sess., 1994), c. 670, s. 1.)

Part 12. Decontamination Standards for Methamphetamine Sites.

§ 130A-284. Decontamination of property used for the manufacture of methamphetamine.

For the protection of the public health, the Commission shall adopt rules establishing decontamination standards to ensure that certain property is reasonably safe for habitation. An owner, lessee, operator or other person in control of a residence or place of business or any structure appurtenant to a residence or place of business, and who has knowledge that the property has been used for the manufacture of methamphetamine, shall comply with these rules. For purposes of this section, the terms "residence" and "place of business" shall be defined as set forth in G.S. 130A-334. (2004-178, s. 7.)

§ 130A-285: Reserved for future codification purposes.

§ 130A-286: Reserved for future codification purposes.

§ 130A-287: Reserved for future codification purposes.

§ 130A-288: Reserved for future codification purposes.

§ 130A-289: Reserved for future codification purposes.

296

Vision Books Order Form

Fax Orders:	1-980-299-5965
Phone Orders:	1-704-898-0770
E-mail Orders:	www.visionbooks.org
Mail Orders:	Vision Books, LLC P.O. Box 42406 Charlotte, NC 28215

Shipp To:
Name_____
Address_____
City_____State_____Zip_____
Phone_____Fax_____
Email_____@_____

Bill To: We can bill a third party on your behalf.
Name_____
Address_____
City_____State_____Zip_____
Phone____(   )_____Fax_____
Email_____@_____

Pamphlet Number ($15.00 Each)	Qty	Total Cost
_____	_____	_____
_____	_____	_____
_____	_____	_____
_____	_____	_____
_____	_____	_____
_____	_____	_____
_____	_____	_____
_____	_____	_____
Full Volume Set 1-92	92 Pamphlets	1,380.00

Free Shipping & Handling on Full Volume Orders
Add $1.00 Shipping & Handling Per Pamphlet $_____

Total Cost $_____

Thank you for your support. Management!

DID YOU ENJOY THIS BOOK?

Vision Books, LLC would like to hear from you! If you or someone you know has been fasely imprisoned, we would like to hear your story. If the 'North Carolina Criminal Law and Procedure' has had an effect in your life or if you have suggestions, we would like to hear from you. Send your letters to:

Vision Books, LLC
Attn: Staff Writers
P.O. Box 42406
Charlotte, NC 28215
Email: staff@visionbooks.org

Order Additional Copies:

Fax Orders: 1-980-299-5965

Phone Orders: 1-704-898-0770

E-mail Orders: www.visionbooks.org

Mail Orders: Vision Books, LLC
                       P.O. Box 42406
                       Charlotte, NC 28215